Keys to Employee Success in Coming Decades

Keys to
Employee Success in
Coming Decades

EDITED BY

Ronald R. Sims
and John G. Veres III

QUORUM BOOKS
Westport, Connecticut • London

658.314
K 44

Library of Congress Cataloging-in-Publication Data

Keys to employee success in coming decades / edited by Ronald R. Sims,
John G. Veres, III.
    p. cm.
    Includes bibliographical references and index.
    ISBN 1–56720–194–6 (alk. paper)
    1. Employee motivation.   2. Success in business. I. Sims, Ronald
R. II. Veres, John G.
    HF5549.5.M63K49   1999
    658.3'14—dc21   98–30539

British Library Cataloguing in Publication Data is available.

Library of Congress Catalog Card Number: 98–30539
ISBN: 1–56720–194–6

First published in 1999

Quorum Books, 88 Post Road West, Westport, CT 06881
An imprint of Greenwood Publishing Group, Inc.

Printed in the United States of America

The paper used in this book complies with the
Permanent Paper Standard issued by the National
Information Standards Organization (Z39.48–1984).

10 9 8 7 6 5 4 3 2 1

Ronald Sims would like to dedicate this book to his wife, Serbrenia, and his children, Nandi, Dangaia, and Sieya.

John Veres would like to dedicate this book to Frances and John George Veres, Jr., who taught him to read and write; to Beth, Erin, Johnny, and Olivia, who provided constant support; and to Wiley R. Bolyes and the late William O. Jenkins, who taught him most of what he knows in addition to reading and writing.

Contents

Figures and Tables   ix

Acknowledgments   xi

Introduction   xiii
John G. Veres III, Ronald R. Sims, and Daniel F. Michael

1. Succeeding in the Next Millennium: Three Skills Employees
   Must Possess   1
   Ronald R. Sims, Serbrenia J. Sims, and John G. Veres III

2. Self-Directed Change and Learning as a Necessary
   Meta-Competency for Success and Effectiveness in the
   Twenty-first Century   15
   Richard E. Boyatzis

3. Making Your Way in the Next Century: Taking the Career
   High Ground   33
   Kenneth L. Murrell

4. Self-Directed Careers   55
   Robert M. Fulmer and Philip A. Gibbs

5. The Telecommuting Life: Managing Boundary Issues
   at Work and at Home   71
   Karen Locke and GiGi G. Kelly

6. Being Successful in Asia: How to Survive and Thrive   91
   Mark Payne and Milano Reyna

7. Managing the New Future Manager: Individual and
    Organizational Perspectives   105
    *M. Ronald Buckley, Danielle S. Wiese, Milorad M. Novicevic,
    and Thomas D. Sigerstad*

8. Foundations of Success: A Life Course Approach to
    Women's Career Success   119
    Ella L. J. Edmondson Bell and Stella M. Nkomo

9. Knowing Yourself: Who? Why? What? How? and When?   137
    Diana Page

10. The Critical Role of Information Technology for Employee
    Success in the Coming Decade   157
    Hsing K. Cheng

11. The New Employer-Employee Contract: A CEO's
    Perspective on Employer and Employee Success   183
    William Donaldson

12. Staying Sane in an Ever-Changing World   199
    William I. Sauser, Jr.

13. Keys to Employee Success: What Skills Are Really
    Important for Success in the Future?   223
    John G. Veres III and Ronald R. Sims

Index   243
About the Contributors   247

Figures and Tables

FIGURES

2.1	Contingency Theory of Action and Job Performance	17
2.2	Theory of Self-Directed Change and Learning	18
4.1	Career Stages	59
6.1	Basic Confucian Principles	94
6.2	Western/Capitalist/Judeo-Christian Values	95
10.1	The Distribution of the U.S. Labor Force from 1860 to 1980	159
10.2	The Structure of a Decision Support System	161
10.3	The General Structure of Business Spreadsheet Models	162
10.4	Economic Order Quantity (EOQ) Model	164
10.5	401(k) Retirement Funds Allocation Model	166
10.6	401(k) Retirement Funds Model Solver Parameters	168
10.7	401(k) Retirement Funds Solver Results	169
10.8	Microsoft Access Main Screen	172
10.9	QBE Screen for Scenario 1	173
10.10	QBE Result for Scenario 1	174
10.11	QBE Screen for Scenario 2	175
10.12	QBE Screen for Scenario 3	177
10.13	QBE Screen for Scenario 4	178

10.14 QBE Screen for Scenario 5   180
11.1   Protean Career Contract   186

TABLES

4.1   Career Anchors   63
5.1   Benefits of Teleworking   75
10.1   Sample Tables Created Using Query by Example   171
10.2   Commonly Used Conditions   176

Acknowledgments

A special thanks from Ronald Sims goes to Herrington Bryce, who has been instrumental in encouraging his professional growth and development. The support of the School of Business at the College of William and Mary is also acknowledged. And finally, Serbrenia, Nandi, Dangaia, and Sieya are always there when they are needed.

John Veres would like to thank Donna Velasquez, Roger Hung, and Daniel Michael for their valuable assistance in preparing the manuscript. Without their help, this book would not have been possible. He would also like to express his gratitude to the contributors, who suffered through revisions without complaint.

Introduction

JOHN G. VERES III, RONALD R. SIMS,
AND DANIEL F. MICHAEL

The need for an increased focus on employee success has emerged in response to a number of changes and challenges in the world of work. More specifically, the ever-increasing complexity of the challenges facing organizations and the pace of change both signal the escalating pressure that will be—and currently is—brought to bear on employees to either be proactive initiators of their own success or be left behind as marginal and unsuccessful contributors. What are some of these other changes and challenges that are contributing to the changing world of work and a call for increased emphasis on employee success?

First there is what some have referred to as "the changing economy." The economy is being reshaped by globalization; technological upheavals, especially in the areas of computers, telecommunications, and information; growth and decline among job sectors; cultural diversity; changing societal expectations; expanding interest in entrepreneurship; and more fickle, more demanding customers.

In Chapter 1, Sims, Sims, and Veres discuss the significant changes confronting the organization of the future and how these changes will affect how jobs and employee work will be performed. The authors then discuss three skills they consider important to employee success in the unpredictable and constantly changing world of work in the coming years.

GLOBALIZATION

Twenty or 30 years ago, national borders acted to insulate most firms from foreign competitive pressures. They no longer do. National borders have become nearly meaningless today in defining an organization's operating boundaries. It has become increasingly irrelevant, for instance, to label a company's home country. BMW is supposedly a German firm, but it builds cars in South Carolina. Ford, which is headquartered in Detroit, builds its Mercury Tracers in Mexico. So-called U.S. companies such as Exxon, Gillette, Coca-Cola, and IBM now receive more than 60 percent of their sales from outside the United States. Mitsubishi of Japan, Siemens of Germany, Nestlé of Switzerland, and Royal Dutch/Shell of the Netherlands are just four examples of the hundreds of multibillion-dollar corporations that operate in dozens of countries throughout the world.

Globalization doesn't just mean doing business across national borders. It also means expanded competition for almost every type of organization. Today's employees must be aware that they face foreign competitors as well as local and national ones. For instance, since 1972, Dennis Marthell has run a profitable business by processing checks for several major banks in the southeastern United States. In recent years, however, he has found himself competing against firms in the Caribbean. Through computer technology and overnight delivery services, the Caribbean firms can provide the same services at better prices owing to lower labor costs in countries such as Jamaica and Trinidad.

In Chapter 6, Payne and Reyna suggest that as globalization of business continues, and as Asian markets continue to grow rapidly, employees will need global knowledge and experience to be successful. The authors present a collection of cultural perspectives to guide the fresh-off-the-plane ex-pat through his or her early days in Asia and suggest that an understanding and appreciation of cultural differences are critical for success in Asia.

CHANGES IN TECHNOLOGY

We often forget that only 20 years ago almost no one had a fax machine or a cellular phone. Until recently, the terms *e-mail* and *modem* were in the vocabularies of perhaps a few hundred people; computers occupied entire rooms rather than eleven inches of lap space; and *networks* referred to the major providers of television programming. How quickly times have changed. The silicon chip and other advances in information technology have permanently altered the economies of the world and the way people work. Digital electronics, optical data storage, more powerful and portable computers, and the ability for computers to communicate with each other are changing the way information is created, stored, used, and shared.

In Chapter 10, Cheng discusses the critical roll of information technology for employee success in the coming decade and the trend of our society moving toward an "information economy" where information technology dominates the majority of economic activities. Opportunities for individual employees afforded by information technology in general and personal computing technologies in particular are explored. The critical role of spreadsheet and database software for employee success is also discussed.

In Chapter 5, Locke and Kelly discuss telecommuting and its potential benefits for the individual and the organization. The authors describe how this new work arrangement not only may change traditional work and family relationships but also may cause those relationships to deteriorate. Suggestions are given for managing this new work arrangement to avoid potential negative outcomes.

TOFFLER'S THREE WAVES: GROWTH AND DECLINE IN JOB SECTORS

Futurist Alvin Toffler (1980) argued that human history can be divided into "waves." The first wave was *agriculture*. Until the late nineteenth century, all economies were agrarian. For instance, in the 1890s, approximately 90 percent of people were employed in agriculture-related jobs. The second wave was *industrialization*. From the late 1800s until the 1960s, most developed countries moved from agrarian societies to ones based on machines. The third wave arrived in the 1970s and is based on *information*. Toffler and others see these waves as essentially revolutions, in which complete "ways of life" are thrown out and replaced by new ones. The second wave, for instance, totally changed the lives of English villagers as they adjusted to life in English factories. The third wave is eliminating low-skilled, blue-collar jobs, while, at the same time, creating abundant job opportunities for educated and skilled technical specialists, professionals, and other "knowledge workers."

In Chapter 9, Page describes the history and significance of work from the employee's perspective and describes the impact of technology on pre- and postindustrial work in order to provide a better picture of the nature of future work and careers. The author then describes strategies for managing work transitions and for determining career direction and work values.

Job growth in the past 20 years has been in low-skilled service work (such as fast-food employees, clerks, and home health aides) and knowledge work. The latter group includes professionals such as registered nurses, teachers, lawyers, and engineers. It also includes *technologists*—people who work with their hands and with theoretical knowledge. Computer technicians, physical therapists, and medical technicians are examples of jobs in this category. By the year 2000, it's predicted that knowledge workers will make up a third or more of the U.S. work force.

In Chapter 7, Buckley, Wiese, Novicevic, and Sigerstad discuss the changing role of managers in managing newcomers in a rapidly changing world of work. The authors examine the nature, dimensions, and potential influence of societal, demographic, and organizational changes on young newcomers and describe how organizational newcomers have changed in terms of their desired relationship with organizations as well as several career issues they must confront. Individual career strategies for newcomers are also suggested.

In Chapter 3, Murrell presents "21 New Rules" for preparing management and organizational leadership for the coming century. Each rule can be used to help prepare employees and managers for the changes that are taking place in organizations and the world of work. The central focus is how best to prepare for the most desirable jobs and careers available, while avoiding the false security of any organization that may offer more than it can deliver.

CULTURAL DIVERSITY

As recently as 1960, only 32 percent of married women were in the U.S. labor force. Today, that figure is close to 60 percent. By the end of this decade, 61 percent of all working-age women in the United States will have jobs, and women will make up 47 percent of the total work force. Currently, women with children under 6 years of age are the fastest-growing segment of the U.S. work force. This trend of women joining the work force, incidentally, is taking place worldwide in industrialized nations. The numbers of women in the labor force are rapidly approaching those of men in Great Britain, Canada, Australia, Hong Kong, Singapore, and Japan.

In Chapter 8, Bell and Nkomo discuss various factors that contribute to the success of women in their work lives. Using a life history approach, the authors attempt to provide an understanding of the factors, conditions, and people who contribute to a woman's career over the course of her life span. Particular interest is shown in discovering how a woman's racial identity shapes her life as she grows into womanhood.

A NEW WAY OF LOOKING AT THE ORGANIZATION

The economy has been undergoing changes. So, too, have organizations. As the following describes, the underlying theme is that the "new organization" is becoming more flexible and more responsive to its environment. The old organization: jobs are permanent; the work force is relatively homogeneous; quality is an afterthought; large corporations provide job security; if it ain't broke, don't fix it; spread risks by being in multiple businesses; hierarchy provides efficiency; workdays are defined as 9-to-5; work is defined by jobs; pay is stable and related to seniority and job level; managers alone make decisions; and business decision making is driven by utilitarianism.

The new organization: jobs are temporary; the work force is diverse; continuous improvement and customer satisfaction are critical; corporations are drastically cutting overall staff; reengineer all processes; concentrate on core competencies; dismantle hierarchy to increase flexibility; workdays have no time boundaries; work is defined in terms of tasks to be done; pay is flexible and broad banded; employees participate in decision making; and business decision-making criteria are expanded to include rights and fairness.

The breaking of the psychological contract that used to exist between employer and employee has accelerated as international competition in the private sector (and calls for reinventing government in the public sector) and has prompted restructuring, downsizing, and rightsizing. This has and will continue to lead to a considerable amount of economic uncertainty, lack of security, and a regression to employee self-interest rather than organizational well-being. In Chapter 11, Donaldson suggests that the terms of the old employer-employee contract have become obsolete and unworkable in response to intense competitive pressures and globalization of markets and have been replaced by a "new contract." The old contract was based on the idea that "I'll take care of you, if you take care of me," whereas the "new contract" is based on the assumption that "I'll take care of me for you, if you take care of you for me." Here, longevity, rank, and entitlement have been replaced with contribution, mutual respect, and fit with values, culture, direction, and goals. He presents a discussion on the implications of the new contract for employers and employees.

SELF-DIRECTED CAREERS

The new contract between employers and employees transfers responsibility for career development from the organization to the employee. So today's employees are becoming more concerned than ever with keeping skills current and developing new skills. They see learning as a lifelong process. At one time, a skill learned in youth could provide a living for life. Now technology changes so rapidly that as soon as an employee has learned something, that "something" becomes obsolete. In this climate, employees are increasingly recognizing that "if you snooze, you lose." There will always be other people out there who are keeping current and who are ready to assume your work responsibilities if you show signs of falling behind.

In Chapter 4, Fulmer and Gibbs discuss self-directed careers and emphasize the importance of employees taking control of their own careers by developing career plans, including mission and goals, assessing individual interests, knowledge, skills, and abilities, and preparing for the achievement of career objectives by obtaining the necessary training and experience. In addition to individual factors, organizational members must consider both organizational and external-environmental changes that have taken place that significantly affect traditional work relationships and terms of employment. In view of the many changes taking place in the working world, a "Ten Commandments" for a self-directed career strategy are presented.

SUCCESSFULLY COPING WITH STRESS

Rapid and unexpected change makes life exciting. It also causes stress. So no employee should be surprised to find that stress, burnout, and the like, will continue to be among the hottest issues in the new world of work. Downsizing and reengineering have resulted in many employees' having to take on new tasks and, very often, having to work harder. To reduce costs, for instance, companies are frequently increasing overtime among their high-skilled employees. When companies combine reduced job security, pressures to learn new skills, and heightened workloads, they create a workplace that is increasingly stressful on employees, a workplace that will continue to present new challenges to employee success. In Chapter 12, Sauser discusses five forces for change confronting today's organizational members and explores why people resist change. A practical strategy is then presented for using these forces for change in providing momentum to one's own career enhancement, reducing stress.

As the psychological contract continues to evolve in accordance with the paradigm shift to new employer expectations, employees will need to continually enhance and update their skills so that when companies restructure, they can find new jobs, whether with the same company or with another firm. This places a premium on lifelong learning, education, and training. If employees take charge of their own employability by keeping their skills updated and varied, they will also build a stronger possibility for their own job security and success. In Chapter 2, Boyatzis discusses the process of self-directed change and learning and how this process occurs, not in a smooth but in a surprising, discontinuous fashion. The practical suggestions presented here for engaging the self-directed change and learning process are provided as a roadmap for improving your change and learning efforts. Lastly, in Chapter 13, Veres and Sims discuss how the traditional functions, roles, and skills of employees are changing in response to the increasing complexity of the world in which they live. A detailed discussion is then presented of the skills considered critical to employee success in the coming decades.

We hope that this book will be useful to readers who are interested in maximizing employee success. The book is written for employees, whether in private, public, or not-for-profit organizations and whether in executive, middle management, or frontline positions. There will be no panaceas in this book, and its contributors make no claim to being experts on everything related to employee success. They are individuals who have experience in understanding what employee success means, and their contributions to this book are based on lessons learned over many years by observing, analyzing, working, and studying both successful and unsuccessful employees.

REFERENCE

Toffler, A. (1980). *The third wave*. New York: Morrow.

1

Succeeding in the Next Millennium: Three Skills Employees Must Possess

RONALD R. SIMS, SERBRENIA J. SIMS, AND JOHN G. VERES III

INTRODUCTION

Organizations are becoming more and more demanding of their employees. Today, it is not enough to stay on top of the latest developments within a rapidly changing organization or discipline. What is required is mastery of a broader set of important knowledge, skills, abilities, and other characteristics (KSAOCs) that enable employees, their work teams, and organizations to succeed.

Being a successful employee has to some extent always been one of the toughest tasks in any organization. Now, and in the immediate future, it will arguably be one of the most complex and demanding challenges for employees. We believe that part of the reason is that employees have been battered by rightsizing, reengineering, downsizing, and an array of cost-cutting measures brought on by increasingly stormy global economic seas and are in urgent need of a revitalized self-commitment to their own success. In a bittersweet way, today's employees sense that they are in tough waters, and they will only survive if they take more responsibility for their own success.

Increasing emphasis on measuring employees' contributions to the profitability of an organization is another reason why the task of being a successful employee will be complex and demanding. Employers will increasingly expect employees to have an immediate and positive effect on company operations as they continue to set higher and higher expectations in response to increased competitive pressures and shareholder demands. As we enter the twenty-first century, a new set of major changes are reshaping the economy, creating organizational challenges, and changing the nature of jobs. These changes are testing the mettle and talents of organizations and their employees. Unless employees develop the skills they need to cope with these challenges, many will not measure up and will become casualties of their own deficiencies. The purpose of this chapter is to discuss several skills that we believe have been, and will be, increasingly important to employee success in the unpredictable and constantly changing world of work. The chapter will look at the organization of the future, briefly discuss how jobs and employee work will change, and explore three of the skills we believe are important to employee success in the coming years.

CHANGING ORGANIZATIONS

Like their host organizations, employees of today and tomorrow need to grapple with a number of revolutionary forces including accelerating product and technological change, global competition, deregulation, political instability, demographic changes, and trends toward a service society and information age. Forces such as these have changed the playing field on which employee organizations must compete. In particular, they have dramatically increased the need for organizations to be responsive, flexible, and capable of reacting rapidly in a global marketplace. Thousands of organizations and their employees are re-creating themselves to fit these new conditions. The typical company will be smaller and employ fewer people (Dessler, 1998). More people will start business for themselves, and many organizations will continue to downsize or break themselves up. Even within large organizations, the operating units will be divided into small, self-contained mini-units.

The traditional organization structure will become more team based and "boundaryless" (Keichel, 1993). The new organization will stress cross-functional teams and interdepartmental communication. There will be corresponding deemphasis on "sticking to the chain of command" to get decisions made. For years at General Electric (GE), Chairman Jack Welch has been talking of the boundaryless organization, in which employees do not identify with separate departments but instead interact with whomever they must to get the job done.

Employees will be empowered to make more decisions. Work will require constant learning, "higher-order" thinking, and much more worker commitment. The result for employees will be more empowerment and less of a 9-to-5 mentality. Experts like Karl Albrecht argue for turning the typical organization upside down. They say today's organization should put the customer on top and emphasize that every move the company makes must be geared toward satisfying the customer's needs. To do so, every organization must empower its employees with the authority to respond quickly to the customer's needs.

Flatter organizations will be the norm. Instead of the pyramid-shaped organization with its seven or more layers of management, flat organizations with just three or four levels will prevail. Many organizations have already cut the number of levels between top management and the lowest level of employees from a dozen to six or less—and with them a large number of managers and other employees. As the remaining employees are left, they have more autonomy and are expected to do more with less.

Work itself will be organized around teams and processes rather than specialized functions. In the manufacturing plant, for instance, employees won't just have the job of installing the same door handle over and over again. Instead, they'll be part of multifunction teams, ones that manage their own budgets and control their own quality (more will be said about this in the following section).

Management specialist Tom Peters says the new organizations will be "knowledge based," the way consulting firms and hospitals are today. Here teams of highly trained and educated professionals apply their knowledge to clients' problems, working in an atmosphere in which they direct and discipline their own activities (Peters, 1992).

The new organization will stress vision and values. Formulating a clear vision and values that employees can commit themselves to will be more important than ever. Organizations will have to communicate clear values regarding what is important and unimportant and regarding what employees should and should not do (e.g., expected ethical behavior).

Employees must be change agents. As GE's Jack Welch puts it, "You've got to be on the cutting edge of change. You can't maintain the status quo, because somebody's always coming from another country with another product, or consumers' tastes change, or the cost structure does, or there's a technology breakthrough. If you are not fast and adaptable, you are vulnerable" (Sherman, 1993, p. 82).

CHANGING JOBS

Almost 200 years ago, very few people had a "job." Sure, they worked, and worked hard, raising food or building things. They did so, however, without scheduled work hours, without bosses and job descriptions, and without employee benefits. Instead, they performed a variety of tasks, guided by the weather or when people would gather at the market to buy what they had made. It was the Industrial Revolution that introduced individuals to large manufacturing organizations, which helped create what we know today as the job—centralized worker locations, formalized job requirements, and being responsible to a "boss." But now, some 100 years after the Industrial Revolution changed America, things have started to change again. Customized production is replacing mass production. Employees today are more likely to be processing information than to be producing physical products. And this is all happening while organizations are facing a more dynamic environment such as increased competition from the global village (Norton, 1996). As a result, the United States is being de-jobbed! And that has profound implications for employees today and in the coming decades.

Employees have traditionally had the luxury of having a job description that defined what work they needed to do. Their tasks were relatively routine—even when they performed "other work as assigned." Employees today and tomorrow, however, may not have that luxury. Tasks change too frequently to be captured accurately in a job description. Sure, job descriptions can be rewritten, but not every week. For many jobs the job description may become obsolete (Thomas & Velthouse, 1990).

Rather than having a routine job, employees will work on assignments as needed. They will not be specialists in one area, but, rather, they will be multifunction/skilled specialists. They will work with other employees for a period of time, then move on to another project. Workers will perform their duties as members of project teams. They will be assigned to these teams because of the skills they possess. They will have changing schedules, work in several places, and perform a variety of tasks. Some of these project team members will be contingent workers—temporary, contractual, and consultant "hired guns" brought in to assist.

Clearly, not all of the employees in the United States are being de-jobbed. Yet the trends are pointing in that direction. Actual numbers of workers might not decrease drastically. Rather, de-jobbing will reflect the degree of connectedness employees have to an organization. There will be a small core of employees, the full-time employees of the organization who provide some essential job tasks for the organization. Employees who hold these core jobs will enjoy a full slate of employee benefits and job security that workers enjoyed 30 years ago. Beyond the core group will be the contingent work force. These individuals will make up the bulk of the organization as long as their performance is satisfactory, as long as a project lasts. Job security for these individuals, then, will last only for the duration of the project on which they work. Survival for many contingent workers will become a function of their entrepreneurial abilities.

SKILLS IMPORTANT TO EMPLOYEE SUCCESS IN A CHANGING WORLD

Change, newness, uncertainty—what do they mean for tomorrow's employees? Although making predictions can be viewed as an exercise in futility, there is some evidence highlighting the issues with which employees will need to concern themselves. The key to success, if it can be narrowed down to one statement is this: be prepared to make adjustments! Opportunities will abound for those prepared to accept and deal with the information age.

Information technology, supported by other changes in our society, has permanently altered employees' lives. The new life requires a constantly evolving list of skills employees must possess. Those who embrace knowledge and continuously learn new skills will be the ones who thrive in the new organization and world. However, regardless of whether employees are permanent or contingent there are several skills (i.e., effective followership, acting ethically, and emotional intelligence) that they will need to develop if they are to succeed in coming years. It is not our intent to say that these are the only skills employees must develop, but for our purposes they are among the most important.

Effective Followership Skills

One of the most important keys to employee success will be their ability to develop effective followership skills. That is, employees will need to be effective team players who partner with other members of the organization to create the organization's vision and to implement goals and strategies successfully. Developing the skills of an effective follower requires that employees learn to act like leaders. According to Kelley (1988), "People who are effective in the follower role have a vision to see both the forest and the trees; the social capacity to work well with others; the strength of character to flourish without heroic status; the moral and psychological balance to pursue personal and corporate goals at no cost to either; and above all, the desire to participate in a team effort for the accomplishment of some greater purpose" (p. 147). Successful followership characteristics (Lundin & Lancaster, 1990) include commitment to the organization's vision and goals; ability to self-manage; a sense of integrity and honesty; credibility, competence, and focus; versatility; work and task ownership; critical problem-solving skills; and the ability to be team players and energetic, empowered individuals. Effective followers will be less the creators of the organizational vision and strategy and more the implementers of it.

Having effective followership skills also means that employees will need to be self-managers. Self-management requires acquiring self-awareness and control of one's own feelings and behavior. It means being nondefensive and taking risks by challenging the supervisor and the organization. In being self-managers, employees will give a cost advantage to their organizations by eliminating the need for supervisory or management levels. This also means that employees who develop followership skills will work as empowered, self-motivated co-leaders who will not always wait to be told what to do.

As effective followers, employees will need to be committed to organizational goals while balancing their personal needs with their loyalty. Being an effective follower does not mean employees will be yes-people. Employees will still need to have high standards in the areas of integrity, honesty, and personal ethics. Alcorn (1992) notes that "followers expect high consistency between what leaders say and what they do. Likewise, leaders will continue to expect agreement between followers' expressed values and values observed" (p. 10).

Tomorrow's effective followers will also need to demonstrate competence and focus. They will also need to search for unsolved problems to solve, take initiative in enforcing quality and performance standards, and ensure that work is aligned to organizational goals. They will also need to take ownership and responsibility for organizational tasks and their work. "Owning the territory . . . means knowing your job very well and taking pride in that expertise. It means working constantly to help you piece and fit into the larger puzzle" (Lundin & Lancaster, 1990, p. 20).

Tomorrow's effective followers will need to be versatile and critical problem solvers. "Versatility involves being able to deal with ambiguity" (Lundin & Lancaster, 1990, p. 20). Being flexible in order to accept and implement needed changes is a critical skill for effective followers. Employees will need to successfully implement change strategies developed by leaders and their work teams. As noted earlier in this chapter, changing budgets, globalization, organizational forms, customer expectations, regulations, and relationships with other organizations are only some of the elements that will require greater and constant flexibility by employees.

By developing effective followership skills, tomorrow's employees will be able to communicate effectively and keep information flowing. As critical problem solvers, tomorrow's employees must be able to seek to understand assumptions and causes of problems. They must not be satisfied with symptoms and quick fixes. Tomorrow's employees will need to be able to increase productivity when they solve problems and develop cost-efficient work methods. In today's and tomorrow's leaner times, this will require that followers recognize problems, design and evaluate alternative solutions, and choose and implement the one that is best for the organization without referring the problem to, or receiving direction from, others. They must strive for organization-wide achievement.

Employees will need to act like leaders and successfully manage and nurture relationships. It will take time and patience to nurture good relationships. Taking the time to develop such relationships will be a valuable resource for the employee, their work team, and organization. Being able to work well with others, possessing good communication skills while displaying empathy for the needs and objectives expressed by others, will be a must for employee success. This also means that employees must be able to move away from viewing situations as "win-lose"—that is, not viewing another worker as "winning" at the expense of others but instead viewing a situation in light of what is best for the overall organization. Employees will need to view such decisions as "win-win" situations by everyone and not evaluate according to how they affect individuals, teams, or departments.

Employees who possess effective followership skills will prove to be valuable to their organizations because they are active contributors and possess four essential qualities. First, *they will manage themselves well*. They will practice self-management and self-responsibility. They will think for themselves. They will work independently and without close supervision. Work can be delegated to them without anxiety about the outcome. Second, *they will be committed to a purpose outside themselves*. They will be committed to something—a cause, a product, a work team, an organization, an idea—in addition to the care of their own lives. Most people like working with colleagues who are emotionally, as well as physically, committed to their work. They will not be self-centered or self-aggrandizing. Third, *they will build their competence and focus their efforts for maximum impact*. They will master skills and acquire knowledge that is useful to their organizations, and they will hold higher perform-ance standards than their job or team group requires. Fourth, *they will be courageous, honest, and credible*. These individuals will establish them-selves as independent, critical thinkers whose knowledge and judgment can be trusted. They will hold high ethical standards, give credit where credit is due, and won't be afraid to own up to their mistakes. A question you need to answer is: *Will you be an effective follower?*

Acting Ethically

There are many who believe we are currently suffering an ethics crisis and that things will get worse before they get better as we move into the next millennium. Attitudes and behaviors that were once thought of as reprehensible—cheating, lying, and covering up mistakes—have be-come, in many people's eyes, acceptable or necessary practices. Some employees have covered up information about the safety of their prod-ucts. Other employees have profited from illegal use of insider infor-mation. Price fixing, polluting the environment, and pirating software are further illustrations of ethical lapses. And some government contrac-tors have overcharged for their work. Even college students seem to have been caught up in this wave. Recent studies have noted the tendency of large percentages of students to cheat on tests and steal (i.e., illegally copy software) (Sims, Cheng, & Teegen, 1996).

Concern over this perceived decline in ethical standards is being addressed in several ways. First, ethics education is being widely expanded in undergraduate and graduate curriculums. For example, the American Assembly of Collegiate Schools of Business, which is the primary accrediting agency for business schools, now requires all its member programs to integrate ethical issues throughout their business curricula (Russell & Scherer, 1995). Second, organizations are creating codes of ethics and introducing ethics training programs (Boroughs, 1995).

Making ethical choices can be difficult for employees; however, acting ethically will be an important skill for employee success in the coming years. Obeying the law will continue to be mandatory, but acting ethically goes beyond mere compliance with the law. It means acting responsibly in those "gray" areas, where right and wrong are not defined. Employees should do the following things to enhance their skills in acting ethically.

Make sure they understand their own values and beliefs. There is no doubt that the personal values and beliefs of individuals play a major role in what they will or will not do. Personal values and beliefs often form the basis for their choices of alternatives when confronted with various ethical dilemmas. Unless employees understand their own values and beliefs, they will not be able to filter through how they view the world, act ethically, and make important ethical decisions.

Make sure they know their organization's policy on ethics. "Organization policies on ethics" describes what the organization perceives as ethical behavior and what it expects employees to do. This policy will help employees to clarify what is permissible and the discretion employees have. This becomes the code of ethics for employees to follow.

Make sure they understand the ethics policy. Just having the policy in hand does not guarantee it will achieve what it is intended to do. Employees need to fully understand it. Behaving ethically is rarely a cut-and-dried process. But the policy can act as a guiding light, providing a basis from which employees will do things in the organization. Even if a policy does not exist, there are still several steps employees can take before they deal with a difficult situation.

Always think before they act. Employees should ask themselves, "Why am I going to do what I'm about to do? What led up to the problem? What is my true intention in taking this action? Is my reason valid? Or are there ulterior motives behind it—such as demonstrating organizational loyalty? Will my action injure someone? Would I disclose to my family or my boss or my coworkers what I'm going to do?" Employees should remember that it is their behavior and their actions. They need to make sure that they are not doing something that will jeopardize their team, organization, or own reputation.

Employees should ask themselves what-if questions. If employees are thinking about why they are going to do something, they should be asking themselves what-if questions. For example, the following questions may help shape an employee's actions. "What if I make the wrong decision? What will happen to me? to my job?" "What if my actions were described in the local newspaper or TV news show? Would it bother me or embarrass me or those around me?" "What if I get caught doing something unethical? Am I prepared to deal with the consequences?"

Employees should seek opinions from others. If it is something major that employees must do, and about which they are uncertain, they should ask advice from others. Maybe they have been in a similar situation and can give the employee the benefit of their experience. Or maybe they can just listen and act as a sounding board for the employee.

Employees should truly do what they believe is right. Employees have a conscience, and they are responsible for their behavior. Whatever they do, if they truly believe it was the right action to take, then what others say is immaterial. Individuals need to be true to their own internal ethical standards and ask themselves: "Can I live with what I plan to do or have done?"

Emotional Intelligence

While possessing skills to be an effective follower, acting ethically, and others (i.e., creative problem solving, being sensitive to diversity, and lifelong learning) are important to employee success in the coming years, emotional intelligence just might be the most important skill an employee will need. This concept encompasses a wide variety of capabilities, including the ability to manage one's emotions, empathize with others, and cope with emotional relationships. Emotionally intelligent organizations of the future will need to be populated by employees with these attributes if they are going to be successful in the twenty-first century.

To be successful in the coming years, employees will need more than academic intelligence. For example, very bright people can be utter failures when it comes to interacting with others in a group or team situation. Very often "smart" may not make up for a lack of social skills. Additionally, it has been recently noted that the characteristic that most distinguishes star performers from average workers is not IQ (intelligence quotient) but emotional intelligence (EI) (Martinez, 1997).

EI, or EQ (emotional quotient), is a bigger predictor of workplace success according to Daniel Goleman, who published a book on the subject in 1995. Goleman believes an individual's success at work is 80 percent dependent on EI and 20 percent dependent on IQ. According to Goleman, there are four basic "people skills" that are separate from academic intelligence but important to success. These components of emotional intelligence are: (1) delaying your gratification, (2) controlling your emotions, (3) dealing constructively with your anger, and (4) reading other people's feelings. Martinez (1997) has noted that EI encompasses five dimensions: self-motivation skills; self-awareness, or knowing one's own emotions; the ability to manage one's emotions and impulses; empathy, or the ability to sense how others are feeling; and social skills, or the ability to handle the emotions of other people.

A very simple test used to assess the ability to delay gratification has been found to relate to success 25 years later. Children are left alone in a room with marshmallows and M&Ms. They can either wait five minutes, or they can eat the candy immediately. They are told that if they wait, they will get more candy. Those children who weren't able to control their impulses and ate the candy immediately were more likely to be in jail 25 years later.

Like the ability to delay gratification, the ability to control our emotions and deal with anger constructively is critical to success. Some people aren't able to control their anger and are prone to fits of temper. However, emotional outbursts usually aren't very adaptive and can cause problems when interacting with others.

While we may not react on it much, the ability to read other's feelings is also a critical skill. People who are better able to correctly read the emotions displayed in the faces of others are more successful in the workplace and tend to have more friends.

EI will continue to be a necessary qualification for being a good team player tomorrow as it is in today's business environment. For example, EI made an important difference in the performance of Bell Labs in New Jersey. Bell engineers whose performance was rated the highest by their peers were found to have high levels of EI. The highly rated engineers were simply better at relating to others.

Research shows that emotions, properly managed, can drive trust, loyalty, and commitment—and many of the greatest productivity gains, innovations, and accomplishments of individuals, teams, and organizations (Cooper, 1997a). Studies also show that it is EI (and the related aspects of practical-creative intelligence), not IQ or raw brainpower alone, that underpins many of the best decisions, most dynamic organizations, and most satisfying and successful lives (Cooper, 1997a). Other research also shows that people with high levels of EI (measured by EQ, the emotional-intelligence equivalent of IQ) experience more career success, build stronger personal relationships, lead more effectively, and enjoy better health than those with low EQ. People with high emotional intelligence motivate themselves and others to greater accomplishment.

Can EI be learned by employees? The answer seems to be yes. EI seems to be more of a set of skills than an innate capacity. As such, it should be something that people can learn and develop. Goleman (1995) believes that EI increases with age and that people tend to have better EI skills in their 40s and 50s, so that means they are learnable. Cooper (1997a) suggests that EI is learnable at almost any age. Goleman also notes that unfortunately the training provided by most organizations does not truly help employees develop their EI skills. Because most training occurs in the classroom (which is fine for reading or math or intellectual things), it doesn't work for EI because these skills are about behavior change and how individuals empathize and manage their own feelings, how well they collaborate and lead a team (Martinez, 1997).

Employees will need to spend considerable time learning how to identify and develop their EI skills in the future. One place to start the process is to review and understand tools currently used to measure EI skills. For example, the EQ-i test; the EQ-Map by San Francisco–based Essi Systems; and other assessments that measure a portion of EI skills, such as Martin Seligman's ASQ (Aptitude Sales Quotient) test used to measure optimism.

Employees should also increase their understanding of organizations that are taking it upon themselves to being emotionally intelligent by identifying the EI skills employees need to succeed and be top performers. For example, Western Union Insurance in Calgary, Alberta, Canada, is using an EI test to establish benchmarks for measuring job applicants' skills. The test the company uses is BarOn EQ-i, the first scientific EI testing instrument ever developed.

Through EI testing the company has discovered that someone in claims should have a high level of empathy (the ability to sense the feelings of others), whereas employees working in underwriting should have a higher level of independence. The company uses the results as their benchmark to rate future applicants. The information is shared with managers to help them understand the competencies the company is looking for, the people skills.

Organizations like American Express have also been trying to figure out the importance of EI skills and how exactly emotion is relevant to their business. Robert K. Cooper, author of *Executive EQ: Emotional Intelligence in Leadership and Organizations* (1997b), notes that companies have built teams, reengineered processes, and even downsized the work force for the sake of profitability and that it's now time to make sure organizations are getting the most efficient, high-performing employees possible—ones that won't "check their brains at the door."

As the latter attitude above becomes more pervasive in organizations, employees must recognize the importance of making an investment in developing EI skills. Organizations will increasingly be analyzing the EI skills of the work force as part of investing wisely in human capital. Employees must realize that EI will be vital to organizations in four areas: selection and hiring, building high-performance teams, career development and restructuring, and work force planning decisions. Major Richard Handley, head of education and training for Randolph Air Force Base, Texas, conducted research on trimming the failure rates of new air force recruiters and found that high-performing recruiters exhibited high levels of EI and that a focus on EI could shed new light on the strengths and weaknesses of teams and how employees are developed (Martinez, 1997).

Employees must recognize that improving their EI skills will provide them with the power not only to control emotions but also to perceive them. Failing to perceive them can be costly. EI skills are exactly those required of employees to effectively work in groups or teams. Employees must learn and be able to persuade, listen, exercise patience and restraint, offer sympathy, and recover from the emotional assaults common to group give-and-take. Failure to develop essential EI skills will limit employees' ability to harmoniously work with others and hinder their effectiveness in navigating the ups and downs of a contemporary career.

Career and life success in the future will undoubtedly be more connected to one's ability to react to a challenging situation with a sense of empathy and respect for others. Employees must engage their emotional intelligence and use the challenging situations as opportunities for education, wisdom, and empowerment. As Cooper (1997a) suggests, emotions are not only wellsprings of intuitive wisdom; they also provide us with potentially profitable information every minute of the day. But it isn't enough for employees to just have emotions. They have to know how to acknowledge and value feelings in themselves and in others and how to respond to them appropriately. Employees who possess and effectively use EI will have the ability to sense, understand, and effectively apply the power and acumen of emotions as a source of human energy, information, trust, creativity, and influence.

As employees form their own EI, they will most likely find that they may also increase these powers: intuition, the capacity to trust and be trusted, a sense of integrity and authenticity, an appreciation of constructive discontent, the ability to find breakthrough solutions in difficult circumstances and make sound decisions, and leadership effectiveness (Cooper, 1997a). In short, employees will be better able to reach and embrace the power of emotions instead of shying away from them.

CONCLUSION

The need for an increased focus on employee success has emerged in response to a number of changes and challenges in the world of work.

More specifically, the ever-increasing complexity of the challenges facing organizations and the pace of change both signal the escalating pressure that will be—and currently is—brought to bear on employees to either be proactive initiators of their own success or be left behind as marginal and unsuccessful contributors. To be proactive initiators of their own success in the twenty-first century, employees must understand that as the economy and their world of work continues to change in response to (1) increased globalization, (2) technological upheavals, especially in the areas of information, telecommunications, and computers, (3) cultural diversity, (4) more demanding customers, and (5) changing societal and organizational expectations, they, too, will have to change.

The intent of this chapter has been to discuss three skills we believe are and will continue to be important to employee success in the coming years. The ability to be an effective follower who can act ethically and possess emotional intelligence will, in our view, improve employees' confidence, overall portfolio of KSAOCs, and their chances of success, regardless of the task, job, situation, or organization.

In conclusion, the new employee—the "redesigned" employee—of tomorrow must understand the importance of, and take responsibility for, their own success. This means that they must go beyond understanding just their area of specialization. They must welcome change—accept it, master it, use it, and deliberately cause it. They must be proactive rather than reactive. They must be innovators rather than imitators. They must be willing to confront all constraints rather than simply accept them and the limitations on action that they impose when accepted. They must be willing to take risks rather than avoid them while striving to continually develop themselves—and manage their own careers—professionally, technically, and personally. They must be effective followers who are ethical and recognize the power and energy of emotions.

REFERENCES

Alcorn, D. S. (1992). Dynamic followership: Empowerment at work. *Management Quarterly, 33*(1) (Spring): 9–13.

Boroughs, D. L. (1995). The bottom line on ethics. *U.S. News & World Report* (March 20): 61–66.

Cooper, R. K. (1997a). Applying emotional intelligence in the workplace. *Training & Development, 51*(12): 31–38.

Cooper, R. K., & Sawaf, A. (1997b). *Executive EQ: Emotional intelligence in leadership and organizations.* New York: Grosset/Putnam.

Dessler, G. (1998). *Management: Leading people and organizations in the 21st century.* Upper Saddle River, NJ: Prentice-Hall.

Goleman, D. (1995). *Emotional intelligence.* New York: Bantam.

Keichel, W. (1993). How we will work in the year 2000. *Fortune* (May 17): 79.

Kelley, R. E. (1988). In praise of followers. *Harvard Business Review, 66*(6) (November–December): 142–148.

Lundin, S. C., & Lancaster, L. (1990). Beyond leadership . . . the importance of followership. *The Futurist* (May–June): 18–22.

Martinez, M. N. (1997). *HR Magazine, 42*(11): 72–78.

Norton, R. (1996). Job destruction/job creation. *Fortune* (April 1): 55.

Peters, T. (1992). *Liberation management.* New York: Knopf.

Russell, L. G., & Scherer, R. F. (1995). Debating ethical issues: Using the forensic model for analysis and presentation. *Journal of Management Education* (August): 399–403.

Sherman, S. (1993). A master class in radical change. *Fortune* (December 13): 82.

Sims, R. R., Cheng, H. K., & Teegen, H. (1996). Toward a profile of student software piraters. *Business Ethics, 15*(8): 839–849.

Thomas, K. W., & Velthouse, B. A. (1990). Cognitive elements of empowerment: An interpretive model of intrinsic task motivation. *Academy of Management Review* (October): 666–681.

Toffler, Alvin. (1980). *The third wave.* New York: Morrow.

2

Self-Directed Change and Learning as a Necessary Meta-Competency for Success and Effectiveness in the Twenty-first Century

RICHARD E. BOYATZIS

Change is occurring around us all of the time. Our social, political, and economic environments are changing. Watching or reading the daily news tells about minor changes and possibly signals major changes. Our organizations, careers, and jobs are changing. Organizations are bought, sold, created, and liquidated. They change their markets, products and services, and methods of operations. Careers change as organizations delay promotions, as technology eliminates or alters jobs, and as managerial philosophy changes. Some of these changes are intentional, such as when managers alter strategy and tactics according to plans or events or in pursuit of goals. Some of the change is unintentional and a consequence of other factors. For example, when a capital crisis hits Japan, it may force a change in plans for those expecting Japanese investments or those expecting to sell capital equipment in the Japanese market. There is evidence that the psychological contract between a person and their employing organization has changed dramatically in the last 20 years. The business press tells us to control our own careers because we cannot rely on our employing organization to do it. All of these conditions in our lives and careers are changing all of the time.

At the same time, we are changing. We change in the knowledge we possess and understand. We develop and use some skills and abilities, whereas others atrophy or lie in wait for some opportune moment. Our attitudes and perspectives change, at times. Some of the changes occur whether we seek, permit, or deny them. We age each day. At some point, our body changes its chemistry, and that affects our behavior, appearance, and mood. There appears some progression through various stages or cycles in our lives and careers. Some of these follow a rhythm, like the likelihood of a midlife or midcareer transition (also known as a *crisis* when we have trouble with the experience). Other changes in our lives appear or happen to us as discontinuous or unpredictable events, such as the birth of a child or grandchild, a heart attack, divorce, or death of a parent or spouse.

With all of these changes, we must adapt or we stagnate, atrophy, and die. Growth and adaptation constitute a key motivating force in life. It contributes to how we choose to expend our energy and how we choose to devote our discretionary effort. In addition, there is a perpetual human desire to take control of conditions in one's life, or at least to want to increase the degree of control, except for those who have lost all sense of hope or efficacy! Desired or intentional change can be said to be self-directed.

SELF-DIRECTED CHANGE AND LEARNING

Although there are some types of behavioral change that are biochemically induced, such as hormonal changes, most behavioral changes are self-directed. That is, if our behavior changes, it is usually the result of a decision or choice we are making. In addition, if we define *learning* as sustainable change with certain awareness of the change, then most learning is also self-directed. *Effectiveness* and *success*, which are not synonymous, require a good "fit" between the person (i.e., his or her capability or competencies, values, interests, and so forth), the demands of a specific job or role, and the organizational environment, as shown in Figure 2.1 (Boyatzis, 1982). In human resource management, common practice is to identify the competencies needed for effective job performance and then either find people with those competencies and hire them for the job or develop them in people already in the organization (Boyatzis, 1996).

Unfortunately, competencies, even those empirically determined to lead or relate to outstanding job performance, are *necessary but not sufficient* to predict performance. They help us understand *what* a person is capable of doing, and what they have done in the past, but not what they will do. In this way, competencies explain and describe *how* we perform but not *why* we perform. We need to know more about people's motivation and values to ascertain how their commitment to the objectives, organization, and work and their compatibility with the vision/mission and culture of the organization will affect their desire to utilize competencies they have or develop or enhance other competencies. In some approaches to competency research, researchers will incorporate "intent" in the definition, such as Boyatzis (1982), Spencer and Spencer (1993), and McClelland (1973). Although this helps make the competency profile needed for maximum job performance more comprehensive, it

Figure 2.1
Contingency Theory of Action and Job Performance

Best Fit = Area
of Maximum
Stimulation,
Challenge, and
Performance

Source: Boyatzis, 1982, p. 13.

still does not address the "will or desire" to use one's capabilities or develop and enhance others. Looking at competency needs for superior performance in jobs and roles in life, we are continually drawn back to the need for intentionality: What is the person's intention or reason for using the behavior and ability?

It is the same with behavioral change. Adults change themselves, especially regarding sustainable behavioral change. In other words, adults decide what or how they will change. This is also evident in terms of learning. People learn what they want to learn. Other things, even if acquired temporarily (e.g., for a test), are soon forgotten. Students, children, patients, clients, and subordinates may act as if they care about learning something, go through the motions, but they proceed to disregard it or forget it—unless it is something they want to learn and change. Even in situations where a person is under threat or coercion, a behavioral change shown will typically extinguish or revert to its original form once the threat is removed. This does not include changes induced, willingly or not, by chemical or hormonal changes in one's body. But even in such situations, the interpretation of the changes and behavioral comportment following it will be affected by the person's will, desire and

Figure 2.2
Theory of Self-Directed Change and Learning

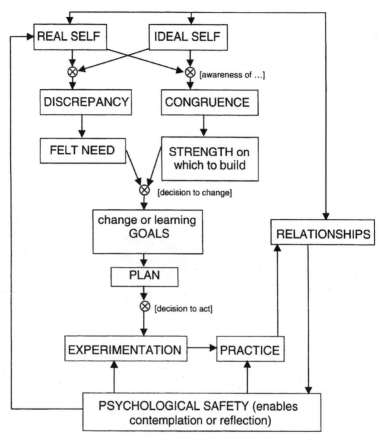

values, and motivations. In this way, it appears that most, if not all, sustainable behavioral change is intentional. *Self-directed change is an intentional change in an aspect of who you are (i.e., the Real) or who you want to be (i.e., the Ideal), or both. Self-directed learning is self-directed change in which you are aware of the change and understand the process of change.*

The process of self-directed change and learning is graphically shown in Figure 2.2. This is an enhancement of the earlier models developed by Kolb, Winter, and Berlew (1968), Boyatzis and Kolb (1969), Kolb and Boyatzis (1970a, 1970b), and Kolb (1971). The description and explanation of the process in this chapter are organized in four sections. Each section starts with a point of discontinuity—that is, a part of the process that may not, and often does not, occur as a smooth, linear event. It occurs with surprise, sometimes seeming to be stuck for long periods of time and then suddenly jumps. This is experienced as a discontinuity.

Throughout the chapter, concepts from chaos or complexity theory are used to organize and describe the model of self-directed change and learning. A person might begin the process of self-directed change and learning at any point but will often begin when he or she experiences some discontinuity that provokes awareness and a sense of urgency.

THE FIRST DISCONTINUITY: DECIDING WHO I AM AND WHO I WANT TO BE

The first discontinuity and potential starting point for the process of self-directed change and learning is the discovery of who you are and who you want to be or the decision among the choices as to what you are or what you want to be. That is, discovery of your Real Self (i.e., Who am I?) and your Ideal Self (i.e., Who do I want to be?).

Catching Your Dreams, Energizing Your Passion—the Ideal

Our Ideal Self is an image of the person we want to be. It emerges from our ego ideal, dreams, and aspirations. The last 20 years has revealed literature supporting the power of positive imaging or visioning in sports psychology, appreciative inquiry (Cooperrider, 1990), meditation and biofeedback research, and other psychophysiological research. It is believed that the potency of focusing one's thoughts on the desired end state of condition is driven by the emotional components of the brain (Goleman, 1995). Relying on earlier research on approach versus avoidance drives (Miller, 1951) and the power of conscious volition (James, 1892), it has been thought that your dreams and aspirations carry with them unconscious drives that are more powerful than conscious thought.

Our aspirations, dreams, and desired states are shaped by our values, philosophy, life and career stages, motives (McClelland, 1985), role models, and other factors. This research indicates that we can access and engage deep emotional commitment and psychic energy if we engage our passions and conceptually catch our dreams in our Ideal Self image.

It is an anomaly that we know how important consideration of the Ideal Self is, and yet often, when engaged in a change or learning process, we skip over the clear formulation or articulation of our Ideal Self image. If a parent, spouse, boss, or teacher tells us something that should be different, they are giving us *their* version of our Ideal Self; they are telling us about the person they want us to be. The extent to which we believe or accept this image determines that extent to which it becomes part of our Ideal Self. Our reluctance to accept others' expectations or wishes for us to change is one of many reasons why we may not live up to others' expectations or wishes and not change or learn according to their agenda!

We may be victims of the expectations of others and the seductive power of popularized images from the media, celebrities, and our reference groups. In his book *The Hungry Spirit: Beyond Capitalism, a Quest for Purpose in the Modern World* (1997), Charles Handy describes the difficulty of determining his ideal.

I spent the early part of my life trying hard to be someone else. At school I wanted to be a great athlete, at university an admired socialite, afterwards a businessman and, later, the head of a great institution. It did not take me long to discover that I was not destined to be successful in any of these guises, but that did not prevent me from trying, and being perpetually disappointed with myself. The problem was that in trying to be someone else I neglected to concentrate on the person I could be. That idea was too frightening to contemplate at the time. I was happier going along with the conventions of the time, measuring success in terms of money and position, climbing ladders which others placed in my way, collecting things and contacts rather than giving expression to my own beliefs and personality. (p. 86)

Awareness of the Real: Am I a Boiling Frog?

The awareness of the current self, the person that others see and with whom they interact, is elusive. For normal reasons, the human psyche protects itself from the automatic "intake" and conscious realization of all information about ourselves. These ego-defense mechanisms serve to protect us but also conspire to delude us into an image of who we are that feeds on itself, becomes self-perpetuating, and eventually may become dysfunctional (Goleman, 1985).

How does this happen in reasonably intelligent, sensitive people? One aspect is the slow, gradual development of the perception of my self-image (i.e., who I am or how I am changing). The often-cited "boiling frog syndrome" applies here. It is said that if one drops a frog into a pot of boiling water, it will jump out with an instinctive defense mechanism. But if you place a frog in a pot of cool water and gradually increase the temperature, the frog will sit in the water until it is boiled! (The author has never tried this, nor wants to, but accepts the story as it has been told.)

These slow adjustments to changes are acceptable, but the same change made dramatically is not tolerated. As a more direct example, people gaining weight or losing their sense of humor often do not see the change in their current, real self because it develops from small steps and iterative adjustments. In the recent action-adventure film *Fire down Below*, Steven Seagal (the hero) is asking a local resident in the hills of West Virginia about smoke pouring out of the ground from an abandoned coal mine. When she tells him that it has been that way for twelve and a half years, he says, "Does that ever concern anybody that the earth's on fire in the ground?" She replies, "No, no matter how strange something is, you give it enough time and it becomes normal!"

The greatest challenge to an accurate current self-image (i.e., seeing yourself as others see you and consistent with other internal states, beliefs, emotions, and so forth) is the boiling frog syndrome. Several factors contribute to it. First, people around you may not let you see a change. They may not give you feedback or information about how they see it. Also, they may be victims of the boiling frog syndrome themselves as they adjust their perception on a daily basis. For example, when seeing a friend's child after two years, you may gasp as to how fast he or she has grown. Meanwhile, the parent is only aware of the child's growth when it's time to buy new shoes or clothes or when a sudden change in the child's hormonal balance leads to previously unlikely behavior.

Second, enablers, those forgiving the change, those frightened of it, or those who do not care may allow it to pass unnoticed. Our relationships and interpersonal context mediate and interpret cues from the environment; they help us interpret what things mean. You ask a friend, "Am I getting fat?" To which she responds, "No, it is just the spread of age or normal effects of gravity." Whether or not this is reassuring to the listener, it is confusing and not providing feedback to the question asked. In a likely attempt to be nice or defend themselves against similar information about themselves, they foster or perpetuate a delusion about your current real self-image. Here is a test: Is there something about yourself that you said, when you were young, you would never let happen but has? Do you find yourself gradually taking on more characteristics and mannerisms of one of your parents? The confusing changes resulting from transitions in life or careers have typically gone unnoticed until they abruptly interfere with functioning or lead to such abhorrent behavior that everyone seeks an alternate explanation.

A third source of this confusion is that our thoughts are significantly emotionally toned by the oldest parts of our brain, not the cortex! With the melange of strange emotions or subtle affective information, we seek to reconcile the discrepant data into an image of a coherent whole person. As a way to interpret these internal states, we often pick up cues from others. In the context of others with whom you work, play, and live, you may not be the paragon of capability you think, or you may be but in the context of others who are also similar paragons—you are just another god on Olympus!

In counseling sessions with chief executive officers (CEOs) and directors of not-for-profits, I have often been surprised by their lack of seeing themselves as leaders—and, of course, I am only referring to the effective ones! They would not use the label of being a leader to describe themselves, but others around them see it as clear. Sometimes humility blocks this perception. Sometimes, it is the context mentioned above. When you are just one of the gods on Olympus, everyone has these powers. (On the planet Krypton, Superman was just another citizen without "supernatural" power.) This lack of admitting that which is obvious to others to yourself can also occur (or the illusion of it) when you have prolonged spiritual blackouts, losing sight of your core values and your philosophy.

Challenges and Paths to Awareness of Your Real and Ideal Self

There are two major "learning points" from this section helpful in engaging the self-directed change and learning process: (1) *Engage your passion and create your dreams* and (2) *Know thyself!* Both of these learning points can be achieved by finding and using multiple sources for feedback about your Real and Ideal.

The sources of insight into your Real Self can include systematically collecting information from others, such as the 360-degree feedback currently considered fashionable in organizations. This is a form of construct validity. That is, in collecting information about how you act and appear to many others (i.e., supervisor, peers, subordinates, clients/customers, family and spouse, and so forth), you are forming a consensually validated image of yourself. Whether this consensus is an image of *the real you* is based on two assumptions: (1) These others see, observe, and interact with you; and (2) you reveal yourself to them. Other sources of insight into your Real Self may come from behavioral feedback through videotaped or audiotaped interactions, such as collected in Assessment Centers. Various psychological tests can help you determine or make explicit inner aspects of your Real Self, such as values, philosophy, traits, motives, and such.

Sources for insight into your Ideal Self are more personal and more elusive than those for the Real Self. Various exercises and tests can help by making explicit various dreams or aspirations you have for the future or your life. Talking with close friends or mentors can help. Allowing yourself to think about your desired future, not merely your prediction of your most likely future, is the biggest obstacle. These conversations and explorations must take place in psychologically safe surroundings. Often, the implicit norms of one's immediate social groups and work groups do not allow or encourage such discussion. In this case, you may want to search for groups who are considering changing their lives in an academic program, career development workshop, or personal growth experience.

THE SECOND DISCONTINUITY: THE BALANCE OF PRESERVATION AND ADAPTATION

The second discontinuity and potential start of self-directed change and learning is to determine the personal balance between the aspects of yourself you want to preserve, keep, relish and those you would like to change, stimulate to grow, or adapt to your environment and situation. The awareness or realization of these components and the balance is your readiness to change.

Strange Attractors of Change and Continuity (Adaptation and Preservation)

The strange attractors of preservation and adaptation, or change and continuity, constitute a yin/yang balance and interaction regarding ourselves. That is, for a person to truly consider changing a part of himself or herself, you must have a sense of what you value and want to keep. Likewise, to consider what you want to preserve about yourself involves admitting aspects of yourself that you wish to change or adapt in some manner. Awareness of these two and exploring them exist in the context of each other.

All too often, people explore growth or development by focusing on the "gaps" or deficiencies. Organizational training programs and managers conducting annual "reviews" often commit the same mistake. There is an assumption that we can "leave well enough alone" and get to the areas that need work. Unfortunately, in the process the exclusion of one's strengths or those parts of yourself you value, enjoy, respect, and are proud of get lost. It is no wonder that many of these programs or procedures intended to help a person develop result in the individual feeling battered, beleaguered, and bruised, not helped, encouraged, motivated, or guided. The gaps may get your attention because they disrupt progress or flow (Fry, 1998).

Exploration of yourself in the context of your environment (How am I fitting into this setting? How am I doing in the view of others? Am I part of this group or organization or family?) and examination of your Real Self in the context of your Ideal Self both involve comparative and evaluative judgments. A comprehensive view includes both strengths and weaknesses. That is, to contemplate change, one must contemplate stability. To identify and commit to changing parts of yourself, you must identify those parts you want to keep and possibly enhance. In this way, adaptation does not imply or require "death" but, rather, evolution of the self.

Your willingness to change, or readiness to change, relies on articulation of this balance and *both* of these factors. In various conceptualizations of readiness to change, Guglielmino (1978) and Gugliemino, Guglielmino, and Long (1987) focus on personal characteristics that precede change and appear to help move the process along. But in the model presented in this chapter, one's readiness to change and even the desirability and commitment to the change are affected by the balancing of articulation of elements of preservation and elements of adaptation.

The model presented in this chapter describes the change process. The noun or object of the model is not "change." Change itself is not the object. The ideal or desired end result is the object of the change process. This desired end result may include aspects of the current Real Self as well as aspects of the Ideal Self not as yet achieved.

This involves juggling the present and future at the same time. That is, preservation and adaptation are present and future oriented, respectively. Preservation is "preserving the core," stability, or in Fry's (1993) terms, the "continuity." This is the part of ourselves that we value, enjoy, and want to keep and that is often built into a part of our identity, self-image (self-schema), persona, and possibly even our public image. It is, in this sense, the present! Our "continuity story" tells us about the core. You can use a life history, or autobiography, to generate your core. Meanwhile, adaptation is "stimulating change," or growth, and, in aspiring toward some Ideal Self, is pursuing something in the future.

Challenges and Paths to Your Readiness to Change

There are two major "learning points" from this section helpful in engaging the self-directed change and learning process:

1. *Identify or articulate both your strengths (those aspects of yourself you want to preserve) and your gaps or discrepancies of your Real and Ideal Selves (those aspects of yourself you want to adapt or change);* and

2. *Keep your attention on both characteristics, forces, or factors—do not let one become the preoccupation!*

Some organizational cultures will, as mentioned earlier, encourage a preoccupation with the "gaps." Some individuals have philosophies, or value orientations, that push them to focus on areas of improvement (i.e., a pragmatic value orientation or philosophy [Boyatzis et al., 1997] or a dominant underlying motive of the need for achievement [McClelland, 1985]). Some individuals have such a low level of self-confidence or self-esteem that they assume they are unworthy and distrust positive feedback and focus on negative issues and the gaps.

To achieve these learning points, build strengths into any development or learning plan on which you are working. At the same time, prevent overuse of a strength as a way to deny or avoid adaptation and change.

THE THIRD DISCONTINUITY: THE DECISION TO CHANGE

The third discontinuity and potential start of the process of self-directed change and learning is the decision to change. Prochaska,

DiClemente, and Norcross (1992) called this movement from precontemplation to contemplation of change. It is the emotional and/or intellectual next step beyond awareness of your strengths and weaknesses, discrepancies and congruencies between your Real and Ideal, that which you want to preserve and that which you want to adapt. It is during this part of the process that the direction and intention of the change effort are articulated and made explicit (i.e., conscious).

The setting of goals and creating plans to achieve those goals have been an integral part of models and theories of change processes and, in particular, self-directed processes for several centuries (Kolb & Boyatzis, 1970a). William James described the importance of conscious volition in helping one to change. Of course, even earlier Benjamin Franklin outlined a process for becoming a virtuous person by setting daily and weekly goals to increase one's virtuous behavior. McClelland (1965) formulated a motive acquisition process that included goal setting and planning, then proceeded to establish the effectiveness of these steps in motive change studies among entrepreneurs (McClelland & Winter, 1969; McClelland et al., 1972; Miron & McClelland, 1979). Kolb, Winter, and Berlew (1968), Kolb and Boyatzis (1970a, 1970b), Boyatzis and Kolb (1969), and Kolb (1971) began to elaborate the points in the process when goal setting and planning are essential for change to occur. Integration of McClelland's steps in motive acquisition and the Kolb and Boyatzis models resulted in a process called the *competency acquisition process* (Boyatzis, 1982; Spencer & Spencer, 1993).

As part of seven longitudinal studies on M.B.A.s who attempted to develop competencies which were found to be characteristics of effective and outstanding managers, development of personal learning goals and a personal learning plan were integrated into a first-semester required course. Studies showed that those M.B.A. students completing this curriculum improved significantly on almost all of the competencies shown to be related to effective and superior management (Boyatzis et al., 1995; Boyatzis et al., 1996; Boyatzis, Wheeler, & Wright, in press). Previous goal-setting literature had shown how goals affected certain changes (Locke & Latham, 1990) but had not established change on the set of characteristics distinguishing effective managerial performance. Leonard (1996) showed that M.B.A.s who set goals desiring to change on certain competencies changed significantly on those competencies as compared to other M.B.A.s.

Challenges to Deciding to Change

The one major learning point from this section helpful in engaging the self-directed change and learning process is: *Create your own personal learning agenda!*

Others cannot tell you how you should change—they may *tell* you, but it will not help you engage in the change process. Parents, teachers, spouses, bosses, and sometimes even your children will try to impose goals for change or learning. People only learn what they want to learn!

The late 1960s and early 1970s were witness to a widespread program in organizations called Management by Objectives. It was so popular that you could find books and workshops on learning by objectives, teaching by objectives, and so on and so forth. In all of these programs, there was one and only one approach to goal setting and planning taught. It specified development of behavior-specific, observable, time-phased, and challenging goals (i.e., involved moderate risk). Unfortunately, the one-size-fits-all approach lacked a credible alternative until McCaskey (1974) suggested that some people plan by "domain and direction setting." Later, Renio (nea McKee) (1990) studied how people planned personal improvement efforts inductively and discovered objectives-oriented planning style, domain and direction planning styles, and task- (or activity-) oriented planning styles. She actually found a fourth style, called "present-oriented," which appeared as an existential orientation to one's involvement in developmental activities and could be considered a nonplanning style.

The major challenge or threat to engaging in goal setting and planning is that people are already busy and cannot add anything else to their lives. In such cases, the only success with self-directed change and learning occurs if people can determine what to say "no" to in their lives to free room for new activities.

Another potential challenge or threat is the development of a plan that calls for a person to engage in activities different than their preferred learning style or learning flexibility (Boyatzis, 1994; Kolb, 1984). In such cases, a person commits to activities or action steps in a plan that require a learning style that is not their preference or not within their flexibility. When this occurs, a person becomes demotivated and often stops the activities or becomes impatient and decides that the goals are not worth the effort.

THE FOURTH DISCONTINUITY: THE DECISION TO ACT

The fourth discontinuity and potential start of self-directed change and learning is to experiment and practice the desired changes. Acting on the plan and toward the goals involves numerous activities. These are often made in the context of experimenting with new behavior. Then following some period of experimentation, the person practices the new behaviors in the actual settings within which he or she wishes to use them, such as at work or at home. During this part of the process, self-directed change and learning begin to look like a "continuous improvement" process.

To develop or learn new behavior or achieve desired changes in yourself, the person must often find ways to learn more from current or ongoing experiences. That is, the experimentation and practice do not always require attending "courses" or a new activity. It may involve trying something different in a current setting, reflecting on what occurs, and experimenting further in this actual setting. Sometimes, this part of the process requires finding and using opportunities to learn and change. People may not even think they have changed until they have tried new behavior in a work or real-world setting. Rhee (1997) studied full-time M.B.A. students over a two-year period, interviewing, testing, and video- and audiotaping them about every six to eight weeks. Even though he found evidence of significant improvements on numerous interpersonal abilities by the end of the second semester of their program, the M.B.A. students did not perceive that they had changed or improved on these abilities until after they returned from their summer internships.

Dreyfus (1990) studied managers of scientists and engineers who were considered superior performers. Once she documented that they used considerably more of certain abilities than their less effective counterparts, she pursued how they developed some of those abilities. One of the distinguishing abilities was group management, also called team building. She found that many of these middle-aged managers had first experimented with team-building skills in high school and college, in sports, clubs, and living groups. Later, when they became "bench scientists and engineers" working on problems in relative isolation, they still pursued use and practicing of this ability in activities outside of work. They practiced team building and group management in social and community organizations, such as 4-H Clubs, and professional associations in planning conferences and such.

The experimentation and practice appear most effective when they occur in conditions the person feels are safe (Kolb & Boyatzis, 1970a). This sense of psychological safety creates an atmosphere in which the person can try new behavior, perceptions, and thoughts with relatively less risk of shame, embarrassment, or serious consequences of failure.

Our relationships are an essential part of our environment. The most crucial relationships are often a part of groups that have particular importance to us. These relationships and groups give us a sense of identity, guide us as to what is appropriate and "good" behavior, and provide feedback on our behavior. In sociology, they are called *reference groups*. These relationships create a "context" within which we interpret our progress on desired changes and the utility of new learning and even contribute significant input to formulation of the Ideal (Kram, 1996). In this sense, our relationships are mediators, moderators, interpreters, sources of feedback, and sources of support and permission for change and learning! They may also be the most important source of protection from relapses or returning to our earlier forms of behavior.

In a study of the impact of a yearlong executive development program for doctors, lawyers, professors, engineers, and other professionals, Ballou et al. (in press) found that participants gained self-confidence during the program. These were people who others would think very high in self-confidence even at the beginning of the program. It was a curious finding! The best explanation came from follow-up questions to the graduates of the program. They said it was the *confidence* to change that was increased. Their existing reference groups (i.e., family, groups at work, professional groups, community groups) all had an investment in them staying the same; meanwhile, the person wanted to change. The Professional Fellows Program allowed them to develop a new reference group that encouraged change.

Based on social identity, reference group, and now relational theories, our relationships both mediate and moderate our sense of who we are and who we want to be. We develop or elaborate our Ideal from these contexts. We label and interpret our Real from these contexts. We interpret and value strengths (i.e., aspects considered our core that we wish to preserve) from these contexts. We interpret and value gaps (i.e., aspects considered weaknesses or things we wish to change) from these contexts.

Challenges to the Decision to Act

The major learning points from this section helpful in engaging the self-directed change and learning process are:

1. *Experiment and practice and try to learn more from your experiences!*
2. *Find settings in which you feel psychologically safe within which to experiment and practice!* and
3. *Develop and use your relationships as part of your change and learning process!*

CONCLUDING THOUGHT

Our future may not be entirely within our control, but most of what we become is within our power to create. Hopefully, the self-directed change and learning process described in this chapter can provide a roadmap and guidance for how to increase the effectiveness of your change and learning efforts. As a concluding thought, I offer a few lines from the 1835 John Anster translation of Goethe's *Faustus: A Dramatic Mystery*. In the Prologue to the Theater, he says:

> What you can do, or dream you can, begin it,
> Boldness has genius, power and magic in it!

APPENDIX 2.A: FORMULAS FOR SELF-DIRECTED CHANGE AND SELF-DIRECTED LEARNING

$SDC = Real^{new} - Real^{old}$ or

$SDC = Ideal^{new} - Ideal^{old}$ or

$SDC = (Real^{new} - Real^{old}) + (Ideal^{new} - Ideal^{old})$

$SDL = SDC (A + U)$

Legend

SDC = Self-Directed Change

SDL = Self-Directed Learning

A = Awareness of the change

U = Understanding the process of change

REFERENCES

Ballou, R., Bowers, D., Boyatzis, R. E., & Kolb, D. A. (in press). Fellowship in lifelong learning: An executive development program for advanced professionals. *Journal of Management Education*.

Boyatzis, R. E. (1982). *The competent manager: A model for effective performance*. New York: John Wiley & Sons.

Boyatzis, R. E. (1994). Stimulating self-directed change: A required MBA course called Managerial Assessment and Development. *Journal of Management Education, 18*(3): 304–323.

Boyatzis, R. E. (1996). Consequences and rejuvenation of competency-based human resource and organization development. In R. W. Woodman & W. A. Pasmore (Eds.), *Research in organizational change and development* (Vol. 9). Greenwich, CT: JAI Press, pp. 101–122.

Boyatzis, R. E., Baker, A., Leonard, D., Rhee, K., & Thompson, L. (1995). Will it make any difference? Assessing a value-based, outcome-oriented, competency-based professional program. In R. E. Boyatzis, S. S. Cowen, & D. A. Kolb (Eds.), *Innovating in professional education: Steps on a journey from teaching to learning*. San Francisco: Jossey-Bass, pp. 167–202.

Boyatzis, R. E., & Kolb, D. A. (1969). *Feedback and self-directed behavior change* (Working Paper 394–69). Cambridge, MA: Sloan School of Management, MIT.

Boyatzis, R. E., Leonard, D., Rhee, K., & Wheeler, J. V. (1996). Competencies can be developed, but not the way we thought. *Capability, 2*(2): 25–41.

Boyatzis, R. E., Murphy, A. J., & Wheeler, J. V. (1997). *Philosophy as the missing link between values and behavior* (Working Paper 97–3(3a)). Cleveland, OH: Case Western Reserve University, Department of Organizational Behavior.

Boyatzis, R. E., Wheeler, J., & Wright, R. (in press). Competency development in graduate education: A longitudinal perspective. *Proceedings of the First World Conference on Self-Directed Learning*, GIRAT, Montreal.

Cooperrider, D. L. (1990). Positive image, positive action: The affirmative basis of organizing. In S. Srivastva et al. (Eds.), *Appreciative management and leadership*. San Francisco: Jossey-Bass, pp. 91–125.

Dreyfus, C. (1990). *The characteristics of high performing managers of scientists and engineers.* Unpublished doctoral dissertation, Case Western Reserve University.

Fry, R. & Srivastva, S. (1992). Introduction: Continuity and change in organizational life. In S. Srivastva et al. (Eds.), *Executive and organizational continuity: Managing the paradox of stability and change*. San Francisco: Jossey-Bass, pp. 1–16.

Goleman, D. (1985). *Vital lies, simple truths: The psychology of self-deception*. New York: Simon & Schuster.

Goleman, D. (1995). *Emotional intelligence*. New York: Bantam Books.

Guglielmino, L. M. (1978). Development of a self-directed learning readiness scale (Doctoral dissertation, University of Georgia, 1978). *Dissertation Abstracts International 38*, 6467A.

Guglielmino, P. J., Guglielmino, L. M., & Long, H. B. (1987). Self-directed learning readiness and performance in the workplace: Implications for business, industry, and higher education. *Higher Education, 16*: 303–317.

Handy, C. (1997). *The hungry spirit: Beyond capitalism, a quest for purpose in the modern world*. London: Hutchinson.

James, W. (1892). *Psychology: A briefer course*. New York: Henry Holt and Company.

Kolb, D. A. (1971). *A Cybernetic model of human change and growth* (Working Paper 526–71). Cambridge, MA: Sloan School of Management, MIT.

Kolb, D. A. (1984). *Experiential learning: Experience as the source of learning and development*. Englewood Cliffs, NJ: Prentice-Hall.

Kolb, D. A., & Boyatzis, R. E. (1970a). Goal-setting and self-directed behavior change. *Human Relations, 23*(5): 439–457.

Kolb, D. A., & Boyatzis, R. E. (1970b). On the dynamics of the helping relationship. *Journal of Applied Behavioral Science, 6*(3): 267–289.

Kolb, D. A., Winter, S. K., & Berlew, D. E. (1968). Self-directed change: Two studies. *Journal of Applied Behavioral Science, 6*(3): 453–471.

Kram, K. E. (1996). A relational approach to careers. In D. T. Hall (Ed.), *The career is dead: Long live the career*. San Francisco: Jossey-Bass, pp. 132–157.

Leonard, D. (1996). *The impact of learning goals on self-directed change in management development and education*. Unpublished doctoral dissertation, Case Western Reserve University.

Locke, E. A., & Latham, G. P. (1990). *A theory of goal setting and task performance*. Englewood Cliffs, NJ: Prentice-Hall.

McCaskey, M. B. (1974). A contingency approach to planning: Planning with goals and without goals. *Academy of Management Journal, 17*(2): 281–291.

McClelland, D. C. (1965). Toward a theory of motive acquisition. *American Psychologist, 20*(5): 321–333.

McClelland, D. C. (1973). Testing for competence rather than intelligence. *American Psychologist, 28*: 1–14.

McClelland, D. C. (1985). *Human motivation*. Glenview, IL: Scott, Foresman.

McClelland, D. C., Davis, W. N., Kalin, R., & Wanner, E. (1972). *The drinking man: Alcohol and human motivation*. New York: Free Press.

McClelland, D. C., & Winter, D. G. (1969). *Motivating economic achievement*. New York: Free Press.

McKee, A. (1991). Individual differences in planning for the future. Unpublished doctoral dissertation, Case Western Reserve University.

Spencer, L. M., Jr., & Spencer, S. M. (1993). *Competence at work: Models for superior performance*. New York: John Wiley & Sons.

Miller, N. E. (1951). Comments on theoretical models illustrated by the development of a theory of conflict behavior. *Journal of Personality, 20*: 82–100.

Miron, D., & McClelland, D. C. (1979). The impact of achievement motivation training on small business. *California Management Review, 21*(4): 13–28.

Prochaska, J. O., DiClemente, C. C., & Norcross, J. C. (1992). In search of how people change: Applications to addictive behaviors. *American Psychologist, 47*(9): 1102–1114.

Rhee, K. 1997. *Journey of discovery: A longitudinal study of learning during a graduate professional program*. Unpublished doctoral dissertation, Case Western Reserve University.

3

Making Your Way in the Next Century: Taking the Career High Ground

KENNETH L. MURRELL

MANAGER'S NEW RULES AND EMPLOYEE COROLLARIES

Written a few years ago and shared with managers and students across the country, the widely circulated monograph "21 New Rules" was formulated to help prepare management and organizational leadership for the coming new century. Each rule reflects considerable changes in the world of work and business and has occurred in less than one generation. The effort to write such a list and define each new rule was in hopes of helping focus the field of management, not on what has been historically true but, instead, on a deeper examination of what is needed in the future. Rule 21, as the last developed in the earlier paper, was that "Interdependency Underlies the Transformation Process" or, in simpler terms, the game cannot be played alone. The significance of this rule should be evident for the purposes of this chapter.

The boundaries between manager and employee are becoming more and more blurred, and the physical distance of anyone to anyone else on the planet is increasingly unimportant in this expanding age of electronic communication. Borders and barriers are falling at an amazing rate, and the world is not likely to revert back to an earlier way of life in our lifetimes. So what this portends for all of us is the necessity to give careful thought to how our individual roles should change and to open ourselves to rethinking what level of responsibilities we should assume. Interdependency is necessary for transformation, as all the evidence has suggested. That will require as much from enlightened employees as from management, maybe even more as the roles continue to blur together and joint responsibilities grow. We are all needed in this new game!

Each rule can be used to help prepare employees as well as managers for the new realities about how organizations and the world of work are changing. But before any of this will have meaning, or a chance to help the employee prosper, serious soul-searching is required to be confident the work chosen is worth doing. That is the basic premise of all the self-help and career development advice and is fundamental to success in any situation. The individual's success is very important, and the organization's long-term survival and growth require it.

What follows will be a focus on each of the 21 new rules in terms of what each could mean for the success and development of the next-century employee. One thing that is fairly certain is that even the term *employee* will undergo serious change. Just as there are many large corporations (e.g., Wal-Mart) that are discarding the old language and referring to their work force as associates, partners, or colleagues, there are many organizations that will resist and even refuse to take seriously any changes in the world or the language to describe it. These companies may or may not survive. Very few organizations live much beyond 30 years. The important issue for the readers of this chapter is to determine how best to prepare for the best jobs and careers available—and to not seek the false security of any organization that promises more than it can deliver. So, no matter the language used to refer to an employee in the future, the crucial question is how to develop the skills and aptitudes needed by those organizations you may want to work for.

THE NEW TWENTY-ONE RULES FOR FUTURE EMPLOYEES

Rule 1: "Improve Quality and Lower Costs"

As the mantra of business today and for the last decade now, the globally competitive world promises no organization long-term survival unless it can continue to meet what was once an impossible standard. Our international high-tech firms are some of the best examples of organizations forcing this new reality onto everyone, and the pressure is only building. Who can deny the ability to buy a better and faster computer system each month at a lower and lower cost? Even the automobile industry is backing off the annual price increases, and without doubt, the quality of their products are improving also. So naturally the employee of the future must also be able to live up to these expectations. This creates two demands.

One is continual learning and could be called the *professional development imperative*. The second, and equally important, is the ability to manage the stress and pressure this puts on the individual (rule 18 will also touch on this later). Required of the new worker will be a sense of professional responsibility to take utmost advantage of all the development opportunities possible, even if necessary at your own expense. In addition, there is an obligation to one's profession to help it improve overall, or it, too, might be replaced, just as many traditional technical areas have that have not changed to keep pace with the world. To maintain a job in a competitive industry the reality that tomorrow's product, be it an object or a service, must be continually better and be sold at lower cost is a very recent way of thinking. In a near-zero inflationary period, particularly given the global source of labor, the pressure is on productivity—*yours*. Every day a concern about how to do more and do it better is expected. Rather than let this be a demoralizing demand, the new employee can reframe this as a way to live with it as a challenge to continually improve. This again reinforces the previously recommended suggestion to find the kind of work you care enough about to want to do it better each and every day. If you can't do this, then this improvement expectation is often perceived as too much of an external demand and stressor. If you care about your work deeply, the improvement in doing it can satisfy you. If not, then it will seem to be an effort only to please management, and there is seldom enough income possible to keep you forever doing what you do not care about. The choice of careers takes on added importance when it becomes clear that you cannot survive doing demanding work that you are not able to receive intrinsic satisfaction from.

Rule 2: "Return Customer and Product to Center Stage"

Organizations have always been very dependent on the customer and product, but for many years after the last world war, the U.S. economy, in particular, was fortunate to have a very large market with much pent-up demand and very few global competitors to share it with. Two to three decades ago, that began to change dramatically with both Japan and Germany taking market share in many major industries. That change became the wake-up call to many organizations, and a return to customer and product concern led a renewal in American competitiveness. This future is the golden opportunity for the employee who is close to the customer and instrumental in production. It is also a warning sign to staff employees and to those not essential to the production side of the business. The new employee must understand this and, to prosper, be able to offer services directly to the customer or get very closely integrated into the production process. Job security in this world depends greatly on what can be delivered to the end user or at least an internal customer who is perceived to be adding value to the process. All staff and most management positions are at risk in this restructuring period. The career tracks that can respond to rule 1 by offering more for less and that meet the requirements of rule 2 by being close to the action are those most needed in this new economy. It is too simple to say, "Only serve the customer or make the product," but in those two roles, the organization, if it is to survive, must put its best people.

No one can guarantee that those will be the highest-paying positions or those with even the most status, but it is clear this is where the needs are and will be for a long time. In both areas, it should also be clear that continuous improvement is essential, and without that dedication, job security will be greatly reduced.

Rule 3: "Organizational Power Is Created, Not Shared"

No matter how many times you hear managers say they want to share power, be careful not to assume they really want to give up the one resource they will always bemoan not having enough of. Everyone in the organization who is trying to do a job wants more power, and there is nothing inherently wrong in that unless you assume that power is a zero-sum game. In organizational life, it is possible to increase levels of influence, for example, have more power, by working together to achieve common goals rather than by competing with each other to direct the actions of the other. It's called *cooperation*, and it is vital to the success of the larger organization. It is not a zero-sum game in principle. We have learned to think of it that way only because so much of what we pay attention to is limited in nature. True, we cannot all be paid mega-bucks, but if we share an increasingly larger pie, as they do at Microsoft, for example, many could retire as independently wealthy before they reach 40. It is also possible to have a group of employees all above av-erage and who help each other and themselves get better each day; in fact, that is what often accounts for firms like Intel, and it's success. Influence is infinite, and so is power if used to respond to the world of needs and not just used to battle over the finite physical resources. Cre-ativity is a natural gift, and so are the productivity gains made by learn-ing to work together. The role of the employee is to demonstrate daily the laws of empowerment, where more is possible with less and people learn to work together better. Managers, in particular, need help in this area because of the often overly political world they have to live in.

Productivity gains do occur, and when that happens, a test of the em-powerment principle of creating power or influence has also occurred. The new employee may do well to keep teaching these lessons to those too far away from the real work to know that this is how progress is made. Managers too often are frightened by true empowerment because they have less experience in working together cooperatively; but given experience, they can learn that not everything happening in the organization is a political struggle over limited resources.

Rule 4: "Progress Is Subjective—Quality Is Not"

In a world of change the idea of progress itself is in a state of flux. The term *postmodern* reflects a serious questioning of what progress is all about and questions the idea that growth is always better. What is less debatable is that each of us, as producers or consumers, both knows and values what quality is. We all want the feel and sense of quality in what we do and what we buy, particularly if it's affordable. In this is the key to another expanded role for the employee of tomorrow. The future will require more candid and timely feedback about the nature of work and the products produced in the organizations of which we are a part. Our voices as employees and central stakeholders in the future of the firm require us to share our views and not hold back. In fact, we may have to take a much stronger role in arguing for quality and build higher expectations on what we can produce to ensure that we have a career in the future. The role of whistle-blower and corporate conscience will be expanded, and smart companies will build in more protections for those who disagree with current actions that threaten future viability of the firm.

As corporate loyalty is waning and fear of job loss increases, it will be necessary to structure in rewards and training for employees so as not to let shoddy products or inferior service be maintained. It is in the best interests of the work force to help develop quality, even sometimes more so than the temporary managers or the fickle stockholders will argue for. Career success depends greatly on organization long-term success. Employees who want to invest in an organization cannot do as well with a short-term attitude, even if it is all the job can promise. Unless the commitment is made to help build long-term quality, the employee not only risks job loss; even worse, he or she may be risking his or her reputation in a field that is unforgiving if someone hurts the reputation of the field itself. Quality of work is what keeps the employee employable and the company in the game for the long term.

Rule 5: "Global Thinking Really Leads Local Action"

As organizations become more and more global in their thinking, so, too, must employees. If for no other reason than to better know their competitors, employees should be aware of who is out there to benchmark against as concerns the development of world standards of work in their field. This is being done around the world as other societies look to the United States to learn from; we also have a lot to learn and should be equally concerned about how quality work is performed around the world. Technological breakthroughs make the competition far more close at hand than it's ever been. The amount of both offshore electronic-aided work and the amount of employee travel make a very different world than existed even just a decade ago. The movement of labor across country frontiers is a quickly emerging trend. Now is the time to learn about worldwide labor conditions while we still have the natural advantage of a well-trained labor force. That advantage is not predicted to last much longer; so tomorrow may be too late to learn how and with whom to compete.

The other part of this new rule is that as a highly trained professional there may be a large market for your skills outside the United States. Selling your knowledge and expertise overseas may be a very good way of learning more about world-class expectations and also provide options if the local market goes into a slump. If a company gains by exporting, why should not you as an employee also test the world value of what you have to offer? In doing this, you also gain significant education and professional development that can easily make you a much more valuable employee.

Rule 6: "Continuous Quality Improvement Seeds Global Development"

To go beyond where we are is the natural human quest and the path of development for both the organization and the society of which it is a part. For the individual employee, this is the journey that can help make meaning out of each day's toil and effort. The commitment to quality, and the continuous improvement of it, is the definition of the principle of *Kaizen* as developed so well by the Japanese following their defeat in World War II. The desire to rebuild their society and to never again suffer through a devastating war keeps them focused and driven as a nation. That same kind of development drive is inherent in all societies, and when organized and used well, it not only changes that single society—it changes the world.

To be a part of that grander vision and to play even a small role in that transformation is what has kept many people growing and expanding their professional potential. This is the vital energy or spirit, if you will, that makes it worthwhile to commit to an organization for a major part of one's week and eventually a large part of one's life. As the work force of tomorrow commits to that effort, the state of the world lies in their hands. Their family and local community are where the value of that commitment is most likely to show. Far more important than the politicians and chief executive officers (CEOs) of the world, this daily work of so many millions, and globally billions, of people is what keeps the world going. Each piece of special effort is necessary to support the whole, and only as each employee reaches for the best level of quality possible will the future prosperity and development of the planet be assured. This may seem like a heavy weight to lay on the working person, but it has always been the case that the world survives only off the effort of the many and not the glory of a few. This reality is not what sells newspapers, but as you travel around the world, the one common experience is that this is a world full of basically good people getting up each day to take care of their family and to do their jobs. The world moves forward based on the positive involvement of the many and not the symbols or images of the few.

Your best efforts as an employee are vitally needed to answer the question of what we need to know about this process and how it will help us better prepare for employment in the next century. The improvement of the whole will only come from the efforts of the many, and your role in this needs to be seen more clearly for what it represents. Take the time to honor and respect your individual efforts and contributions and do likewise for all the other individuals you come in contact with. Appreciate what you have offered and what you can continue to offer as you yourself grow and develop in your job. This continuous process of improvement should not be a punishment but a blessing, as it represents the potential for the evolution of our very fragile species. Enjoy and appreciate each small step in that direction of development and schedule time to celebrate the contribution you and your organization are making.

Rule 7: "Short-Term Thinking Destroys Quality and Delays Development"

If every employee allows himself or herself to get caught by the short-term disease of modern management nonthinking, then the idea of sustainable organization is out of the question. Not only that, but the chance of ever reaching the performance levels desired will be eliminated in all but the shortest of measures. The employee group, often better than anyone, is fully aware when the short-term results are sacrificing the longer-term performance by which the total organization will be measured. Again, management has a difficult role to play in a position where they lack much needed information. Management and executive reward systems also force much of this short-term thinking, and it is more than Wall Street that is at fault. It is necessary for the employee of the future to know enough about business or the economic environment of the organization to be able to express the concerns necessary that reflect a longer-term view of the organization. Saturn Motors as well as other progressive organizations are even today insisting on their work force having an education that in many ways resembles what M.B.A.s are getting. These companies want the employees to have a bigger picture, not only to better understand the larger world but also to help managers see the worlds in which they work better. The only way to break down the walls between managers and workers is to help them understand each other's language.

Employees of tomorrow must become much better at articulating and speaking for the values of a longer-term perspective when it comes to business and other decisions. In the past this would have been frowned upon by many, and the assumption would have been that the workers in no way could know enough to have a voice in determining how the organization should be run. Today that attitude is sadly outdated; the emergence of "open book" management methods, where all the corporate data are shared, and the modern communication revolution that makes that so much more feasible is dramatically changing the expectations of employees.

Rule 8: "Appreciation Precedes Problem Identification"

To look for the reasons why one goes to work creates a very different experience than spending hours trying to justify calling in sick. It is not that there are no good reasons to stay away from work; it's just that the attitude you take in as an employee, more than anything else, will affect the kind of work experiences you are to have. To find and value the intrinsic rewards and challenges of your work life will give you and those around you a much healthier outlook and create a reality you can find value in. From the principle of first looking for strengths in order to gain the ability and commitment to address the limits or problems has emerged a whole field of organizational change. This field is called *appreciative inquiry*, and as it has been practiced by numerous organizations, the results are quite similar. People are able to get excited again about why they wanted to work in the first place. The meaning of the daily commitments to an organization was rediscovered, and from this, the ability to help change the situation was created. The response to problem issues was not then grounded in denial but instead emerged out of an appreciation of what in the organization had been worthy of care and concern. People were much more able to work together, and the spirit of cooperation increased when the blaming behavior of a problem-oriented attack was reduced.

In the experience of a single employee, the ability to work from one's strengths is a much more affirming and empowering position. It is not to deny problems and limits, but it is to approach them from a position of hope and optimism rather than cynicism or despair. It is one of the hallmarks of being able to work well with others in difficult and demanding times. For the next-century employee, these traits can be very essential in career development, as they have been shown to be in organization development.

Rule 9: "Component Optimization May Destroy System Optimization"

A most important lesson for the next-century employee is that the star in the game does not always help the team to win. Team effort is the expected norm for next-century organizations, but in no way is this to diminish the importance of the individual. The issue is context, and the rule is that it is impossible to compete effectively to reach world-class performance if the actions of one detract from the success of the whole. The game is much more complicated than any sports analogy can match, and even the notion of war, which is where strategy and tactics were born, is thought of as more static and slower to adjust to world changes than business. The new realities demand change at all levels, and the optimizing of one part of the organization does not necessarily imply the high performance of the whole. Employees must be able to recognize the organization as the larger team that extends beyond their own operational team. Organizations are very complex, and in order to add value as a single employee or part of a team, the larger picture is often very important to understand.

The role of the new employee is much more dependent on grasping this larger picture, and this is just one more place where an expanded educational background is necessary. So is the notion of a continually learning employee, since there is no indication at all that either the pace or the complexity of the global economy will be reduced. The new employee must understand basic systems theory and the role of the parts in relationship to the whole of the organization. This is not an overly complicated thought, but it does take an ability to look well beyond your individual role and to develop as an employee who can see the whole system and understand the elements of it.

Rule 10: "Flatter Organization Design Can Enhance Power"

As every good manager is learning, the key to next-century high performance is empowerment and the delayering of the organization. What they all do not know, as well, is that this can be a creator of power in that the overall organization can be much more effective only when they and the employees can both become more powerful. New employees need to learn how to show management this in deeds, their own responsible behavior, not in words only. The win-win of empowerment is something as important for the work force to teach management as vice versa. Both groups must be able to learn these lessons and to build on them for the success of the whole. For employees, the goal is to find the type of organization and a corporate culture that allows for them to be successful as well as their managers. In both successes, the organization builds its success.

The key to success in this setting is not working up the proverbial chain of command but instead to create the commands, as in work teams, throughout the organization that provide the challenge and the opportunity for career development via the route of high performance. Being a part of a world-class team and doing the job as well as it is done anywhere in the world constitute the only source of security now outside of inheriting great wealth. The advantage of being able to deliver high performance is that in that arena it is a seller's market, and your success in one organization can easily lead to another if necessary. Your mobility and economic security are tied directly to your levels of performance in your current job. Doing well and building the reputation as world class along with the ability to work with others equally talented are what provide you with options. In the new economic reality, there are no guarantees of lifelong employment, but there are a variety of opportunities where skills and abilities can be developed. That is what is attracting the best employees today, and there is no reason to expect a change in the future. Learn to go after the jobs in flattened structures with development opportunities assured. Create the career power that comes from ability and marketable skills. Consider all that you do carefully from this perspective and help your own children learn this because it is a new world, and the old assumptions of the industrial paradigm don't hold up any longer. Your success depends directly on what you can do and how well you can do it working with others. More than today, those work relationships will be with peers and colleagues, and your experiences of joint success will be the factors that keep you employed.

Rule 11: "Organizational Development Is Moving Horizontally and Bottom Up"

The idea that the worker of the future will not only be far more responsible for organization structure but also very involved with setting the culture of the organization may sound a little far out for many today. However, the trend line is definitely in this direction, and the efforts to get all of the employees involved in the change process are occurring on many different fronts. Large-scale change efforts are being designed today under the titles of "Future Search Conference Design," "Real-Time Strategic Change," and "Participatory Democracy," to name a few. Each of these change efforts is as concerned with moving the change process out and down as it is in getting top-level buy-in.

The goal is to mobilize the employees in the change effort, and few things would more positively impact one's career than a period of time serving a leadership role in one of these change programs. Underlying each of these models of change is an assumption of collaborative work skills and employees with a sense of the potential for positive change in the organization.

The next-century employee should not only be open to change but, even more so, be able to help lead it. This is a fairly radical departure from the old notion of the employee as a set of hands. The emphasis now and increasingly in the future will be on the employee as a total person with leadership skills never before as in demand or as expected. The employees able to meet this type of challenge will be seen as very valuable to the organization that knows it must either change or risk its very survival. An employee would do well to pick up these change skills and develop the attitudes found to be helpful in developing change programs. There are tons of books and articles available on the subject and good training and educational opportunities all over the United States, but the decision to get yourself ready for this dramatically different set of responsibilities lies with you, the future employee. It could well mean a significant difference in one's career to be able to lead change versus the traditional attitude of just waiting to be changed or, even worse, out of ignorance, being positioned to primarily resist change.

Rule 12: "Ambiguity Is a Catalyst for Development"

Many of the new roles for the employee of the future are unknown at this point or at most are only being guessed at. This does not mean the employee today should sit around confused or waiting to be told what to do in specific terms to prepare for tomorrow. One of the first things any professional has to learn is how to deal with increasing degrees of ambiguity and uncertainty, and that demand is now being placed on every employee. The world is changing so fast that rules and roles are also undergoing constant change. What this means is that employees often have to be able to create their own best estimates of what is needed and how to go about getting it with the help of many others. In ambiguity, two things are confused: the goals and the means to achieve them. Professional workers of the future must at least know why they are working, their own goals, and how to develop the skills (means) to accomplish their goals. This, then, is the start of the process to get out of ambiguity and help them and the organization discover clarity. This process starts with every single individual, no matter where he or she is in the organization. It moves out from the individual to the team and to the total organization as the questions are asked and leadership emerges to help guide the discussion of why and how people are supposed to work in this particular organization.

Ambiguity is thus not allowed to detract from the organization's ability to perform. Achieving that state of clarity is absolutely dependent upon individual employees knowing why they are working (goal) and how to continually develop their skills to help both themselves and their organization. In this way and using a process that forces everyone to answer these two essential questions, the threat of not acting in an ambiguous situation is reduced, and the organization is able to move forward while checking its assumptions for success. That is why the questions raised are useful as catalysts to determine both the vision and the mission of the organization, and a valued employee of the future will be able to also do this for himself or herself.

Rule 13: "Conflict and Diversity Are Natural Assets"

The idea that conflict can be an asset is not always easy to relate to, but for the employee of tomorrow, it is a very important concept. In any organization, and in high-performance systems in particular, there are many natural disagreements. Employees with strong views are essential to organizations if their views are based on experience and knowledge. When the inevitable differences emerge, it is critical that employees of the future not back away or give up their responsibility but instead be able to present their views and their different perspectives well. The conflicts over ideas and strategies are potential positive factors given that the employee is skilled at conflict management and dispute resolution. Creativity and new approaches come from differences if handled maturely, and if not, the one better idea or plan may not be developed. Conflict in this case is not about personalities or petty politics but about substantive issues and important differences in the best answers. Very often the final best answer is yet to be discovered, and it cannot be found if all ideas and thoughts are not put on the table. This requires employees who can carefully articulate and explain their or their team's thinking and be persuasive when need be to help the organization make the best decision. This is a valuable skill to have, as, again, one's career can be enhanced if conflict skills are developed as learned abilities and practiced at the right time in the right way.

This potential for conflict and the development of creativity is assisted by the natural diversity that needs to exist in any growing organization. Particularly in this culture, the issue of diversity is very important. Some would argue that one of society's most important assets is its abundant diversity. Diversity is what gives us a rich multitude of options about how to see and how to act in ways the world values. To take the question of differences as challenges to create better options, or what might be called third ways, is very important as developed skill sets for the employee of the future. The employee of the future must be comfortable not only with differences in age, gender, race, and ethnicity but also with political outlooks and spiritual practices. Beyond a comfort with diversity, the employee needs to learn how to thrive and be creative in a multicultural and richly diverse world. In this setting, much can be achieved, and there should be no incentives to take the easy route. Instead, professional integrity should help the employee work with others to develop better approaches and ways of meeting new-world challenges. The excitement of practicing these new skills is that they are exactly the ones needed by the new global realities. The demands are high to be able to work with others who are very different from you but who care deeply about the organization and its potential. This potential is reached when out of the many different ways the better way is forged through long and intense involvement and open sharing of views. In a word, trust across barriers must be developed by the employees who can be confident in their own self and who have the ability to reach out to others for their mutual benefit and service to a greater cause.

Rule 14: "Working Smarter Is Much Smarter"

The old paradigm taught each of us to work hard and an honest day's work for an honest day's pay. That lesson was likely drilled into our heads every day as we grew up. We heard it from parents, teachers, media, and nearly everywhere we turned. We were told this is a sacred fact, and because the same message was given to the generation before and the generation before that, many of us learned the lesson well. We internalized it, and most likely, we have or are trying to instill the same message in the next generation.

Guess what: It is only half the lesson we need for ourselves and to teach the next generation. Now we all must be learning to work smarter as well. Now the operational slogan is, To work smart and be more productive each day. The more productive, the more the pay and satisfaction. This can only occur as we learn not only to work hard but to work much, much smarter.

New ways of doing work or doing less work through efficiencies to be created that improve output are what is important. It is no longer good enough to give good, honest effort. It is now critical to find the ways to do it better and to stop doing it if it is not value added. Efforts that demonstrate thought—not just repeated hard work—are what will be rewarded more and more. In fact, the ultimate reward for many is to take the good ideas and the mental contributions to someone else or organize a new organization that itself has the capacity to work smarter and not just harder. Entrepreneurship is where many of the work-smarter proponents are going—and going fast in many industries where the barriers to entry are low. The old barrier of huge capital costs for plant and equipment is falling fast, and the personal computer revolution linked to the age of the Internet makes much more possible. The work-smarter employees are finding out that it is not necessary to stay employed in a company that is stuck in the age of work hard–only thinking or, more accurately, the shortage of thinking. If one wants a good job, then the skills necessary are to bring to the organization both a work ethic and an ability to improve the organization. This is sometimes accomplished by emphasizing that performance quality is valued more than the quantity of work that is done.

Rule 15: "Training/Education Is the Prime Infrastructure"

To teach managers the importance of continuous organizational learning is easier than to convince them of the need to see training as investing rather than spending the corporation's limited resources. The new employee needs to be able to help management see the importance of training as investing in the company's capacity to learn. This can be done in several ways, from documenting the cost savings and new ideas coming from training to making special efforts to demonstrate the values of cross-training and shared training experiences. Employees of the future must also be able to see themselves as decision makers in terms of how to invest their own limited resources in their continuous learning. Lifelong learning is much more than a saying; it is a philosophy and a way of staying ahead and employable in a rapidly changing world. Employees need to be able to contract and negotiate with their organization for the investments necessary for their development or look elsewhere for the kind of environment where they are seen as worth investing in. In the next century, this will become even more critical as the terms of employment shift from long-term security to enhanced opportunity. Given opportunities the new employees must have the skills and abilities for the success of the organization as well as their own career success.

Viewing education and training as long-term skill building rather than shorter-term credentialing, as it is too often seen, is very important. The employee of the future will be expected to have the skills and experiences necessary, and yet, without help from the organization, that is not always possible. So in addition to becoming a better learner, the new employee must also become a better negotiator. This requires very different skills than a previous generation of employees had, as they could wait for a benevolent company or training office to figure out for them what they needed. Tomorrow's companies are not likely to move out of any motive that is not bottom-line oriented. Since it is very possible that the training office may have been replaced or outsourced, it is employees' job to determine what they need and how to go about getting company support for it. And if company support is not there, employees of the future better size up if they should go for it anyway. Waiting to be told how one should be developing is not an option for the employee of the future. You'd better be proactive, educated about the options, and determined to get what you need, when you need it. Professional development should of course be supported by the company, but don't bet on it. The risk to your own career development is too high to wait for some well-meaning person or office to finally recognize what you should have been able to see all along. You, like everyone else—and that includes those who would like your job—need continual learning and development. It is the investment in *you* that will pay off for years to come. Learn to make it happen in one way or the other. In this there is no other choice.

Rule 16: "Strong Individuals Build Strong Teams"

In this rule it is important to understand that you need not give up your own unique talents and abilities to be a part of a high-performing team. In fact, it is just the opposite. High-performance teams cannot be created by weak individuals or by those who hold back their own capabilities just to fit in. Equally true is that no team can perform well if it isn't able to get the best from each individual. The employee needs to learn these rules not just from the books of theory that explain them but from the experience of working on high-performance teams. This team experience can come from anywhere, with sports or other outside team activities as two good possibilities, but the employee needs the experience of success while part of a strong team. In this way, it is possible to learn how much stronger one can be when on a team of other strong and capable people. Many professional athletes understand this well and even will go so far as to only compete with other strong teams in order to keep their own personal skills and strengths improving.

Teamwork requires additional skills to what you have as an individual, but it should not expect you to limit or sacrifice talents and abilities you are good at. Team success takes much more from you in that you have to be able to see a larger picture. This is very similar to many of the rules that expect additional and new responsibilities from the employee of the future. You will be expected not only to learn from others but also to help create shared leadership systems where everyone is expected to bring all their talents and abilities to the game. In the increasingly competitive world, our potential comparative advantage lies in two areas. First, as discussed in rule 13, diversity is a unique strength that we in North America are blessed with an abundance of. Second, when we can work together as a team and bring out all of the unique strengths this diversity offers, we can put together organizations that can outperform any in the world. With these advantages, strong individuals will be able to offer their talents along with a team of capable others to create exciting careers in areas where we will be able to maintain a leadership role in a very competitive world.

Rule 17: "Managers Are Not Necessary for Success, But Management Is"

One of the most difficult rules for management to accept is that their jobs are important, but their titles are meaningless, and the assumption that employees can't do these jobs is wrong. Management, more and more, is not about titles or special privileges for a few but the shared leadership roles of the many. Layers of managers are not necessary when everyone is made clear about how important the jobs are for everyone to have. This means that the next-century employee better be able to step up to the responsibilities previously reserved for supervisors and managers and to manage in a team environment with others. Working in this way without a lot of close supervision is just one more example of the professionalization of all workers and the reluctance to spend money on one group of people to simply look over, for example, supervise, another group of people. The economics of this old industrial-management model paradigm are not working today and will be even more obsolete tomorrow. Organization can't afford two salaries for the work of one person. Self-management principles after over 30 years of being promoted as the more humane way of managing are now also being accepted as good economic principles.

What this tells the new employee is to get an education in the basics of management and to help develop the kind of organization that will be able to succeed globally by relying on more multitalented and more self-managing employees. This does not mean that there will be no more managers but that their roles will continue to change dramatically and the partnerships between managers and workers in developing the organization will continue to grow. Managers should become allies and the coaches and resources needed to help develop the organization's capabilities. But the job now requires more partnering skills on the part of both management and the new employee. Self-management does not mean autonomy but, instead, an even greater ability to work with others. Those new employees able to learn this will be the ones with options and potential careers in those organizations more likely to succeed in the future.

Rule 18: "Spiritual and Family Support Is Essential for High Performance"

Given all the new pressures on the employee and all the changes expected to be made, the need for considerable support is undeniable.

From the research on change, we know that change is managed better by those organizations that have strong support systems. These are places to go and things in one's life that offer care, understanding, and the help needed in formulating ways to adapt to high levels of stress. The two places where these things are most often found are in the home, as in family, and in a person's own unique spiritual practices and beliefs. In parts of the world where stress levels are the highest, it has been noted that those with the most resilience and often the most success at getting the jobs done are those who have these two support systems firmly developed. In organizations that seek high-performance outcomes the notion of community often plays a very important role in stress management and in helping employees deal with the tremendous changes they are engaged in.

Employees must learn not only to select their organizations well in terms of this supportive community environment but also to be responsible for building their own personal support systems in ways that work best for them. The need for new skills for the new employee places a great deal of pressure on the employee, and for this reason, a strong support base is essential. As with the issue of professional development, new employees will be expected to take advantage of corporate resources to help develop themselves but also to do what is necessary on their own in order to build their own career foundation and stress management program. Both in the family and in the spiritual domain, issues of privacy are to be protected, but the sharing of these values with others in one's work community, as long as it is not coerced, seems to be a natural and useful activity. New employees have a lot demanded of them, and they deserve the necessary support to help them achieve. Much of that support will need to be built, and if it is not, the new demands might create pressures beyond the employee's coping skills. If this occurs, all the other systems will fail, and thus what seems a private issue becomes a priority concern that should be given due attention. As an employee in the future, it will be expected that you can build the support system needed for long-term performance as well as professional growth.

Rule 19: "Leadership Is Learning Focused, But Responsibility Is Built"

No matter where you work in the organization, one of your most important jobs is to learn. This is as true for the senior executive as it is for the newest employee. And in this learning principle is also a new rule for management in that it needs to learn how to develop leadership throughout the organization. In doing this the organization will be strengthening itself for the globally competitive next century. The emphasis must be placed on building the responsibilities again throughout the organization and to prepare one's self for the dynamic changes that will grow even more demanding in the next century.

What this tells the employee to prepare for has been repeated in several earlier rules, but in this one, the emphasis is on building the leadership skills that work best from a collegial or peer level and where influence often comes without formal authority. There have been several good and very popular books written on this subject since it is one of those obvious trends of management that we need to learn much more about (see, for example, Quinn, 1996; Herman, 1994; James, 1996). The opportunity for employees now is to start developing their leadership skills and to start taking on more and more responsibility. In this way, they stand a good chance of setting themselves up as role models for others to emulate. Corporations wanting to practice this rule will be looking for employees who can operate in this manner, and that is where they will be looking to create their shared leadership models. The demands in this role are many, but it can work if it does help create a sense of responsibility for everyone to offer their own leadership capabilities and not to overly rely on just a few leaders in the organization. To learn how to do this effectively is a tremendous challenge to the organization and will need a lot of leadership, particularly at the employee level.

Rule 20: "Transformational Leadership May Be Invisible, But the Results Are Not"

In the development of employees of the next century, the choice of the organization they opt to work for will be absolutely critical to their career success. The hallmark employees should seek in choosing a successful organization is one where its leadership speaks in terms of results and not just a good public relations department. As recent research is indicating, the charismatic and heroic leadership examples are not what explains the success and staying power of what are called *visionary companies*. Those are the companies who have been the most successful over a long period of time, where their leadership has evolved internally and is a core ideology that everyone in the organization believes in. The top-level management is not seen as the reason for the firm's success but only as one part of a larger picture where dedication and skills at all levels are viewed as crucial. In this way, leadership is more diffuse and often far more shared than the one central-figure model of an all-powerful CEO or board chair. In these settings the employee is allowed to offer his or her own best and to develop the unique leadership talents needed to help form a long-term successful career while making the maximum contribution to the organization.

Organizations that develop transformational leadership at all levels are developing the sustaining capacity to grow and develop over the long term and not just during the reign of a particularly charismatic executive.

This offers the employee a special advantage in that the very skills demanded in these settings are going to be more and more sought after by other organizations in the future. Transforming leadership has the additional advantage of changing the leaders as much as anyone, and this again helps to create career strengths that will last. You stand to gain the most in terms of career development by working within organizations that make a commitment to help *you* also develop as a leader.

Rule 21: "Interdependency Underlies the Transformation Process"

As mentioned in the introduction, this final rule summarizes all the new skills and abilities needed by the employee of the next century. That employee must be able to work with others in a shared leadership role to re-create the idea of what an organization is. In fact, the most accurate description for all of this is that the new employee must be able to work with others to create work communities. In these communities, work will be achieved that everyone cares enough about to invest themselves in the process and to develop their professional talents as the organization evolves. The linkage with others and the culture of work created that gives a person back the dignity and meaning of work will be rewards in themselves. The new employee will gain the pride of also being able to create with others something beyond just a job. In this way, the nature of work itself will be transformed, and the experience will be transforming to more than just the individual employee.

It should be clear to everyone that there are some tremendous social problems that we must deal with effectively. This culture needs a transforming experience as it looks beyond the present and develops expectations for a better future. That future can be more easily developed by people with the transforming experiences that new organizations are capable of providing. The new employee model assumes the ability to change, to continue learning, and to be a part of the leadership process that makes transformation possible. The next century offers much in the ways of opportunities and exciting challenges well beyond the narrow definition of a job. The potential exists to work toward the improvement not only of the organization we choose to work within but also the society into which we were born or have migrated. Now we have a chance to help create what we feel is a much better world, not only in our work life but also in society at large.

SUMMARY AND CONCLUDING COMMENTS

Managers have been forewarned that there are many serious changes that will have to occur if their organizations are to remain competitive. They also know there will be less of them and their roles will be significantly different. For employees of the future, the messages are similar, except there will be many more of them and their professional responsibilities will be greatly enlarged. Many books have been written for the new manager, but only a few describe the new employees' roles. To correct this imbalance, this chapter has tried to focus carefully on the new employee role. Some of the major points of concern are as follows:

• Doing more with less will be expected.
• Empowerment will be necessary and for everyone.
• Quality concerns will drive global competitiveness.
• Long-term development requires employee advocacy.
• Organization development and renewal need you.
• Uncertainty, change, and diversity are the givens.
• Leadership and learning is what it is all about.

This summary list cannot reflect all 21, rules but the essence is here—particularly with the last message about the importance of continual learning. The leadership/learning responsibility is the most important message in all of this. The organizations of the future, in this society in particular, will be expected to have much greater leadership capacity throughout the system.

Employees will be expected to enlarge their professional responsibilities and even to take on leadership roles in the changing of the organization. Their voices are needed if companies are to respond to their customers and to build toward long-term success. The empowerment of the work force is not an option, and neither is it something that can be mandated from above. Conditions and reward structures will have to change to reflect the needs of the future and not the paradigms of the past.

Organizations will only survive when they develop the strengths and abilities of all in the system and not just a few. And those are the organizations that employees should be seeking out. Before employees can possibly succeed in the next-century work environment, they must develop the team and interpersonal skills to perform in a complex and fast-changing world. In this way, their technical and other skills will have a chance to be used. The employee of tomorrow will in many ways be expected to understand the larger picture and be of aid and assistance as the organization responds to its changing environment. These, in many ways, are new roles for the average employee, and the important lesson is not only to respond to these changes but to recognize that these new demands are just a few of what will be a very long list of growing responsibilities.

The key to success is captured in the final point above: Keep learning and, in particular, keep learning how to lead and assist with the continual change process. Technical competency is in many ways assumed to be existing in each and every employee; the critical difference now is in *what else* an employee can bring to the system and *how* he or she can work with others to see it used well. Change is the name of the game in this increasingly global marketplace, and no one is predicting this will do anything but increase. As a successful employee of the future, be prepared for the challenges you will be offered. In so doing there is also a good chance you may improve the quality of your work life *and* your personal life.

REFERENCES

Bellman, Geoffrey M. (1996). *Your signature path: Gaining new perspectives on life and work.* San Francisco: Berrett-Koehler.

Herman, Stanley M. (1994). *A Force of one: Reclaiming individual power in a time of teams, work groups, and other crowds.* San Francisco: Jossey-Bass.

James, Jennifer. (1996). *Thinking in the future tense: Leadership skills for a new age.* New York: Simon & Schuster.

Murrell, Kenneth L. (1997). Emergent theories of leadership for the next century: Towards relational concepts. *Organization Development Journal, 15* (Fall): 35–42.

Pinchot, Gifford, & Pinchot, Elizabeth. (1993). *The intelligent organization: Engaging the talent & initiative of everyone in the workplace.* San Francisco: Berrett-Koehler.

Quinn, Robert E. (1996). *Deep change: Discovering the leader within.* San Francisco: Jossey-Bass.

Seiling, Jane Galloway. (1997). *The membership organization: Achieving top performance through the new workplace community.* Palo Alto, CA: Davies-Black Publishing.

Stack, Jack, with Bo Burlingham. (1992). *The great game of business: Unlocking the power and profitability of open-book management.* New York: Doubleday.

4

Self-Directed Careers

ROBERT M. FULMER AND PHILIP A. GIBBS

TAKING CHARGE

> "Cheshire Puss," she began . . . "would you tell me please, which way I ought to walk from here?" "That depends a good deal on where you want to get to," said the Cat. "I don't much care where," said Alice. "Then it doesn't matter which way you walk," said the Cat. "So long as I get somewhere," Alice added as an explanation. "Oh, you're sure to do that," said the Cat, "if only you walk long enough."
>
> —Lewis Carroll, *Through the Looking Glass*

You have to know where you want to go in order to get there. Unfortunately, many of us are like Alice in *Through the Looking Glass*. Frequently, we let the marketplace determine our career choices. "Where are the jobs that pay the best?" "What are the most attractive opportunities?" "What are our friends doing?" These are the questions many ask when considering career options. This is like a company trying to develop its business strategy by looking only to the external environment without considering what its external strengths and weaknesses are and what its mission is.

Every good career plan starts with a set of goals. Just like a business, we need to determine what our personal mission is, what our life goals are, and what interests, skills, knowledge, and abilities we possess or can acquire. First, we must realize that a career is a marathon, not a sprint. To sustain a career in the long run, we need to enjoy what we are doing. The key is to determine what we have fun doing, what makes us feel good about ourselves. Then the challenge becomes figuring out how to make a living doing it. Second, we should realize that life is not too short. In fact, most of us have several different careers in our lifetimes.

CHANGING TERMS OF EMPLOYMENT

Contemporary challenges of mobilization, technology, diversification, and downsizing have provided opportunities and stresses for career management that were unknown a generation ago. Corporate restructuring has resulted in a reduction of jobs in the *Fortune* 500 companies by 25 percent. This means there are 4 million fewer employees in *Fortune* 500 companies today relative to a decade ago. This flattening of the organization means there are fewer management positions available for promotions. Baby boomers who saw their parents work for the same employer for 40 years find such an alternative less attractive and less available. New entrants to the work force challenge the old assumptions and make the competition for the shrinking number of attractive positions more intense.

Like many other companies, . . . GE [General Electric] has had an implicit psychological contract based on perceived lifetime employment. . . . The psychological contract has to change. People at all levels have to feel the risk-reward tension. . . . The new psychological contract, if there is such a thing, is . . . [commitment] to providing opportunities for professional and personal growth. (Jack Welch, quoted in Bartlett & Elderkin, 1992, p. 7)

In today's environment, more than ever before, career planning is far too important to leave to someone else. Through the 1980s many employees worked in internal labor markets characterized by long-term employment with an employer, internal advancement up a company job ladder, well-defined jobs linked in a progression that defined a career, and individual compensation based on merit and seniority. As organizations become flatter and less bureaucratic, more global and diverse, and more networked and flexible, the employment relationship is changing from long term to short term; from vertical internal career ladders to lateral, cross-company careers; from fixed, defined job boundaries to changing, multiskill jobs; from individualistic performance-reward to team-oriented compensation. Thus, the career contract has changed from loyalty and commitment to one organization in exchange for employment security to one of acquiring and maintaining individual skills in exchange for employability.

In the new employment relationship, employees have been empowered and now are expected to take on the responsibility for their employment. The term *lifetime employment* has changed to *lifetime employability*, where knowledge, skills, and abilities of the employee are continuously improved and updated. Many employers will provide training to help keep employees current, but ultimately the responsibility lies with the individual employee.

YOUR ROLE AND THE COMPANY'S ROLE

Every large organization is interested in managing the careers of its employees. From a corporate perspective, the challenge is often viewed as "succession planning." An important part of every senior executive job at forward-thinking companies like General Electric, Johnson & Johnson, or Transamerica is sitting down to do a comprehensive review of each of the key individuals working for them to determine their potential for advancement and their needs for development. At the same time, there is usually a review of each key position in the firm. Who is available to step into this job? What needs to be done to improve the qualifications of a potential successor?

Even in the most progressive organization, this job is far too important to leave to someone else. Career management is a lifelong process of learning about oneself, various job assignments, and the organization(s). It involves setting personal career goals and developing workable strategies for achieving these goals. Most important, it requires a willingness to revise goals and strategies based on feedback as well as work and life experiences.

The responsibility for career management lies with both individual employees and their organizations. In progressive companies, it is a collaborative process. Generally, organizations seem to take this challenge more seriously than do individuals. Surprisingly, many employees seem to think that it is improper to aggressively assume responsibility for managing their own careers or to be sure that the organization understands what their objectives are. For an individual, the wisest assumption is that the organization is not going to automatically take care of his or her career aspirations. At best, the organization must balance the needs and interests of large numbers of individuals. Consequently, all employees should assume responsibility for three challenges.

Objectively assess skills, interest, and potential. This requires what Jack Welch (1992) calls "acuity—seeing the world as it is and not as you wish it were." Not every individual has the potential to be the chief executive officer (CEO).

Identify realistic career objectives and develop a plan to achieve those goals. The process of stating objectives will often help identify areas that need to be strengthened or new skills to be developed. A realistic career plan will recognize improvements that need to be the basis and a process for achieving these objectives.

Prepare for achieving career objectives by obtaining the necessary training and experience. Sometimes an employer will provide training. More often, however, individuals can step ahead of the queue by signing up for developmental courses or programs.

TRADITIONAL CAREER STAGES

Several scholars have identified a series of stages that individuals move through in their working lives. Figure 4.1 presents a career stage model that is largely based on the work of Harry Levinson (1968) and his colleagues. This model suggests that most people will pass through four stages in their careers. These stages are establishment, advancement, maintenance, and withdrawal.

Managers and professionals quite naturally compare their situation in an organization and their prospects with those of other individuals approximately the same age. We should point out that the ranges shown in the figure are approximations. The timing of the career transitions will vary greatly among individuals. Michael Dell, Steve Jobs, and Bill Gates didn't wait until their 40s to become CEOs of major corporations. Paul Terhorst wrote the best-seller *How to Retire at 35*. George Burns was still accepting bookings in his 90s. Despite these exceptions, most people will find that career stage and approximate age are useful for their own planning purposes.

We have slightly modified Levinson's original ages since it appears that the norms seem to have moved to earlier ages during the past two decades. In other words, most individuals no longer have until their 40s to establish themselves in a profession. Unless "advancement" begins in a person's 30s, they are not likely to find much progress in the next two decades. More and more, workers are finding that the period of maintenance may even exist for them as a full-time employee. Once their ability to move up ends, the possibility of "outplacement" and a totally new kind of career may be in store for them. (We will come back to the concept as we look at "the new rules" and the "shamrock organization.")

Establishment

Obviously the first challenge of an individual's career is to become established within a company and profession. This stage usually involves preparation for a specific job, landing that job, learning the specific requirements of the job within the environment of a specific employer, and learning to fit into an organization and profession. For almost everyone, this will last through early adulthood, but by their mid-30s, most people begin to think of themselves as accountants, engineers, managers, or executives.

Figure 4.1
Career Stages

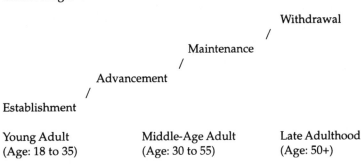

Source: Modified from Levinson, 1968.

One of the adjustments to the working world is the absence of the kind of quantitative feedback provided by most educational programs. New employees seldom get a one-year review that says, "Your overall performance is .7 on a 4.0 scale." This lack of definitive feedback creates a degree of uncertainty and insecurity in all but the most secure, self-confident individual. Most graduates who are hired into a competitive program find there is little in the first few month that they can do to distinguish their performance from other talented, hardworking individuals who have similar responsibilities.

The initial assignment is often a significant stroke of "luck." One former student reported, "When I found out that I was to work in the paper products division at Procter & Gamble, I realized that my future wasn't with this organization. It is a great company, but at its heart, it is a soap company." Obviously, some employees are confident and insightful enough to initiate what their first assignment will be. This exercise of self-determination begins with taking personal responsibility for your most important "subordinate"—the one who looks back at you from the mirror each morning.

Advancement

During their 30s, most people will get a sense of how far they are likely to go in their profession. This period, termed *advancement*, should involve just that. A former company group chairman at Johnson & Johnson explained his strategy for getting promoted every 2 years over a 30-year period.

During the first year on a new job, I worked like crazy to get on top of the demands of a position that I wasn't really comfortable with at first. If it were a good promotion, this would involve a significant "stretch." Usually in eight months are so, I began to feel comfortable with the position and attempted to show some significant improvements in performance. Generally, by the second year in the job, I was looking for ways to expand the position by taking on additional responsibilities. I never asked for a new title or even increased compensation. That always came along as a result of my doing more than as expected. (personal interview, May 3, 1997)

Maintenance

According to Levinson (1968), the maintenance stage finds the individual trying to maintain productivity while evaluating progress toward career goals. In our observations, most individuals cannot enjoy a period of ten to fifteen years of maintenance. We believe that when a person's ability to advance ends, there is a relatively short period before the individual is likely to be offered a "package" for early retirement. It is almost always less expensive to use a younger person to perform a particular task—and it is especially desirable for a corporation to utilize the services of an individual who is still demonstrating an ability to advance.

In today's world, the "maintenance" period of an individual's career may involve more of what Charles Handy (1994) calls "the second leaf of the '*Shamrock Organization.*'" Handy argues that, like the leaves of a shamrock, today's business organization is made up of three very different groups of people. Each group is managed, paid, and organized differently. Each group has quite different expectations for work and advancement. The first leaf in a shamrock organization is made up of core employees. These are permanent employees who are viewed as essential for the ongoing business of the firm. They are expensive, and their number is shrinking. The next leaves of Handy's shamrock consist of part-time and temporary workers—the contingency work force. These are often individuals who had entered the "maintenance" stage of a career and have been "rightsized" into early retirement. Yet by utilizing skills and knowledge developed over many years, these workers may be brought back for "consulting assignments" or contract employment. In some cases, these individuals join the third shamrock leaf, composed of organizations and professionals to whom jobs are farmed out. In either case, the latter two leafs do not have the same commitment from an organization. The cause of the prevalence of jobs in the second and third leaves of the shamrock—the "new rules" that we will discuss later—is becoming increasingly important for progressive career strategists.

Withdrawal

The withdrawal stage has traditionally involved the consideration of retirement options or possible career changes. Eastern philosophy often encourages individuals who have completed their responsibilities as "householders" to enter a more contemplative stage of life where they emphasize spiritual development or "giving back" to society. Many individuals who are moving into what once was "withdrawal" are looking at productive ways to spend the last 20 or 30 years of their lives. In some instances, part-time employment is undertaken for financial reasons. In other instances, it's merely a way of staying mentally and physically alert. One of our friends, an 87-year-old attorney, still works four hours per day answering questions that come into the "State Courts Association" in Williamsburg. His compensation is less than one twentieth what he had billed as a successful lawyer, but the work (and modest paycheck) helps keep him alert while feeling like (and being) a productive member of society.

CAREER ANCHORS

For many individuals, their sense of self-worth rests upon the perception they have about the success of their careers. Based on a twelve-year study of M.B.A. graduates from the Sloan School of Management at MIT, Edgar Schein (1978) developed the concept of career anchors. Career anchors are self-perceived talents, motives, and values that guide an individual in making important career decisions. While Schein found great diversity in the career histories of the graduates, there were significant similarities in the way they explained the career decisions they had made. Based on extensive interviews with these graduates, Schein developed the following five career anchors.

Technical/functional expertise. Individuals who anchor their career in their technical/functional expertise want to specialize and become competent. General management holds no interest for them.

Managerial competence. Individuals who want general management responsibility are anchored in this category. Having an impact on organizational effectiveness is important to them.

Autonomy and independence. Freedom is key to this anchor. Such individuals are uncomfortable working in traditional, hierarchical organizations. Careers with autonomy, such as consulting, writing, and professorships, are attractive to these individuals.

Creativity. These individuals are often entrepreneurs. They have a strong need to create something.

Security/stability. Long-term career stability in a single organization or the same geographic area is of utmost importance to these individuals. Government jobs would fit this type of individual.

Career anchors evolve over time and may be modified by job or life experiences. These reference points help an individual identify what he or she really wants to do. A career anchor can help an individual find a match between themselves and an organization. For example, a person with a strong technical/functional interest may not enjoy a job in sales or management. A person with a strong desire for creativity will probably be unhappy working for the Internal Revenue Service. Table 4.1 is adapted from the extension of Schein's work by Daniel Feldman (1988).

ALTERNATE CAREER FORMS

The concept of steady progress through a series of stages in a career (establishment, advancement, maintenance, withdrawal) as well as the concept of fixed anchors for traditional careers must be examined in light of significant changes taking place in the world of work. Traditional or bureaucratic careers can be defined in terms of a sequence of positions in a hierarchy. But these stages are not as predictable as they were when the original analysis was done. The era of "permanent white water" in corporate management has altered these cycles for most of our readers. Mass "delayering" and company mergers shatter the presumed "passages" and any sense of stability or security.

Increasingly, alternative career forms such as professionalism or entrepreneurship seem to be growing in their popularity and importance. Professionals tend to define themselves by the skill, craft, or socially valued knowledge they possess. Accountants, physicians, plumbers, and philosophers all consider themselves to be professionals rather than traditional employees. Their ability to function within the domain of their specialization is the key to their long-term success, not the requirements of a single employer. While some professionals tend to think of themselves as belonging to an especially elite group, ability and performance are still keys to success. As the founder of Common Cause, John Gardner (1989) once said, "A nation that values a poor philosopher more than a good plumber is in trouble because neither their pipes nor their philosophy will hold water" (p. 9).

Opportunity for advancement in a profession comes from being able to take on more important, significant, or rewarding challenges that require more skill and expertise. Upward mobility takes place by broadening and enhancing one's reputation for skill. The major difference between a "professional" businessperson and a traditional employee is that the loyalty of the professional is to the body of knowledge or practice he or she identifies with rather than to the organization that currently provides employment. An accountant or attorney will work with many clients during a single year, but they always keep their sense of being an accountant or attorney rather than an AT&T or IBM person.

Table 4.1
Career Anchors

Career Anchor	Characteristics	Typical Jobs/Positions
Technical/Functional Expertise	Focus on technical aspects of work High need for achievement Less interested in promotions Uninterested in general management issues Apolitical	R&D Professional/functional specialties Technical consulting Project leaders
Managerial Competence	Wants general management responsibility Impact on organizational effectiveness important High need for power Prefers complex organization/business problems	General management Top management team including heads of functional departments Large, established firms
Autonomy and Independence	Freedom to pursue interests Uncomfortable working in traditional, hierarchical organizations	Management consultants Writers and publishers College professors Unlikely to work in large businesses
Creativity	Strong need to create something Short attention span, changes positions often Prefers small firms and new start-up companies	Entrepreneurs Designers/consultants
Security/Stability	Long-term career stability in a single organization or the same geographic area Conformist/"organization man" High need for affiliation	Government jobs Regulated industries Professional services (e.g., medicine, law, CPA)

CPA = Certified public accountant.
R&D = Research and development.

Source: Feldman, 1988, p. 70.

Kanter (1984) describes the evolution of the entrepreneurial career form. The orientation is based on the creation of new value or organizational capability. Minnesota Mining and Manufacturing (3M) is known for its emphasis on encouraging employees to "bootleg" time and resources to work on new product ideas (like the Post-It Note or "Scotchguard"). However, most individuals with this orientation will be more comfortable starting their own business or contracting their skills to a series of short-term employers rather than trying to carve out a traditional career path. For true entrepreneurs, career growth comes from the increased power and responsibility associated with the growth of their business or organization. This same drive may be satisfied by increasing the volume or territory an individual is responsible for. In many ways, entrepreneurial careers are more risky than bureaucratic or even professional careers. In bureaucracies, people hope for predictability and security from lower income than they might receive if they took the risk associated with having their own business or practice. Both in independent ventures and corporate-sponsored projects, entrepreneurs accept the risk and uncertainty in order to gain autonomy and the potential for higher financial rewards. This concept of self-determination or responsibility seems certain to be a major component of an increasing number of careers.

THE NEW RULES

The Harvard Business School's Class of 1974 entered the work force at a time when economic turmoil was fomenting radical, fundamental changes in the business environment. Professor John Kotter recently reported on the results of a 20-year study of the 115 members of this class, where he identifies the factors that influenced their career decisions and explores the insights and strategies that brought them wealth, satisfaction, and security during a time of intense economic volatility. Kotter's 1995 book is entitled *The New Rules: How to Succeed in Today's Post-Corporate World*.

Kotter's "new rules" describe "how to win success at work" and were formulated after Kotter detected a significant shift in what is required to succeed, but he noticed that many businesspeople are still attempting to use old strategies. He claims that the globalization of markets and competition is driving the shift and that those who do well today have "[capitalized] on globalization by pursuing career paths that are less linear, more dynamic, and more unstable" (p. 57). These often lead to starting and "growing" small businesses, consulting, organizational leadership, and deal making. Kotter also warns that business is demanding more and that in order to succeed one must possess extraordinary competitive drive and take advantage of lifelong learning opportunities. Kotter is one of the few scholarly business writers who regularly blends leading-edge, visionary concepts with the tough-mindedness that most successful executives admire. He disabuses the reader of the notion, if any of us still hold it, that there will be any safety or security in a career based on steady upward mobility in a traditional corporation.

"Settling for good, much less mediocrity is dangerous. Large numbers of people have been taught by big business, big labor and big government that fair-to-good is adequate. . . . [T]en years from now fair-to-good will NEVER lead to success" (p. 59).

In order to get beyond the "fair-to-good" range of performance, Kotter makes a strong case for objective assessment and maintaining a careful, realistic, candid, and ongoing self-examination.

Those who aim to lead large organizations should assume the role of the revolutionary, breaking down hierarchies and replacing them with a "flexible network organization" with many more people taking up the responsibilities for leadership. There is a need, he says, to create "self-confidence in competitive situations" through education in business schools and in business organizations.

Before presenting our own "Ten Commandments" for self-directed career strategy, we will summarize the major new rules suggested by Kotter:

Do not rely on convention; career paths that were winners for most of this century are no longer providing much success.

Keep your eyes on globalization and its consequences; everything is changing, offering both large opportunities and large hazards.

Move toward the small and entrepreneurial and away from the big and bureaucratic.

Increase your competitive drive; high standards and a desire to win are essential today and will be even more so in the future.

Yet most campus placement offices still count on corporate recruiters to hire the bulk of their M.B.A.s. And the majority of graduates continue to gravitate to large firms and Wall Street. Corporations are pitching entrepreneurial opportunities to woo enterprising M.B.A.s, but all too often, large firms do not provide the autonomy most self-starters seek. Even so, an astonishing proportion of M.B.A.s end up running their own shows. For example, entrepreneurs account for 40 percent of the Harvard Business School Class of 1974.

Indeed, one of the most valuable lessons entrepreneurship students learn is how to manage their careers. Berkeley M.B.A. Samara Gutsch found a summer job with a San Francisco start-up that made socially responsible toys. She stayed on part-time and, after earning her degree last June, landed a plum job as marketing manager of the highly successful Wild Planet Toys. "I'm definitely taking a pay cut over what I could make elsewhere, but it's worth it to be in on the ground floor," says Gutsch. "And you don't have to leave your values at home" (Westfall & Westfall, 1996).

TEN COMMANDMENTS FOR SELF-DIRECTED CAREER STRATEGY

An individual's career is too important to be left to his or her employer—important decisions made by individuals with less interest in the outcome than the individual whose career is being managed. Career specialists such as Weber, Schein, and Hall offer advice for career self-management that can be organized into ten general commandments for controlling or managing your own career.

Develop New Career Competencies

Each individual should practice candid self-appraisal and work to enhance skills in goal setting, planning, and problem solving. These activities still provide a foundation for a successful application of other career strategies. In today's environment, developing experience in international settings and a demonstrated willingness to take risks and meet high standards are also important. In *The New Rules*, John Kotter emphasizes the importance of globalization, risk taking, and high standards. Rick Miller, formerly CEO of Wang Labs and chief financial officer (CFO) of American Telephone and Telegraph, recognized early in his career the importance of the experience in general management to broaden his expertise in finance.

Choose Challenge over Income

Any new job has a strong impact on your future career. The challenges offered should be weighed more heavily than the more obvious considerations like location and salary. If your current job does not seem to offer adequate potential for the career aspirations you hold, you should probably try to acquire additional responsibilities—if not with your current employer, then with someone else.

Strive for Mastery, Growth, and Excellence

These attributes are the cornerstones for career success. Good performance is not always recognized. In some organizations, performance is difficult to manage or measure. Sometimes there are other important criteria for advancement. Effective career management demands the ability to recognize the key components of performance that are recognized and rewarded. Objectivity in assessing personal performance against the standards is also a requirement for success in any organization.

Recognize the Power of Politics and Value Alignment

Politics exist in every organization. Some groups, however, are an easier fit because they are more aligned with your own value system. It is always important to establish alliances and fight the essential battles. It is equally important to choose your allies and battles wisely. The ability to interpret power structures or to ascertain the alignment of various interest groups is clearly a survival skill.

Maintain Mobility

Eugene Jennings (1971), a pioneer in career strategy, outlines the concept of "executive chess." This involves recognizing the "rules" for maintaining job and career mobility. The widest possible set of options should be sought. This often involves experience in line positions as well as staff responsibilities and holding both administrative and technical jobs. While most individuals are hired for their tactical specialty, they must maintain balance between becoming overly specialized or technically obsolete. Mobility is always difficult if you are invisible. One of the dangers of an international assignment is that it is easy to be forgotten. During long absence from headquarters, ex-patriots who remain in frequent contact with a sponsor or mentor at home are likely to be more successful than those who allow themselves to be forgotten.

Manage Your Mentor

Your immediate superior isn't the only person in an organization who can be helpful to your career. Any senior manager with a strong record of personal performance can provide essential mentoring assistance. These functions generally include offering advice, information, and friendship while serving as a role model and being a sounding board. Mentor-protégé relationships can be invaluable to younger people seeking professional growth and advancement. These should be maintained throughout your career. While some organizations offer formal mentor programs, natural informal relationships with people tend to be the most effective. The key to success in being a good protégé is to understand that you look good by making your mentor look good.

Recognize the Importance of Integrity

Every employee will face ethical dilemmas. No matter how ambitious you are, compromising basic principles will work against you. A reputation for integrity is an important asset—but one that is easy to lose. From time to time, examine your personal values to determine how much you are willing to sacrifice for the organization.

Plan Your Career with Significant Others

It is common for both partners in a personal relationship to have careers together. Both careers may be of critical importance to the individual and the partnership. Actively managing two careers is more than twice as complicated as managing one. No partners should assume that one career is more important than the other. Mutual support, flexibility, joint decision making, and sometimes sacrifices are required to successfully manage dual careers. Children may also have an important voice in career decisions affecting their parents. Individuals who are not married may also wish to involve other important people in their decision-making process.

Develop Contingency Plans

Despite the best efforts to plan your career, unanticipated events will occur. Just as a business should consider alternate scenarios and strategies for responding to new developments, so should individual managers think strategically. Economic changes, technological advances, and mergers and acquisitions or divestitures all lead to significant corporate reorganizations. Discontinuity presents challenges that, if managed properly, may lead to even greater opportunities.

Continually Reassess and Reinvent Yourself

Career choices are made throughout our working lives. French sociologist Émile Durkheim (1895) talks about "self-rationalization." This is the ability to look at oneself as an object and realistically assess what needs to be changed in order to succeed. Alternatively, it is sometimes important to reassess objectives and recognize that options are reasonable to pursue.

In summary, life is not too short. Take charge of your career. It is never too late!

REFERENCES

Bartlett, Christopher A., & Elderkin, Kenton W. *General Electric: Jack Welch's second wave*. Boston: Harvard Business School Press.

Carroll, Lewis (1921). *Through the looking glass*. New York: Macmillan.

Durkheim, Emile. (1895). *The rules of sociological method*. Translated by W. D. Hall. Newark, NJ: Free Press.

Feldman, Daniel C. (1988). *Managing careers in organizations*. Glenview, IL: Scott, Foresman.

Handy, Charles B. (1994). *The age of paradox*. Boston: Harvard Business School Press.

Jennings, Eugene E. (1971). *Routes to the executive suite*. New York: McGraw-Hill.

Kanter, Rosabeth. (1984). *The change masters: Innovation and entrepreneurship in the American corporation*. New York: Simon & Schuster.

Kotter, John P. (1995). *The new rules: How to succeed in today's post-corporate world*. New York: Free Press.

Levinson, Harry. (1968). *The exceptional executive: A psychological conception*. Cambridge, MA: Harvard University Press.

Schein, Edgar H. (1978). *Career dynamics: Matching individual and organizational needs*. Reading, MA: Addison-Wesley.

Terhorst, Paul. (1988). *Cashing in on the American dream: How to retire at 35*. New York: Bantam.

Westfall, Marylord & Westfall, Ronald. (1996). Running their own show. *U.S. News & World Report* (March 18): 89.

5

The Telecommuting Life: Managing Boundary Issues at Work and at Home

KAREN LOCKE AND GIGI G. KELLY

ORGANIZATIONS, THEY ARE A'CHANGIN'

One doesn't have to eavesdrop long on the conversations we are having about our work lives to figure out that something significant seems to be happening. Look at the language we are using to describe our situation (emphases added): "A *tidal wave of change* is sweeping across the American workplace (Ehrlich, 1994, p. 491); "The last decade, *perhaps more than any other time* since the advent of mass production, has witnessed a *profound* redefinition of the way we work ("The New World of Work," 1994, p. 76); and the *very notion of* a job itself is being questioned (Ancona et al., 1996b). Whether one views the terms in which change is described as dramatic hyperbole or a reasonable representation of what is happening, it does seem that change, dramatic or evolutionary, is indeed taking place. New organizational forms like the "virtual organization," new ways to accomplish work (e.g., the widespread use of task forces), and a "new" character to the work force created by significant demographic changes are but some of the indicators of a transformation in the organizations in which we work. Furthermore, the impetus to change is being felt across a wide variety of organizations, from *Fortune* 500 companies to government bureaucracies and even to the military and educational institutions. Indeed, as educators, we in business schools are increasingly called on to reflect these changes by better educating managers to work in systems that are leaner, flatter, more diverse, more team based, more closely networked with customers and suppliers, more responsive to change, and more globally positioned (Ancona et al., 1996a).

EMPLOYEES' RELATIONSHIPS TO ORGANIZATIONS ARE CHANGING, TOO

As there are discernible changes in the organizational systems in which we work, so too are there appreciable changes in how we, as members of the work force, view the relationship we have to these organizations. An interesting, even ironic, aspect of the changed relationship revolves around the centrality of the individual employee.

Shift in Responsibility to Employee

First, our work and careers are increasingly driven by us, the individual employee, as opposed to the organizations for which we work (Arthur & Rousseau, 1996). The downsizings, restructurings, and growth of a contract and contingency work force that accompanied those organizational changes identified above have fundamentally undermined the idea that organizations can be dependable master agents for our lives. These changes have prompted a basic revision in the implicit terms of agreement that governed the relationship between employees and their employing organizations, the so-called psychological contract (Sims, 1994). The notion that employers take care of their employees has given way to the idea that employers provide the means for us as their employees to take care of ourselves. Thus, the ties that we have to organizations in general have been significantly loosened, and the responsibility for managing and shaping our work lives has explicitly devolved to us.

Personal and Family Life Are Increasingly Salient

Second, issues involving family and personal life have become legitimate subjects in the societal and corporate conversations we have about our work lives. The increasing numbers of professional women in the work force, the attention drawn to family issues by the actions of prominent women, for example, Brenda Barnes's (chief executive officer [CEO] of Pepsico's North American beverage operation) recent well-publicized resignation for family-related reasons ("Woman's Resignation," 1997, p. B1), and the life priorities of America's baby boomers (Sims, 1994) all work to elevate the salience of nonwork dimensions of employees' lives. Consequently, our personal and family lives increasingly manifest themselves within the domain of the employing organization. Family and home issues are expressed in discussions and demands of employees for provisions for family-related benefits, such as child care, elder care, and parental leave. They also express themselves in the increasing demand for flexibility in work arrangements such as job sharing, flexible hours, three- or four-day workweeks, and evening hours (Scordato & Harris, 1990; Vercspej, 1989).

Careers Paths Vary According to Life Priorities

Finally, the loosening of organizational ties and prominence of personal and family issues have prompted a related reconceptualization of what constitutes a career. Rather than viewing careers as linear, and essentially tracked within one or a very few organizations, they are increasingly viewed as progressing in cycles (Mirvis & Hall, 1996). Career paths reflect varying priorities at different life stages and will likely involve relationships with multiple organizations over time. This view of careers legitimizes flexibility and individual choice.

To summarize, changes in work institutions themselves as well as changes in the relationship employees have to their employing organizations have made possible the modification of an organizationally driven model for our work lives to one that is essentially employee driven. In the organizationally driven model, the employing organization provided the vantage point from which to view work and career opportunities and, notably, our personal lives. Through this organizational lens, personal and family life is shaped by workplace demands, for example, when and how much time (outside the basic 9–5, 40-hour-week framework) is available for nonwork involvements. By contrast, in the individually driven model, the particular employee's life now constitutes the framing gestalt, and employment with a particular organization is but one part of our lives. Thus, we may choose to job share, to set up a flextime arrangement, or even to take a sabbatical in order to reconfigure and customize our home and work lives as they reflect our needs and priorities at different points in our lives (Platt, 1997).

TELECOMMUTING: A NEW, FLEXIBLE WORK ARRANGEMENT

One innovation in how work is accomplished that provides increased capacity to reconfigure home and work lives is telecommuting, and it is increasingly being adopted by organizations. Telecommuting constitutes a fundamental change in where, how, and even when work is accomplished. After this brief introduction to telecommuting, we will present the case of Glenn, an account of one individual's and organization's experience with creating this new work arrangement. Following the case, we will discuss the issues that are raised by this window into telecommuting. We hope that the issues raised will offer insight into the implications of this new work arrangement both to individuals and to organizations who might be thinking about the telecommuting option.

Telecommuting, or *teleworking,* as defined by the U.S. General Services Administration (1998), refers to a means of performing work away from the principal office, typically at home or at a nearby telecenter. Telecommuting thus results in increased separation from the principal office, while, at the same time, it increases connection to the home. Telecommuting is not new; it has existed for several decades. In the late 1970s and early 1980s, businesses projected that the physical location of the worker would shift from the central business building to the home. Although there were organizations that were early pioneers in this movement, it was not until the 1990s that telecommuting became a viable, acceptable, and occasionally, preferred work option.

A survey conducted by Telecommute America reported 11 million U.S. teleworkers in early 1997, an increase from 4 million in 1990 (Murphy, 1998). Furthermore, conservative estimates for the number of teleworkers in the year 2000 range from 11 to 15 million (Piskurich, 1996). Interestingly, since the early 1990s, projections for the number of teleworkers working in the United States by the year 2000 seem to increase with each passing year. Thus, there appears to be consensus in business and in government organizations that telecommuting is no longer a fad but a reality that organizations must address. Indeed, when we look closely at the forces driving telecommuting, summarized in Table 5.1, we clearly see the interests not only of individuals seeking to increase the quality and flexibility of their home and work lives but also of organizations focusing on economics, the environment, and technological advancements. With this alignment of organizational and individual interests, the increasing growth in the population of teleworkers is not surprising. Nevertheless, it remains a "new work arrangement," very much in its initial adoption phase.

Let's now turn to Glenn's experience to help us better understand what might happen when an individual completes his work at home, electronically connected to, but geographically distant from, his principal office. This case portrays the real-life experiences and reflections of one teleworker. It is worth noting that this case tells a telecommuting story from one demographic perspective—a teleworker who belongs to a dual-career family with children. Although some issues raised in this case are unique to this particular situation, many of the issues are faced by the mass of teleworkers.

Glenn and ABC Co. Explore Telecommuting

Kelly Watson is the vice president (VP) for information systems (IS) at ABC Co. in Chicago. Kelly was hired five years ago as Chief Information Officer (CIO). In this capacity, Kelly was in charge of the migration of systems from the mainframe legacy environment to a new client

Table 5.1
Benefits of Teleworking

Benefits to Organization	Benefits to Individual
Improve office productivity	More retained income (reduce personal expense)
Increase use of new technology	Increase job satisfaction
Enhance recruitment and retention of personnel	Productive and balanced lifestyle
Increase competitive advantage	Reduce stress and illness from commuting
Reduce central office costs	Integrate work and personal life
Optimize personnel performance	Improved family functioning
Minimize cost and disruption of relocation	Effective time management
Improve environmental reputation	Increase personal safety
Strengthen disaster planning	Control and design of workplace

Sources: Hodson, 1997; "ITD Telecommuting Task Force Report," 1997; U.S. General Service Administration, 1995.

server environment. Kelly faced a number of challenges. First, the IS division was under considerable pressure from its customers to get new systems up and running. Second, even though the IS professional resources in her division had grown tremendously, she has had retention problems. The market for IS professionals is so competitive that Kelly faces the constant problem of having to replace staff who have been lured away by competitors, consulting companies, and vendors.

A Problem Arises and a Solution Is Considered

Kelly's most recent expression of her retention problems is the imminent loss of one of her most senior development supervisors, Glenn. Glenn's wife Vicki had received a very attractive job offer in Cincinnati, where she grew up. Although Glenn really enjoyed his work at ABC Co. and had developed satisfying work relationships with his manager as well as with Kelly, he felt that it wouldn't be fair to Vicki to deny her this opportunity. Glenn received calls from headhunters all the time, so he knew that he'd have little problem finding a comparable position.

Kelly, anxious not to lose yet another experienced development professional—especially someone with Glenn's track record with clients—was prompted to try something new. She called Glenn into her office and broached the subject with him: "Would he be interested in working out a telecommuting arrangement with ABC Co.?" Glenn was at first taken aback, but the idea did have some appeal. Glenn was organized and hardworking, so he felt that he would have little problem working in a less structured format. Additionally, in his role as a development supervisor, most of his work revolved around projects. Glenn believed that during some phases of the project life cycle he would need close contact with the users; however, the project on which he was currently working was a long way from that point. And, right now, at least, his physical presence was not really a necessity. Certainly, he wouldn't miss his daily commute through city traffic. On the other hand, Glenn was somewhat concerned with the implications of his telecommuting with his staff, and he knew this would have to be addressed. Intuitively, he realized that he couldn't work completely remotely, so the issue of how frequently and for how long he would have to return to the office would have to be worked out. Kelly asked Glenn to think it over, to speak with Vicki about it, and they would talk again soon.

In the meantime, Kelly met with Harriet, her development manager. It was Harriet who had first informed Kelly that they might be losing Glenn and had urged her to "do everything possible" to keep him. So while Harriet was uncertain as to how telecommuting would work out— she had never worked under an arrangement like this before—she was anxious to give it a try. She did suggest to Kelly that it would be important to discuss this with the other IS managers. Kelly agreed and convened a meeting with her three managers: Harriet from development, Leo from operations, and Gene from end-user support. She also asked a representative from human resources (HR) to attend.

The Decision to Try Something New

Kelly began the meeting by emphasizing the retention challenges the division faced. She informed everyone that they were confronting the imminent loss of yet another experienced professional, this time, a development supervisor. She told them that she was giving very serious consideration to allowing the supervisor to telecommute in order to keep him at ABC Co.

Leo immediately asked Harriet if she knew about this and if she supported the idea. Harriet responded, "Yes, Glenn is really respected by his clients, and I can't afford to lose him right now . . . and who knows, if this works out, the increased flexibility plus the reduction in commuting time and stress that telecommuting potentially offers might make it a powerful tool for attracting and keeping people."

"But, you're only offering it to Glenn, right now?" Gene retorted, looking at Kelly.

"Yes," Kelly replied. "We've never tried anything like this before, so I want to move slowly on it. I'm sure there will be some bugs we'll have to work out as we go along."

"Right!" Leo jumped in. "How are you going to maintain control over his work quality? What happens when he has to meet a deadline and he's got a sick child at home with him who's lying around on the sofa? For that matter, what is he going to do at home—set up a separate office, or is he going to be working from his kitchen table?"

"And," Gene chimed in, "I know that Glenn's really reliable, but what are you going to do when everyone starts wanting to try telecommuting?"

"Hold on!" Kelly interrupted. "These are all really important points, and they illustrate what I was just saying. We'll have a lot of issues to work out. But, for right now, can we agree in principle that this is something we want to try and that we'll begin offering it to Glenn?" Gene nodded.

"It's definitely something that is in our interest as a division to explore," agreed Leo. "Heck, I might try it myself!"

"What do you think, Bob?" asked Kelly, turning to the HR manager. "You've been pretty quiet during all this?"

"Well, I'm all for trying something new, especially if it's going to put a dent in our hiring and retention problems," replied Bob. "But, as the points people here have raised show, there are going to be a lot of issues we'll have to deal with. We'll need a policy on telecommuting—I'll start looking into what other companies are doing with it."

"Good. Then we have agreement," said Kelly. "We'll move on offering it to Glenn as an experiment. In what kind of time frame do we want to revisit this?"

"How about three months?" Bob offered. Kelly looked around the room; the others all nodded.

"Okay," said Kelly. "Now I only hope that Glenn wants to move ahead with this."

Glenn Tries Life as a Teleworker

There was no problem with that. How Glenn and Vicki would juggle each of their professional careers was one of those recurring topics of conversation in their household. Glenn and Vicki agreed that they should do this if for no other reason than this was a working arrangement that they would definitely have to explore at some point in their careers. So why not now?

Initial Setup: The First Couple of Weeks

Setting up their new home in Cincinnati, Vicki was thrilled with the prospect of Glenn working out of the house. Now Glenn would be home when the kids got off the bus and would be able to help with all the "taxi" and other family duties that she had always had the responsibility of managing. Their lives would change in other ways, too. First, Glenn had to find space for an office. Since the living room was rarely used, this room was designated as his office. Second, the office had to be outfitted. With his own money, Glenn purchased used office furniture and had phone lines run into the living room. ABC provided Glenn a laptop computer with a 56K modem. Glenn had asked for an ISDN (Integrated Services Digital Network) line, but ABC was not set up to receive ISDN communications. (Glenn had two telephone lines, one for the computer and one for voice; a month into the project, however, his wife insisted that they get a third line designated for the family.)

Connecting to ABC's system from his home was more difficult than he originally thought it would be. His first week of telecommuting was pretty unproductive as the kinks were worked out of connecting his computer to ABC's network. There were still times when Glenn had a problem getting connected. Sometimes it was the local telephone company's problems; other times it was problems associated with the corporate telecommunication network. There were also concerns about security, so the networking department was looking into different solutions. For now, Glenn dialed directly into the ABC network. ABC already had an "800" number to support this long-distance connection.

The initial reception of Glenn's telecommuting at ABC had also highlighted just how much of a departure from traditional work practices this new arrangement was. On the phone, Glenn would receive comments that it must be great being able to get up when he wants and do what he wants. Ads running on the TV of teleworkers at home in their pajamas only added to the barrage of stereotypical comments (e.g., "Your golf game must be improving!" or "What's on TV now!"). Some of these comments about the informality of working at home were correct. Glenn did enjoy the relaxed dress code and was often on the golf driving range during lunch; however, these offhanded comments made Glenn realize that he had to justify and make visible the work he was accomplishing at home.

Managing his time was also going to require some structure. Glenn set up a daily agenda of tasks to complete. Because Glenn was a "night owl," he found himself completing tasks in the late evening hours when the house was quiet, and he was not disturbed by the phone. The idea of more flexibility with his time was one of the reasons he was excited about telecommuting. However, he was not sure that his availability between 8 and 5 was lessened by working evening hours. Glenn had always been a hard worker, and this continued dedication to work did not change with his new work venue. Glenn also set up daily lists of the people he needed to contact. He would spend a considerable amount of time on the telephone as well as maintaining contact through e-mail. This proactive management of his "virtual presence" was working.

The Next Two Months: A New Set of Issues at Work

The project Glenn was working on had up to this point been conducive to letting him work at home. During this time frame, he had returned to ABC twice for four days. The cost for travel and lodging was picked up by ABC. These interim visits to the corporate office were going to be necessary at least for the short term and maybe for the long term. In addition, very soon the project would be starting implementation, and Glenn realized that he would have to be on-site more—although, he wasn't sure how much more. This was not all bad. Sometimes, Glenn felt the isolation and wanted to simply go out to lunch with his colleagues. He was also concerned that he was out of the loop on the day-to-day happenings. Maintaining and building information connections were much more of a challenge from afar. Glenn was fortunate that Harriet, his boss, was very supportive of the concept of telecommuting and would act as an advocate for Glenn to keep his name and good work recognizable to others in the organization.

The clients Glenn supported also raised some issues. Over the last month or so, there had been times when end users wanted to have Glenn on-site. To maintain his communications with end users, Glenn audio-conferenced in on meetings; however, no video was being used. And while audio-conferencing provided a connection, Glenn did not always feel as an equal participant. One observation Glenn made was that if all participants were meeting face to face in a room with Glenn present on the speakerphone, he did not feel a real part of the exchanges taking place, regardless of how frequently he "spoke up." By contrast, if everyone "met" on a conference call from their separate offices, the meeting dynamics were more equal and satisfactory.

A more daunting issue for Glenn was learning how to manage his staff from a distance. Glenn's prior management style had been "by walking around." He would stop by his staff's cubicles to chat and keep abreast of their work. Now this was impossible to do from his home. Some of Glenn's employees had no problem adjusting to Glenn's physical absence; however, there were some whose productivity dropped markedly. Glenn knew that a more formal management routine was going to be necessary; so he set up weekly audio staff meetings. He also was very interested in exploring the available groupware technologies to support virtual teams, but little use of this type of software (except for e-mail) had been initiated by ABC. Also, his ongoing management and project responsibilities kept him so busy (he was hiring additional staff) that he simply didn't have the time to investigate the technology. Glenn also felt he needed a fax machine, but at this time, no money had been budgeted for such purchases. He later bought one with his own money.

New Issues Arising at Home

On the home front, issues had also arisen with his family. Glenn started receiving an increasing number of work-related calls in the evening when the family was eating dinner or relaxing together. Additionally, late afternoons when the kids came home from school and Vicki returned from work proved difficult. When the kids got off the bus in the afternoon, they were thrilled that Dad was home and were anxious to talk about their day. Glenn loved being available to hear all the school stories, but occasionally, the children would rush into his office excitedly shouting, "Dad, Dad, guess what?" only to interrupt a telephone call or an urgent task. This disruption was annoying and would lead to conflict as the kids were told: "Leave the room. Daddy's working!" On rare occasions when Glenn was dealing with a particularly frustrating problem, family members would bear the brunt of his frustration.

Glenn and Vicki worked out some "new rules" for Daddy's workspace, including some interaction guidelines. For example, Glenn often listened to the kids as soon as they got home; however, they must follow a protocol: First, check to see if he is on the phone; then ask if he has the time to listen. The situation was not perfect; however, all were learning. Glenn was also exploring the option of adding doors to his workspace to clearly indicate availability.

On the positive side, many of the benefits Glenn believed he would have working from home did materialize. Glenn had flexibility and did do more with the family. Glenn occasionally met with his children at lunch and was available if the kids were ill. Glenn also became more active in his neighborhood and truly did not miss the commute to work. Vicki has also really enjoyed having him around, and this reduced some of the stress she had with her job. However, when Glenn has to return to the home office, new arrangements have had to be made to address after-school care for their children, and Vicki has to single-parent. Having Glenn work from home has been a time for all in the family to learn and adapt to the changing work environment.

After Three Months There Are Mixed Reviews at ABC Co.

Results Inside the IS Division

Three months after Glenn began telecommuting, from Kelly's perspective, the reviews on the telecommuting experiment were mixed. It certainly had taken Glenn a little longer to get set up than either he or Harriet anticipated, and the downtime associated with that put pressure on everyone to catch up the project. Still, once the technology-related bugs were worked out, Harriet and Glenn had both been happy with the latter's overall productivity and work quality. Also, Glenn's current clients were beginning to adjust to Glenn's physical absence and realized that quality products were still being delivered. Some clients did believe that Glenn was going to have to be at corporate more for the upcoming implementation.

Unfortunately, the experiment also created some tensions. Harriet was approached by several other development professionals. And when they were told that it was only being offered to Glenn as an experiment for the time, they wanted to know why Glenn was being singled out for this special privilege. Harriet also received a few complaints from some of the division's other internal clients who wondered why they couldn't find Glenn despite the fact that they had dropped by on several different occasions to ask him questions. Additionally, the concern around "special privilege" also cropped up in the other IS functions and highlighted some stresses in the division. For example, operations staffers—who as a group were prone to feel that they always had to cover for mistakes that the developers made—complained to Leo that it was unfair that it was someone from development who got "to stay home and relax on the sofa."

Predictably, perhaps, new technology issues were also raised. If this was truly the way the company was going to move, then new hardware, software, and telecommunication equipment were going to be necessary. Also, the IS division would have to figure out a way to provide technical support for specific teleworker problems that would be difficult to solve because they would not be able to go to the site.

Results in the Rest of ABC

In HR, Bob was also receiving a lot of inquiries from ABC employees, not only in IS but also in the rest of the company who had heard about Glenn's arrangement and who were also interested in telecommuting. Bob knew that the question of whether telecommuting was going to be a company-wide option would have to be answered fairly soon. Additionally, if the telecommuting option is opened up to other employees, then this would have to be addressed at the company level. For example, exactly how would people be compensated and reviewed? What technology will be supplied by the company? How would worker's compensation work if someone got hurt at home? What new training was going to be necessary?

MANAGING THE SPACE BETWEEN WORK AND HOME: BOUNDARY ISSUES

The preceding case points to a number of issues that center on the altered bounding of work and home created by a telecommuting arrangement. Obviously, Glenn is no longer physically present at work.

Glenn's work arrives at the office electronically, but he isn't there, thus creating some dynamics that require active attention. This separation or unbundling of the worker from the principal work location raises issues not only with regard to immediate work relationships, namely, Glenn's boss, coworkers, and subordinates, but also with regard to more peripheral relationships, those organizational employees who are acquainted with Glenn or simply with Glenn's new work arrangement. Additionally, Glenn's physical absence from corporate offices also has more long-term implications for his development opportunities and advancement. At the same time, the creation of a workspace in the home bundles together home and family life with work life. Boundaries that facilitated the creation of a distinct way of living that was nonwork obliged are no longer present, and their absence raises concerns for work, family, and leisure. All these issues will require attendance and active maintenance on the part of the teleworker. Finally, the technology that allows telecommuting to be viable surfaces new issues that both the organization and Glenn will have to address.

Separation from the Work Group: Getting Work Done from a Distance

The physical distance between and the separation of the teleworker from the organization are immediately felt by all parties involved. Absence from the office creates a void, and the managers, coworkers, and others left behind who are unfamiliar with telecommuting have no experiences from which they can draw to fill it. Consequently, it is easy for the ambiguity associated with what the teleworker might be doing away from the office to be resolved with images of activities that are nonwork associated. Perceptions that Glenn is involved in non-work-related activities (e.g., that he is sleeping until nine, watching TV, or playing golf) are understandable, if inaccurate. Second, Glenn's physical separation from those he supervises requires revisiting how he enacts his role as a manager. The interpersonal, informational, and decisional functions that comprise the traditional managerial role typically include a sizable face-to-face component (Mintzberg, 1973). A new way of enacting these roles will be necessary. Third, the potential for a deterioration in all work relationships must be acknowledged and proactively managed. And, there is, indeed, evidence to suggest that telecommuting does have a destabilizing effect on work relationships that is expressed approximately six months into the new arrangement. The good news is that a recovery and mutual adjustment seems to be possible after about a year (Reinsch, 1997).

These three sets of issues clearly point to the need for a "learning and adjustment" period for those organizational members touched by the new telecommuting work arrangement to discover and establish new ways of working. To manage the fact as well as the perception of his working effectively, Glenn set up a routine at home. This routine not only provided a work structure for Glenn but also helped to paint a picture for those in the office of him working at home. As his tangible work products started arriving at the office at predictable time intervals and as his routine for checking in with others at the principal work site became established, many of the stereotypical perceptions of not working faded away. As the case indicated, Glenn had a strong working relationship with his manager, Harriet, and his ability to continue to provide quality contributions to ABC under the new work arrangement was never in doubt. Nevertheless, the issue of ensuring a teleworker's actual and "visible" productivity is central to this new work arrangement. One common response to this issue is for the teleworker and his or her supervisor to create a contract that clarifies expectations for the teleworker's productivity. While it is critical that these expectations be clearly articulated, it is important that both parties define contribution broadly in terms of the overall productivity and success of the work unit rather than narrowly in terms of task products. Important long-term contributions, for example, assisting in the development of others in the work unit, may otherwise give way to the micromanagement of short-term tasks. In addition to clarifying expectations for contribution, teleworkers may take other steps to educate others in the workplace about their long-distance contributions. For example, they may explicitly take the initiative to explain and publicize work activities, creating ways for what they do to be known, for example, by sending monthly reports to the principal work unit as well as to other relevant parties. They may offer themselves as a resource for other projects and, in various ways, "train" others in the office to telecommute with them (Craumer & Marshall, 1997). And they may cultivate the support of on-site supporters to champion their new work arrangement and underscore the contributions they are making; Glenn's boss does an excellent job of maintaining Glenn's symbolic presence in the office by keeping his name and the contributions he makes in the minds of others.

As indicated earlier, learning how to supervise others' efforts in a distributed mode can be particularly difficult and would seem to require a careful and explicit consideration of both the supervisors' and their subordinates' preferred work styles. As the case indicates, this has been a challenge for Glenn and for his employees. Prior to telecommuting, Glenn ensured the productivity and quality of his department's work through an informal management-by-walking-around style. In order to stay on top of his department's contributions and particularly the efforts of those employees who performed better with closer monitoring, Glenn had to find ways to formalize his supervisory activities. Ways of doing this include: weekly status meetings via audio-conferencing, daily work updates via e-mail, and daily telephone conversations.

The above discussions emphasize the importance of developing new ways to ensure the substantive contributions of the teleworker and underscore the importance of paying close attention to the network of relationships in which any of us organizational members are embedded. One of the benefits of being able to work at home is that much more work can be accomplished without the constant interruptions that are a part of the corporate landscape. There is a temptation to stay disconnected and to streamline one's role in order to get more "work" done. It is easy for the task aspects of making a contribution to be more and more salient and to discover too late the consequences of neglecting the relational components of the work. Teleworkers have to make projecting their virtual presence and developing substitute communication channels to stay connected with their relational network a priority (Bjorner, 1997). Glenn relies heavily on audio-conferencing and e-mail to maintain contact. Other technologies are also available to support social and relational needs, for example, video-conferencing and the formation of so-called electronic water coolers, that ability to share informal information online in a dedicated shared space. However, sharing informal information online is not without its consequences. Online information is recorded, and this leads to the potential issue of electronic communication being monitored and reviewed. Companies need to establish policies telling their workers the rules for e-mail use. However, these rules may restrict the flow of informal information that is so prevalent in conducting business. Establishing the informal communication network for teleworkers is an issue that has yet to be resolved.

Separation from Work Opportunities: Issues of Development and Advancement

Before concluding our discussion of the impact of separation from the principal work site, it is important to raise the question, What happens to a teleworker's advancement opportunities and career path? Certainly the lack of visibility that we have already discussed may cause some problems if not actively managed. As one AT&T teleworker rather crassly put it, separation from the workplace means a loss of "suck-up" opportunities (Hequet, 1996). It is important for the teleworker to take responsibility for charting his development path under this new work arrangement, for example, by actively seeking and initiating new challenging work projects. However, because this is uncharted territory for most organizations, we simply do not know the answers to this. Will the teleworker have to return to the home office to maintain upward mobility, or must the teleworker trade advancement for location flexibility?

Working at Home: Dealing with Confounded Boundaries

Ironically, the muddying of boundaries between work and home that telecommuting potentially engenders is in ways reminiscent of the ways in which people worked prior to the Industrial Revolution when people accomplished tasks that maintained different aspects of their lives across the course of a day. Thus, people could cycle continuously between personal, family, and work-related tasks. Telecommuting provides a potential flexibility not only in where but also, to a degree, when the work takes place. While some aspects of the work, most notably contact and coordination with officeworkers and clients, need to take place during corporate business hours, the independent tasks that make telecommuting a viable option for a given employee can be completed at any time. The 24-hour/7-day week, thus, potentially becomes the frame within which work can be accomplished.

This continuous time frame brings both positive and negative attributes for the teleworker. On the positive side is the flexibility to complete work during times when the teleworker is most productive. For Glenn, who is most productive during the later hours of the day, he now can complete work during this time. Additionally, this potential flexibility of where and when to work opens up opportunities for the teleworker to improve their relationship with family members by permitting a more active role in family life (Hill, 1995; Olsen, 1987)—for example, being available to pick a child up from school or to coach a sports team whose practice would typically begin 45 minutes before the parent could get home from work. Thus telecommuting allows the teleworker to work at some tasks early or late in the day, saving times in between for family.

On the negative side, putting appropriate time boundaries around work and separating and conserving the quality of home life, including relationships with the family, are critical. Indeed, there is a real possibility that unless specific steps are taken to bound off work, for example, by establishing a daily work agenda, that one's work life may overwhelm the home, temporally (there is precious little time that work does not impinge on) and emotionally (family members falling prey to work-related frustrations). As is true with regard to the workplace, a learning and adjustment period is also needed at home.

Putting Temporal Boundaries Around Work

As indicated, telecommuting provides a degree of discretion in controlling our work schedule. At the same time, our preceding discussion has highlighted the importance of staying connected and available. Although Glenn can work when he is most productive, his availability during the day has not diminished, and he is working additional hours.

There is a certain irony in Leo's concerns echoed by others in moments of resentfulness, that teleworkers will shirk their work responsibilities or allow their new increased involvement in some family activities to over-shadow their accountability to the workplace. Given that the option to telecommute is typically only extended to those individuals, like Glenn, who have a track record of contribution and whose commitment to "get-ting the job done" is proven, the opposite seems the most likely danger. And there is reason to believe that the anytime/anyplace worker who works in spurts of activity throughout the day and evening will work a longer day than the 9-to-5 worker (DeVito, 1996) and that such longer hours are a way of proving themselves worthy of the telework privilege. But in doing so they risk burnout (Girard, 1997). Consequently, if tele-workers choose to exercise the option not to strictly conform to the same work schedule practiced by those at the principal office, they may need to keep time logs, at least initially, to monitor and arrive at an appro-priately balanced work schedule.

Once teleworkers arrive at an appropriate temporal schedule, how-ever, the fact that their work site is now at home means that they must enlist the cooperation of the other occupants of the home in order to maintain them. For example, in the case of Glenn, the presence of his school-age children in the house after school when there is still some overlap in his corporate workday creates some problems. The presence of a parent at home has traditionally signaled a degree of availability to minister to their needs. As the case indicates, however, this is not always true. Consequently, the children have to learn to adapt and to help sup-port their telecommuting father's work schedule. The family members must negotiate a new structure in the household. Everyone has to learn new rules and to respect the boundaries that are established in order to create work times within the structure of a 24/7 week. This is not nec-essarily an easy task but one that evolves as everyone in the family par-ticipates in this new work environment. It is important to recognize that it may take some time and be especially difficult for younger children to come to terms with the fact that although Daddy or Mommy is phys-ically present in the house, they are unavailable.

Putting temporal boundaries around the work also becomes salient when the 24-hour/7-day frame is applied by those at the principal office who now assume that Glenn is always "virtually available." Being con-tinuously available and on-call can cause new issues for the family, for example, being able to sit down together to a family meal undisturbed.

Putting Emotional Boundaries Around Work

Working at home on a flexible schedule can bring work problems and the emotions associated with them into the home in real time. For ex-ample, hanging up the phone after a difficult discussion with an under-performing employee just as the children come home from school and opening a "bad news" e-mail message in the evening when different family members are occupied with various routines, such as homework or television, point to instances in which office angst can be directly brought into the home in raw form. And family members may find themselves bearing the brunt of emotions like anger on such occasions. Without the ride home to help the worker process and transition such difficult moments, teleworkers have to develop alternative strategies for effectively processing and partitioning workplace feelings from those with whom they live.

Technical Issues: Connecting the Teleworker

The technology makes it possible to work anywhere, any time, providing the flexibility increasingly prized by so many of us on how, when, and where we get our work done. In order for Glenn to telecommute, the technical environment had to be set up. This requires a negotiation between the teleworker and the organization to fully understand what equipment is necessary. Having the proper technology is essential for successful telecommuting (Artz, 1996). At a minimum, the teleworker must have a telephone, with many teleworkers also possessing a computer and a modem. The Internet has provided a low-cost means to connect the teleworker to the office. E-mail has become a primary tool for communication within organizations, thus facilitating an additional means to keep the teleworker connected. One teleworker made the following comment: "You learn to live by e-mail. That was my water cooler" (Murphy, 1998). Other equipment that may be required include printer, fax machine, copier, pager, answering machine, mobile phone, and additional phone lines. Exactly who is responsible for these costs needs to be addressed. In Glenn's case, an additional phone line became necessary to reinforce the boundaries of work and family in the home environment. New rules emerged—no one in the house picks up Daddy's phone. The cost for this additional telephone line was absorbed by Glenn, not the organization. Also, the slow access to the organization's LAN (local area network) is a constant source of frustration for Glenn. It is important to recognize that the phone line has become an umbilical cord that provides the connection of the teleworker to the organization. When there are technical problems (and there will be), this can render the teleworker lifeless. Solving technical problems remotely are often more challenging and procedures need to be established to address these issues.

TELECOMMUTING: THE FUTURE IS HERE

Our aim in this chapter is to bring into focus the extent of the issues that those electing to telecommute may encounter. As our introductory paragraph hinted, telecommuting involves major change. While important, technology involves the least of the issue. A more pervasive and challenging set of issues that telecommuters must find ways of addressing involves the fundamental redesign of the routines that comprise one's daily work habits. And, simultaneously, it requires a reconsideration and conservation of the elements of home and family. As the workplace continues to rapidly change, it is critical that employees and their employers understand their options and the impact of the choices they make. Today, it seems that we are beginning to identify the issues that this new work arrangement raises, but we are a long way from providing solid answers to help individuals and organizations address these issues.

REFERENCES

Ancona, D., Kochan, T., Scully, M., Van Maanen, J., & Westney, D. E. (1996a). The new organization. In *Managing for the future*. Cincinnati: South-Western College Publishing.

Ancona, D., Kochan, T., Scully, M., Van Maanen, J., & Westney, D. E. (1996b). Workforce management: Employment relationships in changing organizations. In *Managing for the future*. Cincinnati: South-Western College Publishing.

Arthur, B., & Rousseau, D. (1996). *The boundaryless career: A new employment principle for a new organizational era*. New York: Oxford University Press.

Artz, T. (1996). Technologies for enabling telecommuting [Online]. Available: http://www.cba.uga.edu/management/rwatson/tc96/papers/artz/artz/toc.htm [1998, April 1].

Bjorner, S. (1997). Changing places: Building new workplace infrastructures. *Online, 21*(6): 8–10.

Craumer, P., & Marshall, L. (1997). Telecommuting from an electronic cottage: Negotiating potholes and toll booths. *Online, 21*(6): 94–102.

DeVito, M. D. (1996). Blueprint for office 2000: The adventure continues. . . . *Managing Office Technology* (December): 16–21.

Ehrlich, C. J. (1994). Creating an employer-employee relationship for the future. *Human Resource Management, 33*(3): 491–501.

Girard, K. (1997). Hold that (telephone) line. *Computerworld, 32*(1): 31–32.

Hequet, M. (1996). Virtually working: Dispatches from the home front. *Training* (August): 29–35.

Hill, E. J. (1995). The perceived influence of mobile telework on aspects of work life and family life: An exploratory study. *Dissertation Abstracts International, 56*(10), 4161A. (University Microfilms No. DA9603489)

Hodson, N. (1997). Teleworking . . . a different way of doing things [Online]. Available: http://www.teleworker.com/seminar/index.html [1998, April 1].

ITD Telecommuting Task Force Report. (1997). [Online]. Available: http://www.itd.umich.edu/telecommuting/report/ [1998, April 1].

Mintzberg, H. (1973). *The nature of managerial work*. New York: Harper & Row.

Mirvis, P., & Hall, D. (1996). The new protean career. In D. Hall & Associates (Eds.), *The career is dead—long live the career: A relational approach to careers.* San Francisco: Jossey-Bass, pp. 365–380.

Murphy, K. (1998). Web fosters telecommuting boom, and many in the industry take part. [Online] *Internet world.* http://www.internet.com [February 9].

The new world of work. (1994). *Business Week* (October 17): 76.

Olsen, M. H. (1987). Telework: Practical experience and future prospects. In R. E. Kraut (Ed.), *Technology and the transformation of white collar work.* Hillsdale, NJ: Lawrence Erlbaum Associates, pp. 135–152.

Piskurich, G. (1996). Making telecommuting work. *Training and Development, 50*(2): 20–27.

Platt, L. (1997). Employee work-life balance: The competitive advantage. In F. Hesselbein, M. Goldsmith, & R. Beckhard (Eds.), *The organization of the future.* San Franciso: Jossey-Bass, pp. 315–323.

Reichenber, L. W. (1996). The virtual work-place [Online]. Available: http://www.decus.org/decus/pubs/magazine/spring96/virtual.html [1998, April 1].

Reinsch, N. L., Jr. (1997). Relationships between telecommuting workers and their managers: An exploratory study. *Journal of Business Communication, 34*(4): 343–369.

Scordato, C., & Harris, J. (1990). Workplace flexibility. *HR Magazine* (January): 75–78.

Sims, R. R. (1994). Human resource management's role in clarifying the new psychological contract. *Human Resource Management, 33*(3): 373–382.

U.S. General Services Administration, Interagency Telecommuting Program (1998). Moving people to work. [Online]. Available: http://www.usa.gov/pbs/owi/telecomm.htm [1998, August 26].

Vercspej, M. (1989). The new workweek. *Industry Week* (November 6): 16–21.

Woman's resignation from top Pepsi post rekindles debate. (1997). *Wall Street Journal* (October 8): B1.

6

Being Successful in Asia:
How to Survive and Thrive

MARK PAYNE AND MILANO REYNA

PROLOGUE

This chapter is a collection of cultural perspectives to guide the fresh-off-the-plane ex-pat through his or her early days in Asia. It is also a synopsis of a recruitment tool we give our new arrivals, *Confucius Wasn't an Ad Guy.*

In our industry, advertising, where brainstorming, critique, debating with the boss and the client, and standing on the edge with an idea (sometimes alone) constitute the name of the game, we face very interesting challenges in Asia everyday. It is tempting to do business the same way we do "back home." But it is also very dangerous. Building a successful agency requires teamwork and great communication. The good news for a creative agency like ours is that being successful in Asia is like building a great brand. You have to know whom you are working with, how decisions are made, and at the end of the day, respect all the nuances and put your best ideas forward.

To try to capture Asia and all of its peculiarities in one chapter or even a book would be ill-fated, as Asia is a mosaic of cultures, religions, beliefs, and idiosyncrasies. Nonetheless, if you take this chapter in broad strokes, it may well save you a few bumps on the head and let you devote your bar tab to toasting success rather than drowning your woes. So the rest of our discussion goes like this.

First, we want you to think about why you would want to come to Asia. What are your expectations? What are the company's expectations of you?

Then we ask you to think about an Asian coming to your home market for the first time. How would they be treated? How would they see their new job?

And of course, we would be remiss if we didn't talk about Confucianism, probably the most common link, if there is one, across all Asian borders.

Lastly, we leave you with a few tips that will hopefully get you off to the right start, no matter what business you are in.

For starters, why are you considering Asia?

Before you read any further or ask any other questions, knowing your purpose in Asia is important. Hopefully, your primary motive is a quest for adventure and a greater understanding of the world, rather than a calculated desire to advance your career. "Adventure Goals" and "Career Goals" are entirely compatible. But to a large extent, your appetite for understanding and operating around cultural differences (or lack thereof) will drive your career goals. Career advancement does not happen because you come to Asia. You have to succeed here first. To succeed you have a lot of learning to do. Cultural understanding bears on your ability not only to make the right business decisions but also to make things happen when over 95 percent of the people you do business with are Asian. You will have to fit into your company's culture, be able to apply your knowledge to a local setting, and adapt to the geographical culture to be successful.

As globalization of businesses continues, chances are that succeeding in Asia will propel you up the career ladder faster than staying in one place. But again, the operative idea is succeeding in Asia, not being here. A spirit of adventure and curiosity will do much more to make you successful than thoughts of promotions, wealth, or fame.

Think for a moment where you came from. Let us say hypothetically that when you come to Asia, an Asian person of equal experience fills the job you are leaving back home, despite never having set foot in your country. How do you think their early months on the job would unfold? And put yourself in the shoes of the colleagues you left behind and answer these questions.

Would your coworkers back home embrace the new Asian arrival as an asset to lead the local team to higher ground? Probably not. In fact, despite their best intentions, human nature may leave them a tad suspicious of the different-looking and -speaking newcomer.

Would your coworkers back home care about what the new arrival had done in other countries, or would their opinion depend solely upon seeing him or her in action? Sure, they may be curious as to what the new person accomplished back in his or her country—but only as an entry ticket to be a part of the team. More likely, they will be measuring the new person's worth by success on their turf.

Now, what if your Asian replacement strolled in with a swagger and arrogance like he or she knew it all? What if he or she said aloud his or her feelings—that he or she has come from another Shangrila to this new place where people have much to learn? It probably doesn't matter where the person comes from, the East, the West, or even some other organization, the reaction to this type of behavior is probably not going to be accepted well.

How would the local staff feel if every meeting included the phrase, "Well, that is not how we did it back where I came from—we used to do it this way"? Curiosity may work in the person's favor at first. But the real test will be the person's ability to apply his or her international experience to everyday local issues.

Remember that for all the fascinating cultural differences, human nature is essentially no different anywhere. Human nature will make even the best-intentioned people a tad suspicious about a foreign-hired person fresh off the plane.

Be humble. As obvious as this seems, many ex-pats pay lip service to this, but relatively few actually put it into practice. Your new Asian colleagues will be eager to learn from you and to tap your experience. But they will judge you based on what you do in Asia, not on your impressive accomplishments prior to arrival. No matter how good your are, you will need their advice and support every bit as much as they will need yours. Maybe more.

Think about what it would take for a newly arrived Asian to get that support back in the office you left behind, and you will land on a good foot in Asia. If human nature is the same, what is different in Asia? Good question.

- How are decisions made?
- What is valued?
- What experiences and learning influence behavior?

Understanding Asia begins with grasping a few core tenets of Confucianism and understanding who we really are (see Figure 6.1 and Figure 6.2 for comparisons). There is no clear analogue for Confucianism in the West. It is not a religion. Few Asians would describe themselves or their behavior as reflecting "Confucianism." Rather, Confucianism is a way of thought that has over time become a code of conduct. It is the glue that has helped a country as geographically and ethnically diverse as China unite a billion people under one flag with arguably less internal strife and boat rocking than one might otherwise expect.

Imagine how powerful Confucianism is in China today with over 2 billion people or in other Chinese-influenced countries such as Indonesia, Vietnam, Malaysia, Singapore, Burma, Korea, Thailand, Taiwan, Japan,

Figure 6.1
Basic Confucian Principles

When trying to understand the ways many people in Asia learn and what they value, you might want to appreciate and consider the following Confucian principles. Keep in mind that these just scrape the surface when it comes to understanding their values and Asian business decision making. The relevance of these principles varies enormously across age groups, countries, provinces, and even types of businesses. But the bottom line is that all of these principles are still very active in Asian business across all markets in Asia.

The interests of the group come before those of the individual.

    The individual is only as good as the whole group thinks it is.

    The individual should not act in a way that calls attention to him or herself.

    Individualism is an unacceptable form of arrogance.

The family is the most important institution in life.

    When family duty and individual goals come into conflict, family comes first.

    Many Asians provide their elders, parents, and siblings allowances to be used toward mortgages, food, care, and education of family members.

    Most Asians live at home until they are married.

The grass is not greener on the other side.

    The status quo is beautiful; change threatens harmony.

    Unity is important.

The past tells us most of what we need to know.

    The future is uncertain and in the hand of capricious gods.

    There are many superstitions and traditions among Asians, and they vary across boundaries.

Act in a manner that won't hurt the feelings of others.

    This is a "golden rule" and often amplified to far grander proportions.

    What we might call "conflict avoidance" is a worthy trait.

    If conflict occurs, deal with it indirectly as possible; better yet, avoid it.

To reduce conflict, know your place in society and act accordingly.

    Child defers to parent.

    Student defers to teacher.

    Female defers to male.

    Citizen defers to government.

    Youth defers to aged.

Figure 6.2
Western/Capitalist/Judeo-Christian Values

It is easy to think about "them" or "they" when trying to understand other cultures. We often forget the importance of how "you," "me," and "we" think while making deicsions and placing judgments and values. Comparing East meets West thinking reveals some interesting differences. Take a look at how the majority of Western business decision makers' minds have been transformed.

- Individual freedom is everthing.
- Majority rules, but government should stay out of the way of the individual.
- Youth, energy, and innovation drive society.
- Losers go with the flow; heroes speak out.
- The status quo is boring; change is inevitable, healthy, and worth chasing.

Cambodia, and Laos. The numbers and the impact are staggering. So what is Confucianism? Here is an admittedly nonacademic version.

CONFUCIANISM 101

Confucius (Kong Fu Tse) was not a prophet, religious leader, or politician but a teacher. His thinking has over the last 2,500 years, by degrees, shaped the mind-sets of over 2 billion people across China and the Chinese-influenced countries: Japan, Korea, Taiwan, Thailand, Indonesia, Malaysia, Singapore, Vietnam, Cambodia, Burma, and Laos. Confucianism has exerted more influence than the Roman Empire, the Beatles, Michael Jordan, Karl Marx, and Bill Gates (well, maybe) combined.

Confucianism's Core Ideal

The primary goal of society is harmony, because harmony is a prerequisite for prosperity and happiness.

What does all this mean? For one, it is important that we understand how people learn and work with one another before we truly become productive in the Asian environment. And in the same breath, it is also important to know who we as ex-pats really are and why we make decisions the way we do (see Figures 6.1 and 6.2). As you will see, there are some fundamental value differences that affect how we work.

One of the biggest mistakes ex-pats make is to generalize their ideas of best practice to Asia. They can still achieve the greatest business accomplishments, but their methodology may have to be modified to make it happen.

How true are Confucian principles in the workplace today? There are some signs that with time they are changing. Affluence and political tides over the last 50 years have clouded some of the traditional ways of thought, particularly among increasingly individualistic young people. But the important thing to remember is that they are still deeply ingrained and are only changing at a glacial pace. "When in Asia, don't let the 'flash' cars, skyscrapers, and cellular phones or the fact that there are over 1 million Chinese millionaires in China seduce you into believing the East has become the West. It hasn't." It is easy to see where confusion—not Confucianism—between West meets East can take place.

Basic Capitalist, Western, and Judeo-Christian Practices

If we were to lay down an equally concise summary of what values shape the Western employee, it would look quite different from the typical Asian. Let's take a quick look (see Figure 6.2).

The clash between the Western bias toward boat rocking and Confucian bias toward harmony is the most important one you will have to manage as you try to make change happen. Don't try to "become" Asian—just understand and respect the differences, and you will do fine.

ICEBERGS IN ASIA: BEWARE, THERE ARE AT LEAST FIVE

Now that we know a little more about Confucianism and our own basic values as Westerners, it is time to look at where most newcomers to Asia make their biggest mistakes. Here are some important areas to keep in mind.

1. Conflict avoidance
2. Change
3. Deference
4. Relationships
5. Loss of face

Before getting into the details, here's a quick scenario to set the mood. Just when you think you have it all figured out, you hit something. You feel like you are quickly losing control. You overreact, jump right in and fix things without involving others, then take total control and disregard all the sensitivities of the local talent.

Ouch! You just hit an "Iceberg."

Be careful when this happens to you. We say "when it happens to you" because inevitably it happens to the best of us. Take a look at the creative restructuring vignette. This will give you a taste of Confucianism and Asian icebergs happening in a routine business exercise.

Creative Restructuring

In the wake of a number of big accounts leaving the agency, the managing director of a large international agency in Thailand needed to cut staff. He went to his highly regarded Thai creative director and asked him to assemble a hit list of who should be let go. When the creative director came back, he was surprised to find the names of all the agency's best creatives (the heart and soul of an advertising agency). Baffled, the managing director wondered why the creative director would cut loose their best talent. He suspected the motive might be that cutting a few highly paid staff rather than many lower-paid staff would hit the salary targets without breaking the harmony on the remaining accounts. This seemed plausible with a slight Asia spin, but one he didn't agree with. He then got his counterarguments together and went to see the creative director. He was right that "harmony" and "feelings" played a part in the scheme, but he was off on how much it really factored. The creative director explained that the entire creative department had met and assessed who would have the easiest time finding a new job. Naturally, the best creatives could easily get hired elsewhere, whereas those who were not very good would have suffered through extended unemployment.

If the "agency stars" could land better jobs, which by now they were already looking for, firing only the best people would actually add up to no upset creatively at all! The creative director was quite proud of how he and his team had worked this out. The fact that this would devastate the agency's creative capability didn't factor into the creative director's thinking at all.

Conflict Avoidance: Asian Iceberg 1

This is a difficult issue to grasp for most Westerners. Let us take a quick view of it in a nonworking environment.

"Come Over for a Few Drinks!"

Joe (the American): "Hey, Kuhn Oranat, my friends and I are having a little party over at my place tonight. Why don't you come over around seven?"

Kuhn Oranat (the Thai): "Ummm . . . sure, I'll see you there." Ten minutes later she thinks to herself, "I really don't want to go to the party. What will I do there with all those foreign guys? I'd rather be with my friends. I know, I won't go. But I can't tell Joe that. I just won't show up. This way I will have made Joe happy once by saying I would go and only disappoint him once, by not showing up. All things considered, everything will be OK when I see him in the morning."

Imagine how many versions of this scenario you can have in a work situation. Just when you think you have it all figured out, someone throws you a curveball. The lesson here is to recognize it early, so you may respond to it quickly.

Lest we forget, the other side to conflict is losing one's cool (being "conflict explosive"—an ex-pat thing common in Asia), which is generally what happens when an ex-pat finds out something is terribly wrong, compared to the way he or she is used to.

From an Asian perspective, losing one's cool, even if you think it is just being direct and passionate, may be viewed as a lack of self-control, youth, stupidity, poor leadership, or all of the above. So you see, there are at least two perspectives on one behavior. Part of your task is to make sure that neither gets in the way of business.

Change: Asian Iceberg 2

Change is hard to implement in most parts of the world. But in today's competitive environment, it is a criterion for success.

In Asia, *change* can have some very negative connotations. It is often perceived negatively because it is a reflection of poor decision making (you need to change because of your indecisiveness, instability, or even weakness). Remember the vignette called "Creative Restructuring"? This is what happened just months before: "Agency Meltdown."

Agency Meltdown

Background: An international ad agency, driven by a strong local management group, recorded a ten-year run of phenomenal profit growth and creative success with minimal foreign management involvement the entire period.

Situation: After a flat year in 1996, the U.S. home office sent an ex-pat over from one of its other agencies in the region to determine what happened and to see what changes can be made to get the agency back on track. To the local management team, the fact that questions were being asked and that changes were on the horizon, however reasonable and soft they seemed to the unwary ex-pat, was received as an overt challenge to their competence after so many years of success.

Outcome: Many key managers resigned, and staff were so shaken they left in droves. Within six months the agency lost a majority of its accounts and staff. Ten years of huge success were undone because of how needed change was approached. Now, this doesn't mean one can't change things in Asia. The best way to do so is by involving local talent before you implement your change. Spending time with employees and educating and soliciting their buy-in up-front will save you aspirin later. If you are really good, you will be able to work hand-in-hand with your local colleague to drive the changes you both might be looking for. Hey . . . this sounds like the way it should be done anywhere in the world, doesn't it? Again, your success is largely dependent upon your sensitivity to this issue, your ability to listen, and your ability to coach your people along.

Deference: Asian Iceberg 3

A fundamental key to Confucianism is "deference." As hard as it may sound, Confucius left little room for equality. Everyone has his or her place in society, including in the workplace. We are not talking about social status here—that is a completely different subject. What we are referring to is respect for authority and leadership.

In the business of advertising, we are conditioned to think of our clients as equal partners. And it is our job to lead them into buying great work that will build their brands. While Confucius stopped short of defining the relationship between the agency and the client, the cultural bias in Asia is to treat the client as superior and to take orders rather than to boldly lead. The challenge for us is to coach our local staff into this mind-set.

Deference also shows up in the office. The cultural bias is usually for subordinates to support their manager's view rather than challenge it. Imagine the quality of input (or lack thereof) in a typical brainstorming session where the boss speaks his or her mind first. Asking questions before sharing one's position, building trust, and creating an environment in which to share opinions is key if you really want honest input.

Relationships: Iceberg 4

Western business is results driven. This is not to say that Asian business is not. But the terms are different. Western businesses are usually governed by contracts written by lawyers, with specified time frames and loads of terms and conditions. And business communication is often governed by a desire to get to the point as briefly as possible. Business in Asia, while ultimately seeking results, is far more relationship oriented. The Chinese term *guan-xi* literally means "good feeling"; its practical meaning in Western terms can be regarded as "relationship grease"—the emotional stuff that turn the gears of business. Terms of business in Asia are not contract driven, although contracts do exist. Getting the business and keeping business are more like terms of marriage: a flexible pursuit of mutual accommodation, continually open to negotiation with an expectation that both parties will work together "till death do they part."

An ex-pat doing business in Asia can expect many late nights, lunches, or time on the golf course building up good faith and *guan-xi*. This is an important concept in most of the Asian markets. But it appears most sensitive in Chinese and Japanese business markets. What is the lesson here? The American wanting to go home after a hard day's work at 6:00 P.M. can probably expect to spend many more nights and weekends building good relationships than the casual long business dinner back home.

Loss of Face: Iceberg 5

In Asia it's common to hear: "He left his job because he lost face" or "You should not do that because she will lose face." Against this backdrop of your best efforts as an employee are vitally needed "face," Asian business communication and decisions are governed much by respecting people's feelings. Clarity and brevity fall way down the priorities list. It is a different communication game altogether, one that consists in some cases of what a Western eye would describe as muddled messages and indirect hints. Consider the following vignette from a newly arrived senior account director.

"Hey, Let's Change the Client's Strategy!"

As a recently arrived ex-pat, green, eager, and wanting to make an immediate impact, I took my local staff through a concise, commonsense proposal to take a brand with flagging sales in a new direction. I explained that not only was the current campaign strategically shaky; it was creatively not as good as we were capable of. The group's feedback was verbally positive, although they seemed uneasy. Further probing brought only more positives, so I ignored the signals and asked them to set up a meeting to present to the senior clients.

Over the next few weeks, my staff was mysteriously unable to lock in a meeting time, saying the clients' schedules were too tight. Increasingly frustrated, I mentioned the pending proposal to another agency staff member who told me that the senior client had fathered the campaign I was trying to kill, professed his eternal love for it, and resisted past attempts to change it.

I realized that selling the change would take a more hard-hitting, beefed-up proposal than what I had prepared. I added more hard facts to the proposal, which the client ultimately bought. At first, I couldn't help but be annoyed at my staff. The results could have been achieved much more easily and quickly if they had been open and honest in the early review. But I realized later that they were caught between two face-threatening land mines that could have hurt my feelings.

If they had told me outright that the initial proposal was only half-baked, it would have been a direct affront to my seniority (of course, I would have welcomed it, but they could never see it that way). Likewise, if they had let me go forward and present it, I would have endured what to them would be a horrific embarrassment—being pummeled by the client before their eyes (again, no big deal to me, but a disaster to their eyes).

Their indirect maneuvering spared me a loss of face, which was their main goal. To this day, I suspect that the seemingly random tip about the client's views from the other staff member had been orchestrated by my team, probably because they sensed my passion for changing the campaign and realized that stalling the meeting would not deter me from moving ahead.

Once I got through shaking my head at the complexity of doing something that seemed so easy, I realized I owed them thanks. They went through these gyrations because they cared and wanted me to succeed and had supported me the way their culture has taught them.

Face, in an overly simplified explanation, is showing respect for another person's feelings. If you say something negative or disagree about someone's actions in front of that person, it is a loss of face. If you do the same thing in front of the person's peers, then it's a serious loss of face. The consequence in a work environment is probably a resignation without explanation. The worst-case scenarios are mass walkouts without any explanation.

A story goes that every new foreign employee in Asia should be given a box of tissues the day he or she arrives and display it prominently on his or her desk. An ex-pat will probably make an honest mistake and make an Asian lose face, usually in a well-meaning attempt at saying there are better ways to get things done around here. We would like to add that the ex-pat should put $50 in a cookie jar every time he or she thinks, "Gee, that was an overreaction. . . . I was not saying anything harsh. I'm just trying to get things done around here." If the jar fills up, the ex-pat will have enough money for a flight home. And they will probably need it. Because it means they have not figured out how to work in Asia successfully. Many ex-pats think that they are handed a team that's not very clever. They say things like, "My local team can't think out of the box. They don't challenge my ideas or the client. They are oversensitive." Our advice is to rethink your style and reread this chapter. We have learned, and many times the hard way, that Asian and Western paradigms are very different and also the same. The techniques that Asians and Westerners use to get results are different, but the outcome for both is for success.

At the end of the day, an ex-pat's role is to achieve business objectives. To accomplish this, ex-pats need the support and involvement of local staff. They are most successful when they are able to apply their knowledge in meaningful ways to the local context. And they are even *more* successful when they discover local insights with their Asian colleagues that help drive the business further.

SOME TIPS FOR SUCCESS

Most of these you will learn along the way, and many more you will get from your colleagues. It seems most ex-pats have their fair share of stories. Imagine how many tips your Asian colleagues will have to share about ex-pats as well. Building trust, demonstrating patience, and refraining from exploiting your style as the preferred mode are key ingredients for success in Asia. Here are some more to consider.

- Respect cultural nuances in your business decision making.
- Be humble and learn from your mistakes.
- Lead by example, coach, facilitate.
- Involve local people in decision making.
- Create a trusting environment.
- Handle personal performance issues privately.
- Promote change based on benefits, not fear.
- Apply your knowledge to meet local market's needs.
- Recognize that silence or "Yes, I agree" does not necessarily mean agreement.
- Be a world-class observer and learner.
- Remember that losing one's cool is not cool in Asia.
- Be cautious about ignoring indirect messages.
- Remember *guang-xi*.
- Face and results go hand in hand.
- Beware of the heightened sensitivities.
- You will only be successful with the support of your Asian colleagues.

A FINAL WORD

Less than a year ago, John Naisbitt, Tom Peters, Bill Gates, and a host of other great names were telling people all around the world that Asia is where it is happening. They are right. Here is why.

Asia is exciting. Over half the world's population is here as well as all the world's major players—for example, Proctor & Gamble, Unilever, Coca-Cola, Toyota, Hewlett Packard, McDonald's, Pepsi, Motorola—building their strongest brands. Most interesting about these companies is that many of their brands in Asia will exceed their U.S. billings in the next five years, if not sooner. Now, where do you think is a great place to be if you want to be where the action is?

The bottom line for 1999 is that headlines about the Asian economic crisis are real. But in the same breath, it's ironic that the two Chinese characters that come together to symbolize "crisis" individually mean *danger* and *opportunity*. With this current crisis comes much opportunity for the global employee and smart companies.

From an employee's perspective, the Asian region will continue to provide the most exciting challenges ever offered: a chance to participate in the world's fastest-growing region, a chance to apply and learn skills faster than anywhere on the planet, and a chance to immerse and test one's ability to add value quickly while working with people across various cultures. Asia will no doubt test one's stamina and ability to conduct business. The future successful employee will need global knowledge and experience. Asia is a great place to get started.

7

Managing the New Future Manager: Individual and Organizational Perspectives

M. RONALD BUCKLEY, DANIELLE S. WIESE,
MILORAD M. NOVICEVIC, AND THOMAS D. SIGERSTAD

INTRODUCTION

One of the current, trite expressions that is often heard is, "The world of work is rapidly changing." We can easily agree with this statement. What is different now is that, we are told, newcomers have changed considerably in terms of their desired relationship with organizations (Munk, 1998). Webber (1976) has provided a framework for the early career issues that must be confronted by newcomers into an organization. In summary, these issues are:

1. Early frustration and dissatisfaction with organizational reality in terms of poor supervision and incomplete understanding of time horizons in careers.

2. Insensitivity to, and passivity in, the organizational political process.

3. Inability to understand and adjust to the evaluative criteria used in an organization.

4. The natural tension between older and younger employees.

5. Misperception of the implicit social contract between the individual and organization and its ramifications.

In our opinion, these issues continue to pose problems for organizational newcomers, despite many societal, demographic, and organizational changes since the publication of the Webber article. Our purpose in this chapter is to examine the nature and dimensions of these changes and their potential influence on young newcomers. As reported by Berlew and Hall (1968), what occurs in the initial stages of employment crucially influences later performance in an organization. We hope to be able to address these critical issues from both an individual and organizational perspective and recommend some possible courses of action.

TRANSFORMED ROLE OF MANAGER IN MANAGING NEWCOMERS

The new organization is personified by managers who foster fluid operating boundaries to articulate an engaging vision and a set of values on which newcomers can model their careers. The new managers emphasize individual initiative and personal responsibility to trigger the newcomers' activities. Newcomers are expected to question assumptions, propose solutions, and take action. The new organization promotes management based on self-discipline instead of control. The new form of managerial control is indirect, of the "pull" rather than the "push" type, giving newcomers a sense of identity, belonging, and ownership of work. It is new entrant–driven in focus rather than manager-driven.

Newcomers quickly join the responsive front line that is closest to the customer or skillful with technology. Managers foster newcomers' self-discipline by socializing them in routines that set norms in terms of time management and delivery on promises. Empowered newcomers operate within the grounded and measurable behavioral guidelines; defined specific outcome expectations; clear standards of performance; and freedom above mandated minimum when they earn the right to operate with relative autonomy. In this way the old social contract is replaced by a rich cognitive-behavioral contract with their manager, which is based on corporate values, organizational policies, and management practices.

The manager's view of the newcomer has shifted from that of the rational and predictable authority-based organization junior to that of a competent young individual of initiative and personal risk based on available data and information. In the traditional organization, manager's control to maintain power was exercised through privileged access to information and data analysis. In the new organization, data and information are distributed to allow newcomers to exhibit self-control based on legitimate and credible performance standards.

Management in the new organization stimulates challenging and questioning decisions and tolerates failure and risk taking. The new role of managers is to become mentors and coaches in developing people to develop business. Managers as mentors and coaches must be open to challenge and tolerant to well-intentioned failures. They must understand that mentoring and coaching go beyond the traditional mentoring and training indoctrination when dealing with empowered newcomers.

The manager's focus is on continuous learning of the newcomers. Newcomers' capabilities and initiatives can rarely succeed in isolation, regardless of their quality and appropriateness. Beyond a commitment to developing newcomers' initiatives and expertise, the manager must be able to link various initiatives and leverage distributed competence by embedding the resulting relationships in a continuous process of team learning and action. The new manager selects the most talented, provides for their horizontal networking, and supports lateral sharing of knowledge in order to ensure that the organization has the best and continually develops their skills and experience. Building team organization requires a culture based on institutionalized trust. The institutionalized trust is made visible in transparent and open organizational process, fair and equitable management decision making, and a shared set of organizationally established core values.

THE CHANGING DEFINITION OF SUCCESS

Webber (1976) has suggested that there are several definitions of the newcomer's success but assumes that the primary definition for young newcomers is patiently climbing to higher managerial ranks. Today, that objective for young managers has been tainted by workaholic parents who were "rewarded" for their loyalty with a lack of family life and being laid off from their jobs. Their parents were the prototypical examples of Whyte's (1956) "Organization Man." However, the post-baby-boom generations believe that success comes with a balanced life and that career success is defined as continued employment in work that is fun, flexible, and rewarding.

ETHICS AND THE NEW MANAGER

When Webber (1976) wrote about the "ethical dilemmas" of young people just beginning their careers, the focus was that there was not one view of ethics that could guide a new manager down the path to appropriate behavior. The new manager might see the law as the definitive guide to right and wrong. The new manager might reflect upon personal moral principles instilled through parental or religious training. Or, the new manager might look to corporate culture for guidance in determining the appropriate behavior—emulating organizational expectations and culture. Whatever the source of guidance, the new manager would, over time, arrive at a mélange of rationale for a set of personal ethics that they can follow on both a personal and an organizational level.

Perhaps not much has changed in the way new managers try to come to grips with their ethical dilemmas. What may seemingly give renewed concern for this important topic is not so much a change in how new managers seek resolution but rather in that the standard has been raised. Webber pointed out that "ignorance, not immorality" (p. 28) is what caused what we, with the 20–20 vision of hindsight, now question as potentially unethical decisions. Was pollution unethical in a time of un-limited resources and before global warming, decimation of the rain for-ests, melting of the polar ice caps, and holes in the ozone layer? Or are they unethical only now as we realize that the earth may not be a com-pletely renewable resource? As society becomes more aware, or as it adopts new and different values, it raises the standard of what is ac-ceptable and ethical behavior.

Aside from the awareness of ethics as a moving target, there is re-newed interest in business ethics (Kumar, 1995) on the part of new man-agers. What is not clear, however, is whether this trend will be ingrained into corporate America in the next generation. If we seem to adopt new ethical standards in years to come, is it because society is raising the standard or because the new manager is a champion of a new morality? As with so much of the socialization process, will we see the new man-ager's enthusiasm tempered by organizational culture, or will the new manager indeed be successful at bringing a stronger sense of ethics to business? Webber (1976) suggested that "people see no connection be-tween 'ethical' and 'economic' or self-interest" (p. 26). Perhaps the new managers will disagree and find that being ethical is in fact a way to improve image, better stakeholder relations, and in the end, become a more successful organization (Hosmer, 1994).

DISTINCT CHARACTERISTICS OF THE NEWEST ORGANIZATIONAL ENTRANTS

The generations born since 1965 are quite different from "baby boom-ers" (Brown-Hogarty, 1996; Losyk, 1997b). Nearly half came from di-vorced homes, and many were raised by single parents. Of those who had two parents living in the same home, more often than not, both parents worked outside of the home. As a result, these generations spent their early years in day care and their later years at home alone. This created generations of freedom-minded and self-absorbed young people who are individualistic but hungry for relationships. Additionally, the use of the TV as a baby-sitter has allowed these generations to witness more violence and negative events than generations of the past. They are well aware that the average incomes of young people are declining, and believe that their economic futures are suspect. These factors have combined to form a highly cynical group—detached but opportunistic.

Coming generations are more diverse, with more African Americans, Hispanics, and Asians than previous generations—a trend that will, in all likelihood, continue (Losyk, 1997b). They also wait longer to graduate from college, leave home, and marry. Television and mass media in gen-eral have opened up a range of new choices that were unavailable to previous generations. This has resulted in a generation of people who require, and are able to adapt to, more visual than verbal stimuli. They do not identify themselves by what they do but by who they perceive they are (Brown-Hogarty, 1996). Their compensatory concern for family values will probably lead to a request for shorter workweeks, more telecommuting, and more home-based businesses (Losyk, 1997b). Change is the major constant in our lives, and this young generation of workers is an appropriate fit with today's diverse, global, and high-tech environment (Losyk, 1997a).

THE NEW PSYCHOLOGICAL CONTRACT BETWEEN INDIVIDUALS AND ORGANIZATIONS

There are a number of common characteristics of these generations that will change the relationship between the organization and the individual (Losyk, 1997b; Munk, 1998). Owing to all the downsizing of the 1990s, young managers do not believe in the concept of job security (Brown-Hogarty, 1996; Losyk, 1997b). As such, they view jobs as a means to an end—that end being life after work. They do not hesitate to take a better position with another organization because they feel little loyalty or commitment to any particular organization. They also do not hesitate to leave when they feel that work and stress have overtaken their lives (Maynard, 1996).

These generations of the newcomers grew up in a fast and furious world. They began experimenting with computers at a young age and are the first truly computer-literate generation. Their communication style is direct and to the point. They have little patience with climbing the corporate ladder—they do not want to "pay their dues." Many question the position authority of others, while demanding respect for themselves. Looking down on the workaholic, they admire those who are able to balance work and life, succeed quickly, and then "downshift" (Brown-Hogarty, 1996; Maynard, 1996). As managers, they are more flexible, more casual, less authoritative, and more team oriented—strong on technology and weak on politics ("Xens as Managers," 1996).

Because these young workers have expectations that are different from their predecessors, they will need to be managed differently (Munk, 1998). This is a highly creative group, used to solving their own problems. Thus, managers should set specific goals for them, while allowing them the freedom to manage the process associated with achieving the goals (Losyk, 1997a; Tulgan, 1995). Associated with this is allowing flexibility and avoiding micromanaging—employing outcome-based control (Maynard, 1996). By providing them with a variety of tasks, managers may benefit by this generation's apparent ability to multitask (Brown-Hogarty, 1996).

Loyalty may be achieved by involving them in decision-making processes, especially those that affect them directly, demonstrating value and respect for their opinions (Brown-Hogarty, 1996; Losyk, 1997a). They also appreciate specific, accurate, and frequent feedback (Brown-Hogarty, 1996; Maynard, 1996; Tulgan, 1995). Managers need to recognize that these individuals are used to being bombarded with massive amounts of information and are thus capable, not only of gathering information from diverse sources but also of devising solutions to business problems based on this information. This means that successful managers will no longer hide or hoard information and will, in fact, go out of their way to gather and disseminate as much information to their employees as possible (Tulgan, 1995). This generation's creative juices can be stirred by making them feel that they are part of an overall mission; thus, communication needs to be more interactive and less authoritarian in nature (Maynard, 1996). Also, they are used to working together on projects, making them valuable members of teams, yet managers should continue to recognize the individual (Maynard, 1996).

These generations are concerned about learning new skills and maintaining marketability; thus, the more companies invest in training these people, the more loyalty and commitment they will experience (Brown-Hogarty, 1996; Losyk, 1997a; Tulgan, 1995). Corporations can accomplish this by formal training and development programs, mentoring relationships, lateral moves, high-profile projects, and the like (Tulgan, 1995). If corporations give them meaningless busywork, they risk losing this resource to another organization that will appreciate what they have to offer (Maynard, 1996; Tulgan, 1995). These generations are composed of individuals who want to make a meaningful contribution, achieving based on how they perform, not on how well they play the political game (Maynard, 1996; Tulgan, 1995). Finally, in order to keep these individuals motivated and excited about work, managers should attempt to develop a sense of fun in the workplace (Brown-Hogarty, 1996; Losyk, 1997a; Maynard, 1996).

In summary, the meaning of work and the centrality of work in human life are quite different to the new generation of newcomers as compared with those of their parents (Munk, 1998). The current generation of newcomers demonstrate their upfront desire for autonomy, self-dependency, and balance between work and family life (Hall & Moss, 1998). They share an increased desire for involvement and participation in the decisions pertaining to themselves. Furthermore, they believe they are entitled to more meaningful and involved work. To the new generation, work centrality has shifted to the balance point between individuals' interests and organizational needs with increased opportunities for self-development and autonomy.

THE CHANGING STRUCTURAL DYNAMICS OF WORK

The world of work has changed considerably since the post–baby boomers have entered the work force in the 1970s. In addition to the nature of work, the work force itself has undergone major transformations. These transformations include the burgeoning growth of technology, work flexibility, shift toward service orientation, and utilization of empowered teams.

Growth of Technology

The use of technology at work has changed the way many different jobs are accomplished. There are a significant number of jobs that are paced by, and dependent upon, technology. Technology, and the ability to use technology, has become an integral and indispensable part of many jobs.

Further, this has helped create an entirely new field—that of information management. Many jobs today are centered on the entry, analysis, and movement of data sets and capturing value through their qualitative interpretation rather than mere quantitative analysis.

Work Flexibility

In order to become more family friendly, organizations will need to develop novel approaches to worker needs. This will take the form of organization policies that will include: (1) flextime—significant flexibility in hours of work; (2) using temporary workers—to accommodate the need for more family time, organizations will utilize part-time students, homemakers, and retired persons; and (3) telecommuting and other methods designed to allow individuals to complete work at alternative work sites (e.g., home—technology will make it possible to perform many jobs anywhere, creating "anywhere" workspaces of virtual corporations).

Shift Toward Service Orientation

The sectors of the economy that have enjoyed significant expansion over the past decades have been the service sector and the financial services sector. There has been a shift in the economy from a manufacturing orientation to a service orientation (Goldstein & Gilliam, 1990). Many of the positions that are available are those that are deemed "low level." Those sectors of the economy that have been traditional beneficiaries of economic growth (e.g., manufacturing) have not fared nearly as well in generating value.

Utilization of Empowered Teams

Organizations have moved toward using teams in complex tasks. It has been reported that teams typically perform at a higher level than the best member of the team. This will be useful in that work promises to become even more complex in the future—there will be a need to develop cross-functional competencies. In addition, teams will facilitate the integration of diverse groups into the work force. As the demographics of the work force evolve, more creative solutions to today's business problems may be developed.

THE CHANGING STRUCTURAL DYNAMICS OF ORGANIZATIONS

Organizations have undergone considerable evolution, congruent with the generational and work changes over the past two decades.

Distribution of Line and Staff

Organizations have tried to develop a more lean approach to staffing. The ratio of staff to line has lowered over the years. Commensurate with this has been a decrease in the number of management positions available in organizations. The future promises many rounds of downsizing and reengineering; so we believe change will be a primary order of business in the future.

Anecdotal Data on Outcomes

Many have bemoaned the changes in the organizational commitment and loyalty of individuals. Many in the older generation see those in the younger generation as significantly less dedicated to organizations, considerably more interested in selfish pursuits, and less committed in their relationship with organizations. In many cases, this phenomenon was brought about by organizations who found that it was less expensive to replace skill sets than to retain and train current employees.

Satisfied with Less

A few years back, *Fortune* labeled this generation as the first generation that would be unable to duplicate or exceed the living standard of their parents. Organizations can no longer provide the upward mobility that has been enjoyed by previous generations. The difficulty faced by organizations is developing individuals and keeping them satisfied with less. This does not set well with the post–baby boomer generation.

Globalization

Organizations have come to the reality that they no longer exist solely in local markets. In order to be successful, organizations must be able to operate on a more global scale. This will influence both the type of employee required and the educational preparation necessary to compete effectively. This trend toward globalization has yet to reach its zenith.

Emphasis on Corporate Social Responsibility

Organizations will continue to pursue a social agenda through their efforts in corporate social responsibility. Organizations have been involved in literacy programs, nutritional efforts, and other forms of philanthropy. Whether trying to engage in social engineering or just attempting to do good deeds, organizations will, in the future, develop strategies to distribute corporate largesse in a manner consistent with organizational philosophy.

ADVICE FOR INDIVIDUAL CAREER STRATEGIES

1. *Continually develop marketable personal competencies.* Newcomers must learn to quickly add skills both to themselves and to their organization, balancing between developing their general knowledge and specific specialization. (Broad general education + advanced knowledge and skills = portable across companies and industries.)

2. *Learn self-management techniques.* Because companies are less able to provide career sponsors and counselors, newcomers will have to learn how to manage their own careers by themselves. Through networking, they must find their own career "agents," "mentors," and "confidants."

3. *Keep yourself mobile by developing a set of options.* Job insecurity means financial insecurity. Career mobility requires conservative investment and liquid resources for a year of expenses. Ownership will switch to leasing. A boundaryless career requires minimum fixed investments. Work will penetrate into every facet of life; residence will also serve as home office and training center.

4. *Team up!* Work continuously on strong team skills development to be able to function effectively from the very start of the team formation. Teams foster high performance levels, members learn to be good team members.

5. *Learn the soft art of professional mingling.* Develop a network of pro-

fessional relationships with creative leaders, efficient administrators, functional boundary spanners, and proactive socializers. The portfolio of your relationships should match the portfolio of roles needed for critical leadership and participation in the team environment.

6. *Learn the politics of tolerance but never sell yourself short.* Since most teams are becoming cross-functional and global, always select your appropriate communication media for your diverse audience. Teams have both democratic and bureaucratic dimensions. Enjoy the relaxed democracy, but never forget that all your data belong to the owner of the server—learn your liability boundaries. Employ soft communication and hard negotiation style—keep your domain within your boss's perception field. First learn the boss's values, norms, and fears. Remember that you are always virtually unemployed, creating the need for referrals.

ADVICE TO MANAGERS FOR EFFECTIVELY MANAGING NEW ORGANIZATIONAL ENTRANTS

1. *Focus on organizational core competencies.* Clarify your organization's core competencies and reasons for operation. After identifying the vital "core" competencies, outsource the rest. Core competencies mean core people—of unique social and technological competence. Expand the time and scope base of future talent identification: from labor market to high school level, and from local level to global level. Hire and make a commitment to those newcomers who have the potential to enhance the core competencies of your organization.

2. *Provide continuous computer-based training.* As continuous training is becoming the norm, the training offered represents the most valuable benefit for newcomers. Expect the technology to play an increasingly important role in the delivery of the training, particularly with the growth of telecommuting.

3. *Retain talent.* Talented newcomers will be more committed to their professional guild and discipline than to your organization. To retain them the organization should provide: respect, interesting and challenging work, opportunities for professional development, resources to use their talent, set of negotiated liberties in their work, and equitable reward based on their contributions to the organization.

4. *Be specific in determining performance goals.* A talented newcomer will require specific and explicit performance goals for team projects. Use all available technological intelligence for comprehensive, sophisticated, and objective performance measurement. Reward results above activities. Remember: The organization's value = people × competence. However, be aware of security issues and safeguard your specific assets.

5. *People make the place.* Talented new team members will commit only to a shared vision coming from inspiring leadership. The leader's uni-

fying vision links the team through clear mission statements and specific team goals. These have to be continuously communicated to avoid dysfunctional team conflict about resources.

6. *Assure quality of team performance.* A team is an organizational option. It becomes a competency only if assembled quickly and at the highest quality and commitment level. Such organizational ability requires extraordinary managerial qualities within the organization. In order to be the best, the team must first be whole.

7. *Create effective work environment.* An effective work environment includes: (a) alternative formats to traditional office (telecommuting in the "virtual" corporation space); (b) environmentally friendly space—physical and social environment for effective work behavior (conference rooms, quiet areas, and equipment areas; (c) ergonomic programs; (d) stress management programs including physical fitness programs; (e) programs directed toward individual coping and health.

8. *Make career resources available to newcomers.* Organizations should provide a career development plan that encompasses the sequence of steps necessary for advancement. This can take the form of providing milestones for newcomers. This should help newcomers understand the time horizons and evaluative criteria involved in progressing through the organization. Even if they leave the organization, keep them as optional contract workers. Do keep a good relationship with past talent; it may become your *future* talent.

CONCLUSION

We recognize that change is omnipresent in today's organizational environment. In spite of this, the problems of new managers are probably not very different than when Webber (1976) published his assessment of "career problems of young managers." Part of the search for differences is an age-old phenomenon of every generation thinking it is different from previous generations. The older generation is sure that the newer generation has different attitudes toward work (most likely opining that the newer generation has deteriorated in some important manner). The younger generation is sure that the older generation suffers from misplaced priorities (most likely that they lacked proper balance and were taken advantage of by their organization). This generational fog obscures the reality that individuals probably are different to some extent and that organizations are different to some extent but that the interface of new managers trying to find success in organizations is the same today as it has always been.

That said, where is our contribution? New managers have always had to determine the lay of the land, size up the playing field, and determine under which set of rules they had to operate. Will the new manager have to deal with a uniquely structured organization, the foreknowledge that they have to manage their careers based on how many jobs they will have, that they have to be proactive in seeking opportunities to build an asset base of knowledge and skills? Will the new manager be frustrated with organizational politics, unclear templates for success, and interminable time horizons with too few opportunities for gratification and development? Before we answer these, let us look at the organizational side. Will organizations and supervisors have to understand the needs of the individual and what makes them most productive? Will organizations and supervisors have to provide opportunities for promising new managers in order to develop their potential and entice them to devote their productive efforts to the organization long term? It should be obvious that the answer to all these questions is yes. The new manager has a responsibility to manage his or her own career, just as the organization has a responsibility to manage the productive return potential of the new manager. Understanding that the playing field has changed and the rule book may be different is the beginning of our recognition that we might be playing a slightly different game. We have pointed to some of the differences. Now it is up to the new manager and the new organization to carry out their respective responsibilities.

REFERENCES

Arnett, E. C. (1989). Futurists gaze into business's crystal ball. *Washington Post* (July 20): F1–F2.

Berlow, D. E., & Hall, D. J. (1996). The socialization of managers: Effects of expectations on performance. *Administrative Science Quarterly* (September): 207–223.

Brown-Hagerty, D. (1996). The young and restless. *Working Woman, 21*(7–8): 27–28.

Goldstein, I.L., & Gilliam, P. (1990). Training system issues in the year 2000. The *American Psychologist, 45*(2): 134–143.

Hall, D. T., & Moss, J. E. (1998). The new protean career contract: Helping organizations and employees adapt. *Organizational Dynamics* (Winter): 22–36.

Hamilton, M. H. (1988). Employing new tools to recruit workers. *Washington Post* (July 10): H1–H3.

Hogarty, D. B. (1996). The young and the restless. *Working Woman, 21*(7–8): 27–28.

Horowitz, F. D., & O'Brien M., (1989). In the interest of the nation: A reflective essay on the state of our knowledge and the challenges before us. *American Psychologist, 44*: 441–445.

Hosmer, L. T. (1994). Strategic planning as if ethics mattered. *Strategic Management Journal, 15*: 17–34.

Kumar, K. (1995). Ethical orientations of future American executives: What the value profiles of business students portend. *SAM Advanced Management Journal* (Autumn): 32–47.

Losyk, B. (1997a). Generation X: What they think and what they plan to do. *Public Management, 79*(12): 4–9.

Losyk, B. (1997b). How to manage an X'er. *The Futurist, 31*(2): 43–44.

Maynard, R. (1996). A less-stressed work force. *Nation's Business, 84*(11): 50–51.

Munk, N. (1998). The new organization man. *Fortune, 137*(5): 62–74.

Rauch, J. (1989). Kids as capital. *The Atlantic* (August): 56–61.

Stern, G. M. (1996). Young entrepreneurs make their mark. *Nation's Business, 84*(8): 49–51.

Tulgan, B. (1995). Managing Generation X. *HR Focus, 72*(11): 22–23.

Webber, R. A. (1976). Career problems of young managers. *California Management Review, 18*(4): 19–33.

Xers as managers. (1996). *Nation's Business, 84*(11): 51.

Whyte, W. H., Jr. (1956). *The organization man.* New York: Simon & Schuster.

8

Foundations of Success: A Life Course Approach to Women's Career Success

ELLA L. J. EDMONDSON BELL AND STELLA M. NKOMO

Scan through the pages of any magazine serving the needs of professional women and guess what you will find? Tons of advice on how women can succeed in today's work world. A recent article in *Working Woman* featured a story entitled "Second Chances."[1] The article was about three high-profile women "who rose to the top of their professions, and just as spectacularly they fell," only to eventually "[master] the art of comeback" (p. 5). In the same issue, Bernadette Grey, the editor in chief, gave tips for "on-the-job training" (p. 6).[2] Her advice to women wanting to climb the corporate ladder was to continue their education and to consider obtaining formal educational credentials. Networking, finding a mentor, strengthening their leadership skills, knowing how to crunch numbers, and—let us not forget—mastering the game of golf are common solutions given to women in steering their careers toward the top.

A major cause for this proliferation of information for working women is their steadily increasing numbers in the work force. They are making significant gains across industries, both in blue- and white-collar jobs. According to a report issued by the federal Glass Ceiling Commission, "two-thirds of the new labor force entrants will be women and minorities by the year 2000." Over half of these new employees will be women. The Bureau of Labor Statistics indicates that in 1990 there were 6 million women in executive, administrative, and managerial positions, as compared to 9 million men. The Glass Ceiling Commission also reported the overall work force demographics for 1994: Women represented 45.6 percent.[3] The number of women making strides in the professions will continue to grow way into the twenty-first century.

After reading these statistics, you may get the impression that women have, for the most part, broken through the proverbial glass ceiling. This is not altogether true. Many women still perceive the glass ceiling is very much intact. While their numbers are increasing, the percentage of women still remains low in the upper echelons of management. A few women are reaching the upper ranks, but they are far from breaking record numbers. Which is another reason why there is countless advice on how to succeed. Still, much of the information available to working women is based on what we call the *parachute theory*. Based on the parachute theory, women simply "drop" into a company without a history, without preconceptions of the work world, and without prior life experiences that inform their values, attitudes, and beliefs toward their careers. Imagine, if you will, women parachuting their way into companies. They are dressed in business suits, armed with a briefcase in one hand and an M.B.A. degree in the other hand, landing in offices where they undertake assignments ranging from dull to risky, until they finally work their way into the executive suite. This is great material for storybooks, but it is far from reality.

What factors contribute to women being successful in their work lives? What suggestions can we offer them? Our intention in writing this chapter is to provide some answers to both of these questions. Rather than taking a parachute approach, however, we prefer to employ a different perspective. Ours is a life history approach. We believe this perspective takes into account the depth, complexity, and richness of women's lives. Our perspective attempts to understand the factors, conditions, and people who contribute to a woman's career over the course of her life span.

The main goal of our research has been to inquire into the professional and personal lives of successful, career-oriented women. We were particularly curious to discover how a woman's racial identity shapes her life as she grows into womanhood. A majority of the career development literature on career-oriented women is based on the experiences of white women. Professional African-American women have remained invisible.[4] Our research was designed with the intention of bringing the stories of professional black women from out of the shadows. We wanted to make the career experiences of both black and white women explicit. We thought it was important to learn the ways in which a woman's racial identity shapes her life, in terms of her family background, the community where she was raised, her educational background, her considerations in selecting a career, and her work experiences.

The insights and suggestions offered in this chapter are based on ten years of research. We conducted biographical interviews with 120 women: 80 African Americans and 40 European Americans. Ours was an inquiry into the women's "lives in progress," over the course of their lives until the present.[5] A woman's story begins with her earliest recollections of childhood and continues through time, each experience building on the achievements, disappointments, struggles, celebrations, relationships, and social contexts in which her life is embedded. Using a life history approach allows us to determine those factors throughout her life span that are critical to a woman's career advancement.

We intentionally oversampled African-American women to establish a large database of their life stories. A cross-race interview team was employed in order for black women to be interviewed by a black female researcher and white women to be interviewed by a white female researcher. Interviews were conducted in two- to three-hour sessions, with each session lasting three to four hours. We interviewed the women in their homes and at their offices, early in the morning or late into the night, depending on the women's hectic schedules.

The participants for this study were recruited through different professional women's networks and referrals from participants and alumnae from educational institutions. Selected participants demonstrated a positive motivation for self-exploration, a willingness to share their life stories, and a commitment to the research project by giving their time. Participants lived in the Northeast and Southeast regions of the country. A majority of them were born in what Gail Sheehy[6] identifies as the Vietnam Generation, born between 1945 and 1955. However, a small number of the women were from the Me Generation, being born in the late 1950s. These women held jobs in a wide range of industries. Most of the women held middle-management positions, although there were a substantial number in executive positions.

In this chapter, we identify the significant relationships, conditions, and institutions that have made a positive difference in a woman's professional life. We will learn what a woman receives—socially and emotionally—from her family, community, and organizations that enables her to move forward in her career. Our approach is to share the women's stories throughout their life course, starting with their childhood experiences and leading right into the positions they held at the time of our interviews. The stories selected for this chapter best illuminate the strategies, relationships, and social supports that contributed to women's career success. We have changed the names of the women whose stories are told in this chapter and disguised other distinguishing facts of experiences in order to protect their identities.

CHILDHOOD EXPERIENCES

One of the powerful antecedents determining a woman's success in the workplace occurs long before she enters a company's front door, lands her first job assignment, and begins to establish her career. Childhood relationships, the community where a woman grew up, and educational experiences all contribute in shaping a woman's perception of the occupational world and her place in it. The salient themes occurring during childhood years were relationships with fathers, being armored for black women, the importance of being a person for white women, and developing a sense of self-reliance for women of both races.

Daddy's Girls

A consistent characteristic resonating throughout the interviews of both the black and white women was their strong identification with their fathers. The phrase "daddy's girl" was voiced time after time by the women as they talked about their fathers. These women spent a good deal of time with their fathers. Their fathers were the ones who exposed the women as young girls to the world of work. Fathers took an active role in initiating their daughters to the work ethic, mentoring them on how to be politically astute, and grooming them to enter the professional world. Fathers were typically the ones with whom the women went to discuss college decisions.

The relationship between Patricia Triggs and her father is an excellent case in point. Patricia is a substantial African-American woman, in terms of her wit, intelligence, and size. Her sentences are colorfully spiked with profanity. She is a woman who is extremely comfortable with herself. In her role as strategist for a *Fortune* 100 company, Patricia consults on product marketing with the company's top-ranking executives. Arthur Triggs, her father, was director of sales for a black-owned company and took an extremely supportive role in fostering his daughter's intellect and curiosity.

When Patricia was a sophomore in high school, she expressed an interest in following in her father's career footsteps, pursuing a career in marketing. Tapping into his professional network, Mr. Triggs scheduled a series of lunch meetings with his colleagues, selecting men and women who were employed in both large white corporations and black-owned companies. Patricia, dressed in her Sunday best, accompanied her father to lunch with a branch manager, a vice president of marketing, and a district sales manager. During each lunch she was able to ask questions about their careers: how they got started, what they did in their jobs, and anything else she wanted to know. These lunches expanded Patricia's career horizons. Mr. Triggs literally guided her earliest career aspirations, and in doing so, he gave her a vision of what her life could be, fueling the fire of her dream.

The Armoring Process

One theme found over and over again in the black women's stories was a process through which a black girl child learned what it meant to

encouraged one another to value this vision of womanhood that clearly challenges prevailing notions of femininity" (p. 109).[8]

Owing to poverty, racism, and economic conditions that prevented black men from being active members of the labor force, lessons on being independent take on a different meaning for black women. Historically, black women are socialized very early in their lives to recognize the reality that they will be jointly responsible in assisting in the financial security of the family. This reality becomes even more pronounced for women from working-poor backgrounds. Several of the black women raised in the rural South lived under conditions of dire poverty. As young girls, each woman struggled just to survive from one day to another. They learned early on in their lives to be self-reliant, mature, and responsible. Many of the women who grew up in the Deep South started working at very early ages. The meager wages they earned helped to support their families.

Eliza Washington is a middle-level manager in her mid-40s in the financial industry. She is matter-of-fact in telling of the days when she worked in the tobacco fields. Eliza Washington started picking cotton when she was 7 years old. "It was messy, it was dirty and involved real long hours." Because she was so little, she had to stand on top of two or three soda crates to reach the leaves at the top of the tobacco plant. During the summer months, Eliza was expected to work all day; she was paid $.50 an hour, all of which she gave her mother to help with household expenses.

White women learned lessons of being self-reliant differently. The social and economic context in which they lived was not tainted by institutionalized racial discrimination. Lessons of independence for white women were not grounded in the expectation or necessity that one day they would assume financial responsibility not only for themselves but also in part for their family's well-being. Take the story of Sandra Martin, a senior vice president in capital markets for a top bank. Sandra grew up on a farm in the flat spartan landscape of western Kansas. On the farm she learned to shoot guns, drive a tractor, and do the physical work required on a farm. Her mother ran two businesses in addition to helping her father run the farm. Sandra and her younger sisters were expected to do the hard physical labor required on the farm. "Dad demanded a lot of us. We loaded hay. If there was hard, physical work he expected us to be able to do it." Her most fun times were spent with her grandfather, who ran the barbershop in town. "I would sit around with him while he chewed the fat. . . . He'd drag me downtown with him and show me off because I could read the newspaper at age 5." At 5 Sandra was independent enough to ride the train by herself to stay with her grandparents, who lived 30 miles away. The conditions of the farming community and living a farmer's life forced Sandra to be more responsible at an early age.

Education

The women we interviewed attended elementary and secondary school during the late 1950s and 1960s. The historical time span is important to understanding the kinds of experiences they had in school. For the women who grew up in the South, segregation was commonplace before the effects of the 1954 *Brown v. Board of Education* Supreme Court decision permeated deeply rooted segregated school systems. Segregation was important in shaping educational opportunities, aspirations, and identities. Interestingly, black women shared more stories on ways teachers influenced their lives than white women.

Eliza Washington's phrase "tough love" best captures what the African-American women who attended all-black schools in the South received from their black teachers. Teachers pushed them to do their best, and they often played a pivotal role in supporting the educational aspirations of the women we interviewed. We found many examples where black teachers were instrumental in the development of leadership skills, the decision to go to college, and selecting a college. Encouragement often went way beyond words. Eliza Washington's guidance counselor paid for her to visit black colleges. Her counselor even loaned Eliza her car so she could visit colleges that were in close proximity. Eliza's counselor also served as a role model, as to what it meant to be a professional woman. "She introduced me to a world of things that I'd never known about. She was the first person I saw that lived a totally different lifestyle." Her guidance counselor influenced Eliza's vision of possibilities while affording opportunities to further her development.

EARLY ADULT EXPERIENCES

Career Choice

One of the major tasks facing the women in our study in their early adult years was making a career choice. Choosing a career involves committing to a career identity and planning how to pursue one's chosen career.[9] An overwhelming majority of the women, both black and white, graduated from college without specific career plans. Most felt no immediate pressure to marry, although nearly all expressed a desire to marry at some point in their lives. The general absence of career specificity we found among the women should not be construed as a lack of motivation and achievement orientation. It was indeed just the opposite. These women were high achievers, smart, and extraordinarily motivated.

Most, however, held a rather naive expectation that a successful career would somehow unfold.

Julia Smith, who graduated from a predominantly white, highly regarded women's college in the Northeast, told us, "I was 20 years old when I graduated from college and assumed that I would go to graduate school. The whole career orientation I didn't have, frankly. I think I came largely from a very naive presumption things would just sort of fall in place in some kind of way. I had no idea of the kind of active assessment that needs to go into choosing a career. It's not that I dismissed it; I didn't even realize it needed to be done." We found similar expectations among the white women. Maxine German, who is today director of corporate affairs for a *Fortune* 500 communications company, recalls her thoughts at the time she graduated from college: "I thought things just happened out there. I just came out of college not knowing what to expect at all out there, but I knew it was only going to be good." We believe the women's lack of career focus in early adulthood reflects the general lack of career counseling they received throughout adolescence and early adult life. Both the black and white women reported receiving little formal advice or help in seriously exploring career options.[10] For the most part, they were left on their own to make a career choice.

In contrast, the very few women with specific career plans in their early adult years seemed to have been most influenced by parental involvement and influence. A hallmark of the women with defined career choices were well-planned paths from college to career. These women took what we describe as a straight path from college to their chosen career. Specific plans and strategies were used to gain entry into their chosen career. Most did not leave things to chance but systematically took the steps necessary to reach their goal.

No one could have been more determined and systematic than Pat Triggs. When Pat was told by campus placement officials that she could not interview with the company she eventually landed her first job with because she was not a graduate student, she was not deterred. Pat describes in animated detail how she got both the interview and her first job in marketing.

But I knew I wanted this job, and this is all I wanted. It wasn't like well, "I'll just go on another interview or change my career plans." This is what I wanted, and I felt I had to have it. On the day the company came to campus, I went there suited up, resume in hand, and just sat outside the reception area. When the interviewer came out to let one student go and pick up the next one, I intercepted him and said, "I know you're not here to interview undergraduate students, but I have a particular interest in your company and here's why. Here's my resume. I live on campus, and I will be at this number all day, so if somebody is 5 or 10 minutes late or you want a cup of coffee, call me ∧ nd I'll be there in 5 minutes."

He said okay. I went back to my room and sat by the phone. He called me. I was there in 5 minutes. We interviewed, and he invited me to visit the company's headquarters. I went to corporate headquarters and had dinner with a branch manager and two other managers. The next day they made an offer on the spot.

Pat progressed quickly on a career path designed to lead from an assistant to a managerial position in the company. This type of behavior and focus were typical of the women who had made a choice to pursue a career in management.

So how, indeed, did the majority of the women without well-defined career goals come to their careers in management? Most of the women took what we call a meandering path to their managerial careers. Often, as one woman put it, "sort of wandering into it." Many of the women started on other careers and, after a number of false starts, ended up in a management career. They were not systematic in their search for jobs, nor did they engage in elaborate strategies or tactics. Their entry into a management career was often serendipitous.

Julia Smith took a meandering path to her entry into a management career. She drifted aimlessly after graduating from college. Seven years and two master's degrees later, she finally "fell into what would become her career." A chance conversation with an acquaintance sparked Julia Smith's interest in business management. As she tells us, "So she started me thinking about it. I said, well, maybe I ought to take the GMAT— the aptitude test for admission to business school. So I sort of just walked in two weeks later and took the test." She did well, with scores in the 97th percentile. Julia was accepted to an Ivy League business school. After graduation, she was highly recruited and landed a job in a *Fortune* 500 company.

For many of the white women in our study the meandering route often started with positions as secretaries or administrative assistants in corporations even though they held college degrees.[11] This is not a pattern we found for the African-American women. After graduating from an elite private women's college, Jean Hofbrau attended a secretarial school so that she could learn how to type. She ended up working as an administrative assistant to a president of a company for a number of years. Eventually, she decided to get an M.B.A. degree and made the commitment to a career in management. It was only at the point she started her first management job that her career goals crystallized: "Well, the day I arrived at the company I knew I wanted to become one of the very few female officers. There was no question in my mind that's what I wanted, and I was positive I was capable of doing it."

Career Entry

While career choice is a major task in early adult life, the next developmental task is being successful in the early stages of one's career. For the women in our study, this required rapidly learning the essential knowledge, skills, and abilities needed to perform well in their first business positions. All of the women identified significant experiences during their career entry that accelerated their learning. For the majority of the women this occurred when they faced a particularly challenging job assignment or being placed in a position where they were no longer in a learning mode but in one that required them to produce results. Both the black and white women left these experiences with important lessons about what it meant to be a successful manager.

Perhaps Dawn Briggs, a high-level marketing manager in the manufacturing industry, best captures what we heard from a number of the women about the transition to becoming a manager.

Coming up the line you have to manage relationships and getting the work done with other resource groups. But then once you get into a managerial role, you have your own assistants and associates reporting to you. It was big. I mean it was scary. A nonmanagerial position had to do with knowing your own capabilities. You know you can get the work done and get it done right. But in a managerial position you have to worry about your staff doing what they're supposed to be doing. . . . You don't have time to go through all of the detail. So you learn to ask questions, set priorities, and trust people to get things done with enough guidance. It's very different.

Gaining self-confidence in their jobs bolstered the women's commitment to a career in management. Sandra Martin "learned that I like managing people. I felt like I had a knack for it. I learned from my early work experience that you have to face the tough issues. You cannot let them go. I also learned I liked the decision process involved in being a manager."

Performing well in the job was not the only important task for these women as they entered management careers. We found other important learning tasks grounded in race and gender. These tasks took on different dimensions for the black and white women in our study. For African-American women the tasks were tied to both their race and gender. The African-American women in our study entered corporate America in the 1970s, representing the first significant cohort of black women to assume authority positions managing white men and women. Eighty-five percent of the African-American women we interviewed identified themselves as the lone African-American woman at her level. "I never felt so disadvantaged as a black woman," recalls Brenda Boyd, as she talked about her first position in a manufacturing plant of a *Fortune* 500 company.

So it was very difficult. I entered a company where the whole language was the world of men. Everything was white male culture. They used different language and had different mores. I had to learn white male culture. I had to learn the culture of baseball and football. None of my analogies, none of my metaphors were appropriate. They didn't understand what I said. They could not believe I was good for the business. It was just a brutal environment. . . . it was a lonely, demoralizing experience sometimes. I never had peers to talk with. So I had to learn how to be particularly diplomatic; otherwise, I would be misunderstood.

The bicultural skills the African-American women developed in their childhood were needed to help them successfully navigate the corporate cultures they encountered.[12]

The African-American women also had to develop a way of maintaining a sense of worth and self-confidence in an environment that constantly reminded them they didn't belong. What comes through clearly in their narratives about early career experiences is learning to distinguish between experiences resulting from their own capabilities and those reflecting racism or other external causes. We use the term *defensive efficacy* to capture this trait.[13] The women learned to protect their self-esteem and not internalize negative racial experiences.

For the white women in the study, overcoming the intimidation of working with men was a significant learning experience. Jean Hofbrau had to overcome feeling intimidated when making presentations to her male colleagues. "I learned I could get through it. However frightening it was, you could get through it. They weren't going to ask you every single thing. I was terrified they would ask, but they were basically on your side and wanting to like the idea rather than wanting to criticize or rip it to shreds. It was not as hard as I feared it would be. Preparing thoroughly, I mean intricately, was absolutely necessary. I memorized my stuff."

Career Mastery

What almost all of the women in our study discovered was making a successful career entry was only the beginning. Once the women had learned the basic requirements of their positions and felt comfortable with their careers, concerns shifted to mastering increased levels of competency and a desire to progress in their careers. Career mastery and getting ahead in their careers presented a whole new set of challenges and behaviors. While career development theorists recognize the challenges faced by individuals during the advancement career stage, women and minorities often face a different set of tasks due to what has been called the *glass ceiling phenomenon*.[14] All of the women, both black and white, consistently cited one important factor: To advance in their careers, they had to excel in job performance to counter stereotypes about women's capacity for significant management responsibilities.

While gender represents a barrier to the advancement of all women, we found race and gender simultaneously created qualitatively different barriers to the advancement of African-American women compared to the white women in our study. Consequently, we found differences in the strategies and actions used by each group to overcome the factors blocking their advancement and performance.

The African-American women who were most successful in advancing in their organizations developed creative responses to the barriers encountered. A common element in the career paths of these women was *outspiraling* career moves—changing employers or functions to gain upward mobility.[15] These moves often turned into a quantum leap propelling the women into a job with greater responsibility and visibility. We found two primary reasons explaining outspiraling moves by the African-American women. One prompt was recognizing that mobility was limited in a current job. In the case of Pat Triggs, when she could not get a fair review despite her outstanding performance, she left. She took a position in a new company that "doubled my salary and at that point I was making more than I ever thought I would ever see in my life. I finally had my dream job. I'm in charge. I'm reporting to the head guy. He's taking my advice. I'm traveling around the world doing marketing strategy. I had realized my plan." Other times the African-American women moved on when they realized they were working for a manager who was prejudiced. They realized the need to move on to a more receptive environment.

In addition to outspiraling strategies, the women developed other creative responses to gain mastery of their careers. One of the formidable barriers to advancement for the African-American women was exclusion from informal organizational networks. We found that the most successful African-American women invented other ways to tap into the informational networks in their organizations. Instead of using the informal, social networks that excluded them, they turned to more formal mechanisms. A typical example was the use of a formal luncheon to brief another group of officers or important clients.

Another important tactic used by the women was volunteering for additional assignments that would enable them to gain additional skills. As one woman told us, "I had to develop myself by expanding my job out. I went to other department heads and said to them, 'I would like to work on one of your projects.'" Seeking additional assignments helped the women to broaden their technical skills and increase their visibility in other parts of their organizations.

We found that very few of the African-American women in our study had mentors. But what they did identify were supportive bosses who championed their career, not just by being a good boss but by actively fighting for them. Part of the developmental task for the African-

American women was recognizing and getting to work for the "right" boss. Pat Triggs captures this need:

Black women have to be lucky or astute enough to work for people who make sure they get credit for their work and make sure the value of their work is understood among their peers. . . . So you have to work for a special individual who says, "Excuse me, but so-and-so did this—not helped me but drove me. Did it, presented it." . . . So working for somebody who is honest and fair isn't enough. They will generally have to go to bat to get what the black woman is due because she is black.

There were two other behavioral dimensions significant in the women's continued achievement in their careers. First was being able to accurately read company culture and to maneuver within the culture without sacrificing their identity. The most successful African-American women were adept in functioning in predominantly white corporate cultures. These women were also keenly aware of the highly political nature of the organizations in which they found themselves. Second, over time the women developed what we call *refined sassiness* as part of their business persona. Treading a very fine line, they were able to be assertive and forthright without crossing the line to impertinence. These women learned how to make their directness work for them in their organizations.

We found among the white women in our study a different set of strategies to address the barriers affecting their career advancement. One tactic used by the women who felt discriminated against was to carefully pick their battles and to use their power wisely. Gloria Goldberg, who rose to the level of partner in an investment banking company, told us, "You learn to keep your mouth shut a little longer. You learn who to trust. Sometimes you're right and sometimes you're wrong. At certain levels you overcome it [sexual discrimination] because you have power." While the African-American women mastered the art of forthrightness without crossing the boundary to impertinence, the white women we interviewed seemed to rely more on accommodative behaviors.

Finally, many of the white women spoke of the instrumental role of mentors in advancing their careers. Linda Butler still recognizes the men who mentored her in her rise to a senior executive in the utility industry. "For whatever reason they had, or whether they thought I was the daughter they didn't have or the granddaughter or whatever, they were very supportive."

LESSONS FOR THE FUTURE

What lessons can be gleaned from the women's stories told in this chapter for women managing their careers in the coming decade? We believe there are several important lessons. In the coming decades, we will need to think about both career success and failure in a much broader context.

Too much emphasis has been given to thinking about careers only during the adult years. This is a mistake. A woman's chances for success in the occupational sphere are enhanced when she is supported by those institutions where she regularly interacts. The experiences, learning, and relationships over the course of a woman's life have a definite influence on how she comes to understand the work world and her position in it.

Based on our research, we believe it is the cumulative aspects of a woman's life that in part determine the degree of success she experiences. Under these circumstances, we should not underestimate the powerful effects of messages a woman receives during her childhood. Family and communities where a woman is raised shape a woman's fundamental sense of self, including her career aspirations. They instill in her the fortitude to move her life beyond traditional boundaries and expectations usually attributed to women.

The black women in our study represent the first generation of black women free to pursue a professional career without the expectation of assuming a domestic role. Their parents, extended kinfolks, and members of their communities joined together in giving them unconditional love, armored them to do their best in the white world, encouraged them to be achievement oriented, and told them stories of their people's painful struggles to achieve racial equality. A resounding theme throughout the black women's narratives was that they were expected to use their talents, skills, and education not only to advance their own status but to help those in the black community who were less fortunate.

White women, particularly those raised in middle-class families, grew up amid family settings that gave them high expectations and fostered a notion of self-help and individual achievement in spite of sexism. It is a theme reflected in their attitudes about advancing in their professional careers. They were taught to believe in the spirit of meritocracy: Individual hard work is rewarded.

While there are critical lessons about career success early in the life cycle, there are also insights to be taken from adult life experiences. A major factor in the success of the women in our study was their ability to quickly read the work environments they entered. Both the black and white women developed strategies to advance and leverage their careers. But we cannot dismiss the role of individual will and resilience. A number of women displayed the ability to pick themselves up despite overwhelming odds against them. They persevered and, in some cases, even thrived from the adverse conditions of their early lives to become self-actualizing, achieving, and self-reliant women.

It should be remembered that these women entered corporate America during a time of relative stability and calm. Well-defined career tracks and job security are things of the past, not the future. The world is changing rapidly and will only continue to do so in the next decade. Turbulent and often unpredictable changes in the political, technological, and sociocultural environment of organizations are having profound effects in the workplace and on the nature of careers. While women will continue to have unprecedented opportunities for nontraditional careers, they will have to be entrepreneurial to achieve success. Flatter organizations mean fewer opportunities for hierarchical advancement. Career resiliency will happen for those women who are flexible and willing to constantly reinvent themselves. They will need to engage in continuous lifelong learning to gain new skills. They will need to be flexible risk takers as they adapt to new roles. Turbulent environments are not just affecting the workplace but all spheres of women's lives.

In his life history study of women's lives, Daniel J. Levinson contends, "To a much greater degree than is usually recognized, women and men have lived in different social worlds and have differed remarkably in their social roles, identities, and psychological attributes" (p. 38).[16] *Gender splitting* is the phenomenon where the domestic sphere is relegated to women and the public sphere is relegated to men. Women's lives are more complex than ever, because they are assuming multiple roles in both the private and domestic spheres. Successful career women will be required to reinvent themselves as they renegotiate their roles as wives, mothers, and daughters of aging parents.

A reinvention of life requires women to think of their lives more holistically. Such reinvention means a new way of being with oneself, with others, and with one's work. It will mean integrating the multiple dimensions of a woman's life—career, personal relationships, leisure, and spiritual—in ways that will bring energy, meaning, and focus. Building relationships with other women and men is an important key. In this context, we are not talking about the usual rhetoric associated with networking. Rather, we mean establishing deeper, authentic, and trusting relationships, where a woman can be open about her vulnerabilities, her fears, and her hopes. Successful women need people in their lives who will push them to move ahead but who will also help them up when they fail. It is not women alone who will have to reinvent themselves. Men will also need to rethink their relationships and how they think about work and other dimensions of their lives. It will necessitate redefining their roles in personal relationships and in their families. We leave this topic to be explored by other scholars.

NOTES

1. "Second Chances," *Working Woman*, April 1998, p. 5.
2. Bernadette Grey, "From the Editor," *Working Woman*, April 1998, p. 6.

3. In 1994 there were 58.4 million women in the work force. The actual demographic breakdown for working women based on 1990 census data is as follows: white women, 77.2 percent; African-American women, 12 percent; Hispanic American, 7.2 percent; Asian and Pacific Islander American, 3 percent; and American Indian, .7 percent. See the report *Good for Business: Making Full Use of the Nation's Human Capital* (Washington, DC: Glass Ceiling Commission, March 1995).

4. Many of the classic studies of women managers did not include African Americans in their samples. See, for example, M. Hennig and A. Jardim, *The Managerial Woman* (New York: Pocket Books, 1978); L. Larwood and M. Wood, *Women in Management* (Lexington, MA: D. C. Heath, 1977). Ann Morrison, Laurie White, and Marian M. Van Velsor only included one African-American woman in her sample for *Breaking the Glass Ceiling: Can Women Reach the Top of America's Largest Corporations?* (Boston: Addison-Wesley, 1987).

5. The term *lives in progress* was first conceived by Robert W. White in his book *Lives in Progress* (New York: Dryden Press, 1952).

6. Gail Sheehy, *New Passages: Mapping Your Life across Time* (New York: Random House, 1995).

7. The term *armor* has been used in the psychotherapy literature to describe an adaptive mechanism for coping with racial oppression. See, for example, B. Greene, "African-American Women," in *Women of Color: Integrating Ethnic and Gender Identities in Psychotherapy*, ed. L. Comas-Diaz and B. Greene (New York: Guildford Press, 1994), pp. 10–29. In her group work with women involved in interracial relations, Faulkner used the concept of armoring when referring to "specific behavioral and cognitive skills used by Black and other people of color to promote self-caring during direct encounters with racists experiences and/or racists ideologies." Faulkner believes young women of color are taught by their families to armor themselves against racism at a very early age." J. Faulkner, "Women in Interracial Relationships," *Women and Therapy*, 2 (1983): 193–203.

8. For additional references on black women's self-reliance, please refer to the following: P. H. Collins, *Black Feminist Thought: Knowledge, Consciousness and the Politics of Empowerment* (Boston: Unwin Hyman, 1990); L. W. Myers, *Black Women: Do They Cope Better?* (Englewood Cliffs, NJ: Prentice-Hall, 1980); G. Joseph, "Black Mothers and Daughters: Their Roles and Functions in American Society," in *Common Differences*, ed. Gloria Joseph and Jill Lewis (Garden City, NY: Anchor, 1981); and F. C. Steady, "Black Women Cross-Culturally: An Overview," in *The Black Woman Cross-Culturally*, ed. Filomina C. Steady (Cambridge, MA: Schenkman, 1981), pp. 7–12.

9. For a detailed description of the elements involved in career choice of successful women, see Barbara White, Charles Cox, and Cary Cooper, *Women's Career Development: A Study of High Flyers* (London: Blackwell Publishers, 1992).

10. Other research supports the view that many school counselors, teachers, and even professors provide little support and encouragement for women to explore careers, especially nontraditional careers. For example, see the research reported by E. E. Gordon and M. H. Sorber, "Initial Observations on a Pioneer Cohort: 1974 Women MBAs," *Sloan Management Review*, 19 (1978): 15–23; N. E. Betz and L. F. Fitzgerald, *The Career Psychology of Women* (Orlando, FL: Academic Press, 1987). For a general discussion on the unique career development issues

facing women, see B. Gutek and L. Larwood, *Women's Career Development* (New-
bury Park, CA: Sage, 1987).

11. It should be noted that this port of entry to a management career was
nonexistent among the African-American women in our study. During the time
these women entered corporate America (1970s), secretarial positions were not
readily available to African-American women and were dominated by white
women. So not only were secretarial positions gendered, but they were also
racialized. For a good discussion of the racial nature of women's occupations,
see T. L. Amott and J. A. Matthaei, *Race, Gender and Work: A Multicultural Economic History of Women in the United States* (Boston: South End Press, 1991).

12. In an earlier study, Ella L. Bell found that professional black women found
themselves living in two distinct cultural contests, one black and the other one
white. The women compartmentalized the various components of their lives in
order to manage the bicultural dimensions. See E. L. Bell, "The Bicultural Life
Experience of Career-Oriented Black Women," *Journal of Organizational Behavior*,
11 (1990): 459–477.

13. This concept reflects one of the defensive mechanisms of a well-developed
black identity described by William E. Cross in his work *Shades of Black: Diversity
in African-American Identity* (Philadelphia: Temple University Press, 1991).

14. For further elaboration on the unique barriers to advancement for women
and minorities, see E. J. Smith, "Issues in Racial Minorities' Career Behavior," in
Handbook of Vocational Psychology, Vol. 1, ed. W. B. Walsh and S. H. Osipow
(Hillsdale, NJ: Lawrence Erlbaum Associates, 1983), pp. 161–222; J. H. Greenhaus,
S. Parasuraman, and W. M. Wormley, "Effects of Race on Organizational Expe-
riences, Job Performance Evaluations, and Career Outcomes," *Academy of Management Journal*, 33 (1990): 64–86; S. M. Nkomo and T. Cox, Jr., "Factors Affecting
the Upward Mobility of Black Managers in Private Sector Organizations," *The
Review of Black Political Economy, 18* (1990): 39–58; E. Bell and S. Nkomo, "Barriers
to Work Place Advancement Experienced by African Americans," in *Good for
Business: Making Full Use of the Nation's Human Capital*; Morrison, White, and
Velsor, *Breaking the Glass Ceiling*; B. Reskin, "Sex Segregation in the Workplace,"
in *Annual Review of Sociology*, ed. J. Blake and J. Hagen (Palo Alto, CA: Annual
Reviews, 1993), pp. 241–270.

15. For a discussion of the concept of outspiraling, see White, Cox, and Cooper, *Women's Career Development*.

16. D. J. Levinson, *The seasons of a woman's life* (New York: Alfred A. Knopf,
1996).

9

Knowing Yourself: Who? Why? What? How? and When?

DIANA PAGE

INTRODUCTION

Good-bye, "job." Hello, "work." The first part of this chapter describes the history of work from the employee's perspective. When you read this part, you will gain an understanding of what work meant to employees, how they felt about their work role, and why work was so important to their lives.

Historically, freedom from work has been the ideal. It was the ruling classes who established societal rules, made decisions about labor for others, and lived comfortable lifestyles mainly from the labor of their employees. Throughout history, the masses of populations have provided the labor that sustained societies. Work habits and standards of behavior were vastly different in the preindustrial era than in the postindustrial era. Personal reputation, family ties, and strong interpersonal relations characterized preindustrial work activities, whereas routine, structure, and largely impersonal relations characterized postindustrial work activities. Propelled by technology and globalization, the turn of our century will chronicle another major transition in the work world.

Although tomorrow's workers will have more options than workers will in the twentieth century, information about future work and value of knowledge and skills will be more critical than they were in the past. The chapter will first provide an explanation as to why work transitions may be traumatic. Next, the chapter describes Who? What? Why? How? and When? strategies to help you manage work transitions and to determine your career direction and work values.

HISTORY AND DEFINITION OF A "JOB"

Labor and the economy are interwoven and impact three essential groups: the agrarian, manufacturing, and service sectors. Fundamental changes in the way the manufacturing and service sectors do business are taking place today. Significant changes in the agrarian sector continue to emerge. However, since the agrarian sector is the oldest of the sectors, the technological impact is more apparent, and thus its progress is easier to recognize.

Therefore, to unfreeze current beliefs about what jobs are, and reframe beliefs about what jobs will be in the future, let's examine the transition of labor in the United States from farming to manufacturing, including a few important sociological factors, and broadly apply those concepts to the prospects for the future of work.

A job in the eighteenth century referred to a task, an undertaking, or a single piece of work (Bridges, 1994). People didn't have jobs; they *did* jobs. Out of necessity, work was defined as what people did, and farming was the primary type of work done by an individual. Controlled by patriarchal figures, individual families worked as a unit for economic necessities. The span of generations within families often included both young and old and male and female members. The nuclear family included a husband and wife, their parents, children of the married couple, and any unmarried brothers and sisters. Family members recognized prescribed roles and accepted a progression of status from one role to another (Brown & Harrison, 1978). The large number of family members and the large number of working family members maximized family security in an era of economic uncertainty that pervaded the preindustrial era. These numbers also brought prestige to families inasmuch as the family unit could cultivate the soil and reap the harvest for food products. Who you were was determined largely by family ancestry, religious affiliation, and personal character.

Work patterns of the preindustrial era (Brown & Harrison; 1978; Zuboff, 1988) were notably different from today's patterns. Because most preindustrial work activities grew from the home, patterns of work were integrated with family life and social activities of the community. Families working side by side depended upon each other to complete specific tasks and activities. In addition to agrarian jobs, innovative trades and crafts such as metalwork, shoemaking, and weaving were developed. Those who worked were guided more by individual necessity rather than by acquisitive ambitions (Zuboff, 1988, p. 31). Moving from an agrarian to an industrial society was thus traumatic for workers.

Effects of "Industrialized" Jobs on Lifestyles

Machines, modeled after human beings and organized in assembly-line formations, were built to meet the increasing demand for products. Ironclad giants resembling elbow and knee joints, configured to automatically produce goods in great quantity with only limited requirements for human labor, gave definition to the Industrial Revolution. Mechanized creatures manually operated by employees with one-dimensional skills produced goods such as metal and lumber products. Manufacturers in the late 1800s, wanting to increase production and eliminate the amount of labor needed to make a product, devised ways to maximize the output of these great machines. More important, these first machines required workers to perform physically demanding or uninteresting tasks on a repetitive and continuous basis. The interface of workers was important only as a function of production.

Further exacerbating this phenomenon were the organizational rules and regulations developed to sustain production levels. Factories employing large numbers of employees who were not socialized to attend work regularly or to arrive at work on time proved costly and inefficient. Intending to provide direction and consistent organizational rules to follow, factory managers developed formal working relationships and communications patterns.

Hierarchical structures grew in response to the classical approach to management. The classical management approach assumed that workers needed to be controlled and added layers of supervision and management to the structure of the organization. The rapid horizontal and vertical growth in the numbers and kinds of factory workers spawned the bureaucracy. The division of labor was crucial, and employees occupied boxes on an organizational chart. They were responsible for specialized tasks and accountable for their work to those immediately above them on a triangular hierarchy. Interpersonal relations addressing social rights and non-work-related issues became less of a priority for management.

The Industrial Revolution produced an extensive change in the patterns of the work. Workers who used to regulate their own work schedules in harmony with the seasons and personal needs were not prepared for the confinement of work activities in factories. Supervisors required workers to perform physically demanding or uninteresting tasks on a repetitive schedule, which came into conflict with workers used to generating their own schedules. Workers felt dehumanized; they resented the confinement and discipline required in the new factories and worked only long enough to purchase necessities. Workers, then, did not readily choose the rigidity and physical indignities of factory discipline as their favorite alternative. Tardiness and absenteeism became standard behaviors as workers struggled to cope with their changing work environment.

The traditional "cottage" industry that produced a few products was replaced by mass production, which produced more products.

Technological Factors Impacting the Past and a Future Agrarian Employment Sector

Reviewing the technological impact on the agrarian and manufacturing labor sectors allows the future of the service sector to become more clear. The mechanization of agriculture from 1880 to 1916 reduced the number of man-hours required to harvest an acre of wheat by 63 percent and 20 years later, by an additional 16 percent (Rifkin, 1995). In a little more than 100 years, the contributions of modern technology further reformed the nature of the farming industry. The farming population in the United States now is less than 3 million, but it sustains a food industry employing more than 20 million workers (Tosterud & Jahr, 1982, in Rifkin, 1995, p. 309). Large agricultural companies have replaced the family farms because of "economies of scale." Chemical and pharmaceutical companies in the future, using genetic engineering technologies, could convert food production into a totally industrial process. Thus, farming as we think of it today would be eliminated.

Sociological Factors Impacting the Growth of Industry and Jobs

Cheap labor and a wealth of natural resources catapulted the United States to economic supremacy by the middle of the twentieth century. Factories and plants developing new products continued to progress through the 1960s. Three factors that critically impacted organizations during this time frame were aggregation, differentiation, and rationalization (Caplow, 1954). *Aggregation* refers to the diversity of social groups brought together in the workplace. *Differentiation* refers to the number of occupations and, in this case, to the increasing number of specializations within these occupations. *Rationalization* occurs when "formal control of behavior is substituted for informal, personal, and spontaneous" actions (p. 24).

The interplay of these factors resulted in complex, highly differentiated organizational structures bursting with prescribed external and internal policies, procedures, and rules. Size and complexity of the organization were closely related with more rigid expectations of human behavior. While rationalization allowed managers to more closely predict certain outcomes, it rejected personal relationships that lay the groundwork for important ethics, responsibilities, and ingenuity. Nevertheless, the industrial labor force multiplied so intensely that by 1960, 35 percent of the total labor force was employed in the manufacturing sector (Heilbroner, 1995, Foreword, p. xii).

Organizational structures approximating great pyramids redefined earlier "jobs." Instead of an activity, the meaning of *job* changed to "position." This was a period of "Camelot," where the myth of the "job" was accepted and "position" became a substitute for "job." Employees identified with, and were distinguished by, their position, or job title. Precise job descriptions detailing expectations of employees and describing reporting relationships were developed. Additionally, human resource personnel developed entire functional career paths, suggesting specific series of jobs leading up the hierarchical corporate ladder.

Psychological Factors Impacting Twentieth-Century Jobs

Generally, the old implicit work-world contract consisted of an agreement of obedience and diligence in exchange for security (Hammer, 1996, 156). Some of the more stable companies even advertised that they "hired for life." The cost of this contractual arrangement became too expensive. Unionism grew, federal regulation increased, and bureaucracies developed as layers of supervision and management were added to organizational structures to measure and control performance. All of these factors added to the cost of doing business in an ever-increasing competitive market. Each of these elements added degrees of specificity that changed the once psychological contract to a formidable requisite for employers.

After many years, this characterization of work offered comfort to institutionalized workers who knew exactly what to expect from their employer and what was expected of them. Nevertheless, "the more attached we've grown into prescribed positions, the more we've lost touch with the inner resources that energize and feed our souls" (Pulley, 1997, p. 24). For example, it is generally the employer who is in the driver's seat. Employers have developed some fairly sophisticated tools and strategies to recruit and select employees. These tools and strategies are designed to attract potential employees who add value to the organization and who "fit" organizational behaviors and philosophies. Such a fit is contrived at best. The assumption here is that the organization is in control, not the employee. Since it is human nature for us to want to be in control of our lives, at least to some degree, this loss of control results in increased feelings of helplessness and stress. Too many employees in the 1990s are part of a negatively inclined psychological spiral. Chasing the American Dream means holding on to the myth of the "job." Preserving the job allows us to acquire material wealth and to live a certain lifestyle. These acquisitions, however, do not necessarily include satisfaction, inner peace, and family harmony.

Thus, workers progressing from the agrarian to the industrial society dealt with dramatic changes in the very nature of work, as work became jobs. These cultural work changes caused a lot of stress and anxiety. Self-reliant, hardworking, agrarian workers with strong family and friendship ties, unable to compete with mass-production methods, felt obsolete. Moving into factories to work required work styles that were very different from preindustrial jobs. Defined social rights and obligations were no longer part of the work culture. In these factories, other people, called supervisors and managers, were responsible for making decisions once made by the workers themselves. As layers of management grew vertically, more and more of the decision-making responsibilities moved upward. By the time the decisions made by upper management reached lower levels of the organizations, the interpretations were so ambiguous, different, or untimely that many of the decisions were counterproductive. Employees who wanted to do a good job were often frustrated. Unable to overcome the momentum of the bureaucratic process, frustration reigned over drive and creativity. Often, the result of this frustration for employees was fear and chaos. Thinking about organizational structure in this context, it is easy to see why organizations during the last fifteen years have either downsized or "rightsized" their work force. Once again, "job" is being redefined. Chaos and turbulence have modified jobs, once thought of as specific and permanent.

Organizations developed a variety of strategies in order to survive and compete. Some strategies included reorganizing and downsizing, and mergers and acquisitions. More than 8 million people lost their jobs to downsizing between 1980 and 1993 (Hubiak & O'Donnell, 1997). Understandably, employee morale was low. One author suggests that the physical sweatshops of the earlier industrial days have been replaced by the 1990s psychological sweatshops (Brown, 1996).

JOB/WORK/CAREER OF THE FUTURE

Futurists describe work and careers quite differently than work in either preindustrial or industrial times. Downsizing has reached its ebb, and organizations are phasing in new employees. However, employee relationships with employers will differ greatly from past relationships. The following are a few examples of future work patterns.

- *Outsourcing*—using outside services or independent contractors or other businesses.
- *Temporary work*—paying an outside agency to provide workers when needed.
- *Independent contractors*—hiring outside independent individuals to carry out or complete a particular project.
- *Gainsharing*—calculating employee pay based on worker contribution and cost.
- *Commission*—paying workers a percentage of what they've sold or saved.

The term *permanent employee* will be appropriate to a much smaller percentage of the work force. Employees who do make up the permanent work force will possess core skills. Examples of core skills are intellectual capital, communications skills, appropriate technological skills, and relevant professional skills for the specific occupation. Hammer (1996) describes three elements that characterize core skills: customer orientation, process orientation, and results orientation. Future workers will need to understand the big picture, business goals, customer needs, and process structures. Rewards will be based on results rather than the performance of specific tasks.

Instead of pursuing the American Dream that worked well for your parents, you need to cultivate your own dream. Where do you start?

Develop an attitude. "Get an attitude"—one that is appropriate for future work. This means you will need to develop new metaphors about your work life. Future work does look challenging. The very nature of work is shifting, and changing metaphors will help you to develop positive, realistic work patterns. For example, the chart below, modified from Edwards and Edwards (1996, p. 42), examines the new and old metaphors that describe attitudes toward work.

Nineteenth-Century Work Attitude	*Twentieth-Century Work Attitude*
After work there is life	In work there is life
Work is what you do	Work is part of who you are
Work is often an unpleasant means to an end	Work itself is enjoyable and satisfying and gives your life meaning
What you do is assigned based on what the boss wants, or company politics dictate	What you do is an expression of yourself and what your clients need
Financial gain is fixed	Financial gain depends on personal results
Freedom comes later	Freedom comes now
You work at the direction of others	Your work is self-directed
Others control the work environment	You control your work environment
Self-expression is sacrificed for economic security	Economic security comes from self-expression
Working on a team is too difficult	Working in a team can increase your personal effectiveness

Future work, then, has the potential to bring you a stronger sense of self-worth and a more solid integration with yourself than with any particular job or career. Rather than organizational control, scheduling your own time, making your own decisions about what you will do and when you will do it, will govern your behavior. Additionally, more opportunities for self-expression that are related to work will emerge.

There are a few elements of the old "job" that are eroding. Fewer, if any, traditional benefits such as health insurance and pension plans will be offered. The stability and security promised by yesterday's jobs are gone. Retirement options will be personal choices, and employees will opt in and out of the labor force in a wider array of patterns than are currently exercised. But developing a new attitude about work will require a transition. Let's talk about the transition from "old" to "new" attitudes.

Managing transitions. Well, if future work is as exciting as it sounds, then why are so many people stressed about the upcoming work patterns? Why do we cling to the old patterns? The answer is, Most workers do not want CHANGE! It's true some people actually do prefer change more than others. But when change is ambiguous and affects us personally, we prefer things stay the same. Lack of self-knowledge and fear of failure are also reasons why we resist change.

Nevertheless, the very nature of work is reforming, and jobholders are experiencing major changes. The psychological impact of having or not having a job is tremendous. Most people in our society define themselves in large part through their job. Job tasks and activities define our roles and to whom we speak and structure a large portion of our life. Driven by the broader societal push to "do a job," and "do a good job," many people have dedicated their lives to their work or a Company. Such employees may have forsaken their families and lives outside work in an attempt to be loyal employees. For those with unhappy lives or no family lives, a job may be the only activity from which they derive any recognition or self-esteem. As the old idea of jobs as fixed positions in organizations changes, how can we kick the work habit?

Let's examine briefly the difference between change and transition as outlined by Bridges (1991). Then we'll discuss what transition means to us personally and discuss ways of dealing with transitions.

Change is situational and external (Bridges, 1991). It refers to a specific activity, thing, or circumstance. Changing necessarily means giving something up or exchanging one thing for another. For example if you leave one company and move to another, you'll have to leave a network of professional and personal relationships. These established relationships are important to your comfort level. Naturally, we don't want to leave this comfort zone for the unknown. But an important first step to continual change that is part of all of our lives today is to let go of the past and plan for the future.

In contrast, transition is action oriented; it means moving from one position, subject, and the like, to another. Transition refers to the internal, psychological process people go through to come to terms with a new circumstance (Bridges, 1991). Using the transition process will help you to develop your own work paradigms. The transition process includes three steps: letting go, acknowledging the indefinite zone, and adapting to new situations.

In step one, letting go, it is necessary for you to openly acknowledge your losses. Denial, anger, bargaining, anxiety, sadness, disorientation, and depression are the coping mechanisms used to deal with the impact of losses. Expect to experience some of these emotions. But instead of ignoring these emotions, deal with them openly with family members and other members of your support group. Recognize your felt losses. You will miss old habits, haunts, and friendships. Give yourself enough time to grieve over your losses. The time frame may be a couple of days or weeks.

In step two, acknowledge the indefinite zone. Old patterns and habits have stopped, and we have not yet developed new ones. In this in-between zone, it is natural to feel confused and somewhat alone. Easing these feelings can be accomplished by redefining the new situation or by assigning a new metaphor. This is a great opportunity to create new metaphors, dream of what you would like to do, break the rules, and empower yourself to think differently.

Step three means starting something new. Adapt to the new situation. People want and fear new beginnings. New beginnings reactivate old anxieties, perhaps because beginnings confirm an end to the old, comfortable way. Beginnings may provoke old memories of past failures. To triumph over this pattern, clearly define your purpose and objectives. This helps differentiate the current from past situations. Then reinforce your behavior by applauding yourself for each small step you take toward the desired change. Get to know yourself: Understand who you are, what you would like to become, and how and when you can achieve your goals.

Goal setting gives direction to the Who? Why? What? How? and When? of knowing yourself. Translating these questions into concrete goals dramatically increases the likelihood that change will result. The rest of the chapter will focus on setting goals that will help you define your work life goals, professional attributes, and long-term career plan.

GOAL ONE: CLEARLY DEFINE *WHO* YOU ARE

Today defining who you are means describing your abilities, characteristics, and desires. A few activities that may help you to define or reinvent yourself include the following: Attend a class or seminar, seek professional career counseling, write a journal, discuss who you are with family, friends, and colleagues, or read and learn about some of the psychological and career-related materials and apply them yourself. Each of these activities will help you gain valuable information and insights about who you are and who you would like to become. You may gain a more total picture of yourself by using more than one of these tools.

Recognizing your uniqueness is the purpose of engaging in the activities mentioned. Different ways of thinking, acting, and feeling comprise your personality. Helping someone to define who they are is a complex process. Thus, competent counselors and instructors use more than one tool to assess personalities. Some of the tools used by instructors and counselors include personality, skill, vocational, and values assessments.

One widely used personality assessment, the Myers-Briggs Type Indicator (MBTI), is a personality assessment that helps us to appreciate differences in the way people perceive information and make decisions. The psychological processes are concerned with two personality variables, perceiving and judging, and the way individuals prefer to use their mind. Perceiving refers to the way we take information into our conscious about things, people, activities, or ideas. There are two distinct ways of perceiving, Sensing (S) and Intuition (N). When we use our S preference, we gather information through the five physical senses: sight, smell, touch, taste, and hearing. These senses deal with present reality. When we use our N preference, we rely on a sixth sense, intuition. We think about possibilities, relationships, concepts, theories, and alternative meanings. We focus on possibilities and a future orientation.

Judging describes how we decide, or come to conclusions, once we have acquired the information. There are two distinct ways of judging, Thinking (T) and Feeling (F). When we use our T preference, we make connections between ideas and concepts in a logical, analytic, and impersonal manner. We make judgments based on facts and according to their rightness or wrongness when we use this preference. When we use our F preference, we make judgments based on values and subjective activities. It is based on what we believe is important. We would make judgments based on the worth of something.

The two personality variables, perceiving and judging, form dichotomous characteristics. For example, when we use the S (perceiving) preference, we cannot at the same time use the N. So when we are becoming aware of information through our senses, we will not be thinking of possibilities and patterns. The theory suggests we each have a predisposition very early in life to two distinct patterns of perceiving and judging. Since we use our preferred patterns more often, we naturally tend to acquire more skill in these areas.

The perceiving/judging preferences influence our satisfaction with particular occupations. For the perceiving preference, S types may prefer security and stability, whereas N types may prefer fulfillment, preferably by doing something creative. Sensing types are drawn to occupations that allow them to deal with a lot of facts; intuitive types instead are drawn to occupations that allow them to deal with possibilities. For the judging preference, T types may prefer occupations where they can apply their skill in handling matters that deal with inanimate objects, machinery, principles, or theories—all of which can be dealt with logically. However, F types may prefer occupations where they can use their skills in matters dealing with people, what they value and how they can be persuaded or helped (see Myers with Myers, 1980, for a more complete description).

Fundamental Interpersonal Relations Orientation: Behavior (FIRO-B), another personality assessment, measures self-perception of how people characteristically relate to others. FIRO-B addresses three dimensions of human relations: inclusion, control, and affection. Inclusion is related to whom you would like to take a boat ride with; control has to do with who is operating the engine and the rudder; and affection is concerned with close relationships that may develop between individuals on the boat. The expressed score indicates what you think you do with others in given relationships. Wanted scores reflect what we want from others in relationships (see Clawson et al., 1992, p. 80).

Values or goals the individual would like to achieve during his or her lifetime are an important part of personality. The Rokeach (1968) Value Survey measures instrumental and terminal values. Terminal values, such as a sense of accomplishment, happiness, pleasure, salvation, and wisdom, describe what life is all about. On the other hand, instrumental values, such as ambition, honesty, independence, affection, and obedience, are fairly good predictors of behavior.

The Strong Interest Inventory (SII) is based on John Holland's (1985a) Theory of Vocational Personalities, a career theory that measures interests and occupational themes. The inventory, a computer-generated assessment, includes more than 300 questions about individual preferences, likes, and dislikes about occupations, school subjects, activities, and types of people. Holland suggests all occupations can be clustered into six major categories: Investigative, Social, Conventional, Enterprising, Artistic, and Realistic. Inclusion in each category means each occupation shares common characteristics. See John Holland's (1985b) Self-Directed Search (SDS), a layperson version of the SII, or write to Consulting Psychologists Press (577 College Avenue, Palo Alto, CA 94306), where you may, for a fee, obtain an SII and have it scored through their career counseling service.

The theory suggests that individuals have a predisposition toward one or more of these clusters. For example, Investigative types prefer activities involving thinking, organizing, and understanding. Their personality characteristics might be described as analytical, original, curious, and independent. Possible occupations for Investigative types might be biologists, economists, mathematicians, or news reporters. Social-type personalities prefer activities that involve helping and developing others. Their personality characteristics might be described as sociable, friendly, cooperative, and understanding. Social types might be social workers, teachers, counselors, and clinical psychologists. Conventional types prefer activities that are rule regulated, orderly, and unambiguous. Their personality characteristics might be described as conforming, efficient, practical, unimaginative, and inflexible. Conventional types might be accountants, corporate managers, or bank tellers. Enterprising types prefer verbal activities and other activities where they can influence others and attain power. They might be described as self-confident, ambitious, energetic, or domineering. Enterprising types might be lawyers, real estate agents, public relations specialists, or small business managers. Artistic types prefer activities involving unstructured, ambiguous activities that allow creative expression. They might be described as imaginative, disorderly, idealistic, and impractical. Possible occupations for artistic types might be painter, musician, writer, or interior decorator. Realistic types prefer physical activities that require skill, strength, and coordination. They might be described as shy, genuine, persistent, stable, conforming, or practical. Possible occupations are those involving hands-on activities such as mechanics, drill press operators, or farmers.

Combining any three of these categories—such as Realistic, Investigative, and Social—is indicative of an occupational direction. Holland's research suggests that individuals are most satisfied with their work where personality and occupation are compatible.

Whether you are just beginning your career or want to establish a different career direction, assessments like the Myers-Briggs Type Indicator, the Strong Interest Inventory, and the Rokeach Values Survey will help you determine who you are today. Once you've defined or taken a fresh look as to who you are, you can begin thinking about what you would like to become. For those of you interested in assessing your own personality and skills, Clawson et al. (1992) have pulled together a variety of tools that help you figure out your own career profile. Let's look at a brief explanation of some of the more popular personality measures used today.

GOAL TWO: DESCRIBE *WHY* YOU ARE INTERESTED IN CHANGING

Education may have given you the tools to be a bookkeeper, accountant, or certified public accountant (CPA), but if you are unhappy with the structure that accompanies such an occupation, you may want to change. Your salary may provide you with a fine lifestyle. But is your lifestyle worth the stress and dissatisfaction your job or occupation brings? Perhaps experience is your greatest asset, and without education, you can expect to stay where you are. Maybe it's time to pursue courses or a certificate or degree program. Perhaps you have dedicated the past 10 or 20 years to helping someone else—the children, your spouse—live their dream. You may have recently married, decided to have children, divorced, or changed some situation in your life that requires you to rethink whatever you are currently doing. Perhaps you're tired of working with negative people. A negative atmosphere can deplete your energy and ravage your self-esteem. Maybe your work is not fulfilling. You may have achieved a good position through a series of structured moves but are no longer challenged by the work, the industry, or the people. Trying something different could energize you.

Dwelling on our dissatisfactions, for the most part, is not productive. However, thinking about why we feel unhappy about certain elements of our work life can point to a need for change. Discontent is demonstrated through our attitudes, the work we produce, and our everyday behaviors. These feelings and behaviors are indicators that it's time to look around for other jobs or careers. Begin by acknowledging your feelings throughout your work and nonwork day.

If you need a little help, in *Finding Your Perfect Work*, Paul Edwards and Sara Edwards (1996) offer a more in-depth look at why you might be changing. In addition, they have developed a number of short exercises to guide you through the process of assessing your values and reasons for wanting to change. You may want to initiate change in your life if these phrases describe your feelings.

_____ Losing interest in things that once interested you

_____ Nagging doubts about yourself and the course of your life

_____ Feeling bored and restless

_____ Wishing you were someone else

_____ Overeating, using alcohol and drugs to feel better or escape

_____ Feeling chronically tired, de-energize

_____ Difficulty motivating yourself to do routine tasks (p. 59)

Feelings such as these are symptoms of discontent. Recognizing such symptoms in your life can help prod you to think about new paradigms and possibilities. When you are feeling great, Edwards and Edwards (1996) suggest the following.

_____ You feel energized and vibrant

_____ Time flies or is suspended

_____ You feel in control of your fate

_____ You experience a sense of mastery having accomplished something

____ Nothing much seems to distract you

____ You discover what you didn't know you could do

____ Everyday concerns drop away (p. 65)

Before you try to figure out what you could or should do, ask yourself: What am I looking for in life? Just because you can do something doesn't mean you *should* do it. Understanding who you are, and why you want to make a change, makes it a lot easier to determine what you would like to do for the next few years or for the rest of your life.

Barbara J. Winter (1993) offers a few helpful suggestions to help think through some of life's issues.

• Where do you want to live?
• How much time would you devote to working?
• What nonwork activities are important to you?
• What terminology would you like to use? Or are you comfortable with (e.g., horticulture, art, management, etc.)?
• Where would you volunteer your time?
• What causes or community issues are important to you?
• How would your daily life become richer?
• What rewards other than money would you expect to receive from your work?
• What skills do you enjoy using?
• What material things would you acquire? Give up? (p. 20)

You may also want to determine the source of your motivators. Here are a few, modified from Winter's (1993) suggestions. First, look over the following list and check off those items that are most important to you. Feel free to add your own items to the list.

____ More time with family and friends

____ Less structured lifestyle

____ Opportunity to try own ideas

____ Wealth

____ Satisfaction with work

____ More nurturing relationships

____ Exploration of the unknown

____ Sense of being responsible and in control

____ Better use of talents

____ Time for personal reflection

____ More independence of thought

_____ Recognition

_____ Less stress/job demands

_____ Variety in work

_____ Adventure

_____ More creativity

_____ Able to carry out more of my own plans

_____ More time for travel

When you have checked off six or seven that are most important to you, rank them from most to least important. When you have completed these exercises, you will have a better idea of why you are thinking about a change in your life. Or you may give yourself permission to make a change in your life. Either way, the next step will be easier, once you have identified why you want to change what you are doing.

GOAL THREE: DESCRIBE *WHAT* KIND OF WORK YOU PREFER

Enjoying your life and your career are responsible activities. Give yourself permission to do what you want to do in life. Pursue your passion. Doing what you want to do is energizing; it propels you to further action and provides you with a sense of satisfaction. One way to discover your passions is to think about the kinds of activities you do when you are not working. Or if you are passionate about your existing work, think about those activities that are particularly exhilarating for you. Try the following exercise (Richardson, 1994) to get you started.

Write a brief description of five accomplishments in your adult life that meet two criteria:

1. You did it well
2. You found it enjoyable or satisfying.

Describe exactly what you did to make this happen. Be specific.
These accomplishments may come from work or nonwork activities in your life. For each activity, describe what you were doing, the people with you, the feelings associated with the activity, and why you enjoyed it so much. Whether this activity impressed someone else is not important. Instead, focus on the events that were meaningful and satisfying to *you*. When you finish writing your stories, share your stories with someone else. Ask someone whom you respect to read your stories and help you to see patterns. Explain that you are trying to decide what kind of work you would like to do, and you are trying to assess your individual skills and abilities.

In addition, ask yourself the following questions about your stories: Why did you find the activity enjoyable? Were you more satisfied with the process or the outcome? What kind of accomplishment is this—new skill, mastery of a skill, helping others, entrepreneurial, exceeding expectations, planning, organizing, troubleshooting? What does this accomplishment say about you?

Give yourself time to reflect. Once you have completed your stories, put them aside for a few days or weeks. When you pick the stories up later, you may be better able to see patterns yourself. From there, you can translate those patterns into meaningful skills and abilities.

For example, you may have prepared computerized spreadsheets to be used for bidding on government contracts for members of your organization. You may have led a group of people who raised $200,000 for the United Way. Or perhaps you instructed coworkers in the use of various computer software programs. Other examples of abilities might be interpersonal abilities, scheduling, working well independently, problem solving, writing, managing time, managing projects, or researching. Employers could appreciate each of these abilities.

Once you have clearly identified your abilities, think about where you would like to use your abilities. Bolles (1995) calls this your *career language*. Bolles suggests that wherever you work, people use specific jargon. In a law firm, there is a lot of talk about legal procedures. Working in the health field, the discussions may be about nutritional problems, addictions, or preventive health care. If you enjoy the field, you will enjoy the language you are dealing with all day long and have a better chance of being happy in your career. What is it that you think and talk about? That may provide a big clue to the field in which you are most interested. If you enjoy talking about a particular field, you will be more inclined to learn more about it.

There are additional issues that will help you to determine satisfying career patterns and career fields. The author of one of the most popular job-hunting books—*What Color Is Your Parachute?*—suggests you think about: the kinds of organizational problems you know about, your favorite things to work with, your favorite people to work with, your favorite job outcomes, and your favorite physical settings (Bolles, 1995). Approaching your career choice from this perspective makes sense since the purpose of finding work you are passionate about means deciding what you like to do most and fitting work around that pattern.

Thus far we have discussed who you are, why you want to change, and your specific abilities. Next let's discuss how to develop goals so that you can integrate your work life with who you are and your work patterns.

GOAL FOUR: DESCRIBE *HOW* AND *WHEN* YOU WILL PULL THIS TOGETHER

Accurate self-knowledge about your desires and abilities will enable you to establish clear goals and objectives. The importance of developing goals and objectives is well documented. Goals provide you with a source of motivation and commitment to your dream. They reinforce your connection to your desires and reduce uncertainty. They will help you to focus on specific outcomes and provide important guides for your actions. Day-to-day decision making is a lot easier once you develop your long-term goals.

Take a step toward achieving results you want by writing out your future dreams or aspirations in goal-oriented, concrete terms. There are three important elements of a well-defined goal. Goals, defined in most every basic management text you read, should be appropriately constructed, specific and measurable, and realistic. First, effectively written goals should start with the word *to*, followed by an action verb. The achievement of a goal should result in some sort of action. Next, a goal should be *specific*. For any goal to be effectively measured, it should describe a singular result to be accomplished. Next, the goal should be *realistic*. That's not a contradiction to achieving your dream. Remember, you are developing the steps to achieving your dream, so the steps are real and achievable. Once completed, you should have achieved—or at least be closer to—your dream work or life.

Let's look at a couple of examples of effective goals.

1. To develop and prioritize a list of the ten most important elements in my life by February 2.
2. To attend a seminar class or career counseling session that will give me feedback about my personality, particularly concerning selection of an occupation of interest to me by September 15.
3. To conduct information interviews by calling (or writing) to several people who are connected to an occupational area of interest to me by October 12.

Each of these goals begins with *to*, followed by an action verb. The verbs describe very specifically what you will do and, further, by a *certain date*. Take the first step in achieving your ideal occupation or lifestyle by writing your first goal.

SUMMARY

Hello, work. Good-bye, job. You will someday look back on your past jobs in the same way that the people one century ago looked at agrarian workers. Jobs will be idealized as never before. The oppressive, hierarchical structures that became synonymous with big business may be remembered the way Weber (1947) intended, simply as objective, routinized, rule-oriented establishments that differentiated organizations in finite terms to enhance production. Organizational stressors associated with unwieldy structures and chaotic changes will be trivialized; people will remember the elements of a job that brought them happiness. However, it is likely that as you read this chapter you may identify elements of dissatisfaction associated with your current job or position that you would like to change. Begin the transition from job to work and become the master of your occupation, responsible for fulfilling your life's desires.

Now is a good time, then, to take stock of who you are. Career counseling, completing personality and vocational assessments, reflecting upon your past and present, and journaling are a few of the tactics discussed that may open up new ways of thinking about a new career and a new lifestyle. Allow yourself to see how you have changed and deal with how you would like to change in the future.

Managing your transition from past to future oriented, from an old to new career pattern, should be a conscious decision. For many, the transition may be gradual. For others, the transition may have been thrust upon them. Either way, developing new attitudes and metaphors brings a much more positive outlook that will help you cope with the uncomfortable elements change can bring.

Because work patterns will be so different from yesterday's jobs and positions, people will behave in different ways. Workers will take their cues from specific tasks and projects rather than from job descriptions and superimposed rules and supervision. Future work patterns have the potential to bring a stronger sense of self-worth and self-imposed control and more opportunities for self-expression than before. All of this accentuates the need to *know yourself*. Evidence suggests that when people are clear about their own abilities and desires, they tend to be more satisfied with life. One presumption of this point is that people act on that knowledge. Self-knowledge is an important element that will help you recognize and take advantage of networking and career opportunities as they arise.

Why do you want to change? The answer to this question is inside you. There are a few hints in the chapter that may bring some satisfactions and dissatisfactions to the surface, but essentially this response requires some reflection. If you are unsure of your feelings, write a journal that describes your feelings about work and nonwork activities you find enjoyable or dissatisfying. When you are clear about why you want to change, you may begin to define what it is you want in a career or in your life.

What are the activities you most enjoy doing? Who are the people you most want to be with? What are the things you most relate to? Where are the places you most want to be? These are the elements that describe what you enjoy doing most. When you can clearly identify those elements you feel most strongly about, you can establish the appropriate goals to incorporate these elements in your life or career. There are several advantages to writing these goals down. You will more clearly see what you want; you will be more motivated to go after what you want; and your commitment to your goals may be stronger. Achieving your dreams is more likely when you develop *effective goals*. Clearly, it is worth your time to assess, or reassess, your abilities and desires and develop a few meaningful goals that will help you achieve your aspirations.

REFERENCES

Bolles, R. N. (1995). *The 1995 what color is your parachute?* Berkeley, CA: Ten Speed Press.

Bridges, W. (1991). *Managing transitions, making the most of change.* Reading, MA: Addison-Wesley.

Bridges, W. (1994). *Jobshift: How to prosper in a workplace without jobs.* Reading, MA: Addison-Wesley.

Brown, D., & Harrison, M. J. (1978). *A sociology of industrialization: An introduction.* London: Macmillan.

Brown, T. (1996). Sweatshops of the 1990s. *Management Review* (August): 13–18.

Caplow, T. (1954). *The sociology of work.* New York: McGraw-Hill.

Clawson, J. G., Kotter, J. P., Faux, V. A., & McArthur, C. (1992). *Self-assessment and career development.* Englewood Cliffs, NJ: Prentice-Hall.

Edwards, P., & Edwards, S. (1996). *Finding your perfect work: The new career guide to making a living, creating a life.* New York: G. P. Putnam's Sons.

Hammer, M. (1996). *Beyond reengineering: How the process-centered organization is changing our work and our lives.* New York: HarperBusiness.

Heilbroner, R. L. (1995). Foreword. In J. Rifkin, *The end of work, the decline of the global labor force and the dawn of the post-market era.* New York: G. P. Putnam's Sons, p. xii.

Holland, J. L. (1985a). *Making vocational choices: A theory of vocational personalities and work environments* (2nd ed.) Englewood Cliffs, NJ: Prentice-Hall.

Holland, J. L. (1985b). *Self-directed search.* Palo Alto, CA: Consulting Psychologists Press.

Hubiak, W. A., & O'Donnell, S. J. (1997). Downsizing: A pervasive form of organizational suicide. *National Productivity Review* (Spring): 31–36.

Myers, I. B., with Myers, P. B. (1980). *Gifts differing.* Palo Alto, CA: Consulting Psychologists Press.

Pulley, M. L. (1997). *Losing your job: Reclaiming your soul.* San Francisco: Jossey-Bass.

Richardson, D. B. (1994). *Networking.* New York: John Wiley & Sons, pp. 38, 39.

Rifkin, J. (1995). *The end of work, the decline of the global labor force and the dawn of the post-market era.* New York: G. P. Putnam's Sons.

Rokeach, M. (1968). *Beliefs, attitudes and values.* San Francisco: Jossey-Bass.

Smith, S. (1991). *Is there farming in agriculture's future? The impact of biotechnology.* Presentation at the University of Vermont, November 14, 1991; rev. October 21, 1992, p. 1.

Tosterud, R., & Jahr, D. (1982). *The changing economics of agriculture: Challenge and preparation for the 1980's.* Washington, DC: Subcommittee on Agriculture and Transportation, Joint Economic Committee, Congress of the United States, December 28.

Weber, M. (1947). The Theory of Social and Economic Organizations (T. Parsons, Ed., &. A. M. Henderson & T. Parsons, Trans.). New York: Free Press.

Winter, B. J. (1993). *Making a living without a job.* New York: Bantam Books.

Zuboff, S. (1988). *In the age of the smart machine: The future of work and power.* New York: Basic Books.

10

The Critical Role of Information Technology for Employee Success in the Coming Decade

HSING K. CHENG

INTRODUCTION

The past decade has witnessed the profound impacts of information technology on almost every aspect of human society. As futurist John Naisbitt correctly predicted in 1982, "Of the ten major transformations taking place right now in our society, none is more subtle, yet more explosive, than the megashift from an industrial to an information society" (Naisbitt, 1982, p. 11). "In particular, the U.S. economy has sustained unprecedented growth in the last three years since the 1960s at an average rate of 4% per annum, while the unemployment rate and inflation both remain checked. The major driver of this remarkable economy is due to improvements in worker productivity resulting from the now-pervasive use of information technology" (Mandel et al., 1997). The implications of information technology for individual welfare are not insignificant. High-tech jobs and industries have accounted for roughly 20 to 25 percent of the real wage and salary growth in 1996 (Mandel & Reinhardt, 1997).

In addition to information technology's contributions to the overall economy and individual welfare, we further observe an astonishing rate of information technology advancement since its inception. A famous quote from *Computerworld*, a popular information technology trade weekly, expresses such advancement in a dramatic way: "If the auto industry had done what the computer industry has done in the last 30 years, a Rolls-Royce would cost $2.50 and would get 2,000,000 miles per gallon of gasoline" (Brynjolfsson, 1993, p. 73). As information technology continues to progress relentlessly, understanding how to take advantage of information technology is absolutely essential to enhance the success of both nations and individuals in the next decade.

The objective of this chapter is to explore the opportunities afforded by information technology in general, and personal computing technologies in particular, from an individual employee's perspective. Specifically, we focus our discussion on the critical role of two common productivity enhancement tools, spreadsheet and database software, for employee success. Specific examples are provided to illustrate how the creative use of these two software tools can greatly improve individuals' decision-making effectiveness. Although most discussions and examples are managerial oriented, they are straightforward and amenable to most people with a basic understanding of personal computing.

This chapter is structured as follows. The next section will discuss the shift of our society toward an information economy with an emphasis on the relevance of information technology to individual welfare and success. The following two sections are devoted to demonstrate how spreadsheet and database software can greatly enhance one's decision-making effectiveness, thereby ensuring one's success as an employee in the work force. Illustrating examples are created for Microsoft Excel and Access on the Windows 95 platform owing to their overwhelming popularity in business.

INFORMATION ECONOMY

The best way to understand the shift of our society to an information economy is to study the trend of labor force distribution. Figure 10.1 shows the distribution of the U.S. labor force from 1860 to 1980 based on U.S. Department of Labor statistics. Figure 10.1 is often cited by economists and social scientists to explain the move of our society toward a so-called information economy in which the information sector employs a majority of the work force. As evident from Figure 10.1, we can conveniently partition the evolution of our economic activities into three stages. In the first stage, the majority of the labor force was in the agricultural sector. The time when the industry labor force percentage surpassed that of the agricultural heralded the arrival of the industrial age. Without a doubt, we are currently in the third stage where the information sector dominating economic activities is an irreversible trend.

The shift toward an "information economy" is not only unmistakably evident but also overwhelmingly favorable. The growth rate of the U.S. economy has doubled to an average rate of 4 percent in 1996 from 1995, whereas unemployment has fallen to 4.9 percent, the lowest level since 1973 (Mandel et al., 1997). On the inflation side, inflation has fallen since 1995, shattering the conventional wisdom that the United States could not sustain growth in excess of 2 percent or 2.5 percent without trigger-

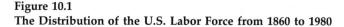

Figure 10.1
The Distribution of the U.S. Labor Force from 1860 to 1980

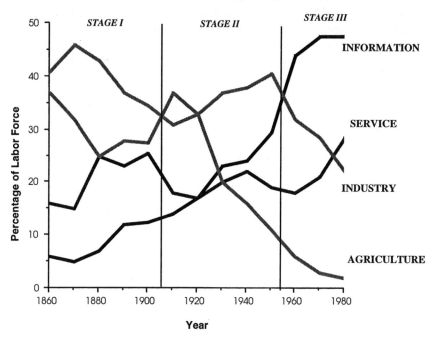

Source: U.S. Department of Labor Statistics, 1986, p. 4.

ing inflation. Such a remarkable achievement of faster growth, lower unemployment, and less inflation than economists ever believed possible is attributed to rapid improvements in productivity (the major driver of economic growth and standard of living) and the unique nature of expansion led by the high-technology sector. There is further compelling evidence that the now-pervasive use of information technology throughout the economy is behind this unprecedented economic prosperity (Mandel et al., 1997).

From individuals' career perspective, the implications of the information economy are too significant to ignore. For example, the number of high-tech jobs rose by 4.9 percent in 1996 versus a 2 percent increase for the rest of economy, according to *Business Week*'s calculations (Mandrel and Reinhardt, 1997). In the same report, the growth rate of real weekly wages for nonsupervisory and production workers in the high-tech sector was 2 percent in 1996, more than four times that of the rest of the economy. Furthermore, according to Princeton University economist Alan B. Krueger, "workers who use computers earn an average of 10% to 15% more than those who don't, even for the same job. Secretaries who use computers enjoy a premium of up to 30%" (Gleckman et al., 1993, p. 68). This phenomenon also applies for M.B.A. graduates from the top 20 business schools. At the University of Texas, Austin, where 25 percent of new M.B.A.'s left school in spring 1993 without a job, the 25 graduates of the B-School's Information Systems Management program averaged 3.5 offers, most of them in the $50,000 range. Nowadays, the 50 graduating Information Management students, the "techno M.B.A.s," at the University of Texas, Austin, received an average salary of $69,000 and an average total compensation of $80,900 (Dyer, Lasdon, & Ruefli, 1998).

Given the shift of society as a whole toward an information economy, it should be apparent that individual employees today, whether choosing information technology as their career or not, need to take advantage of information technology to ensure their success tomorrow. The rest of this chapter describes how individual employees can benefit from using information technology to become successful in the workplace. Specifically, the discussions with illustrating examples focus on how to exploit key features of today's spreadsheet and database software in business settings.

BETTER DECISION MAKING WITH INFORMATION TECHNOLOGY

Employees of all levels face difficult business decisions at all times. The success or failure of both the organization and its employees hinges on the quality of decision making. To make sound decisions, one needs to understand the human decision-making process and how to utilize information technology to enhance decision-making quality.

Herbert Simon (1960) theorizes that human decision making typically undergoes four phases: intelligence, design, choice, and implementation. The first phase of decision making, intelligence, involves "searching the environment for conditions calling for decisions. Raw data are obtained, processed, and examined for clues that may identify problems" (p. 40). Essentially, the intelligence phase is the problem identification phase. As soon as problems are identified, subsequent actions are "inventing, developing, and analyzing possible courses of actions" (p. 41) in the design phase. This includes processes to "understand the problem, to generate solutions, and to test solutions for feasibility" (p. 41). The next phase, choice, consists of choosing among solution alternatives. Finally, the solution is put into effect in the implementation phase. Proper use of information technology clearly improves the quality of decision making. For instance, information systems can track the quarterly performance of a business division against predetermined goals and report the excep-

Figure 10.2
The Structure of a Decision Support System

Interactive
Decision Support

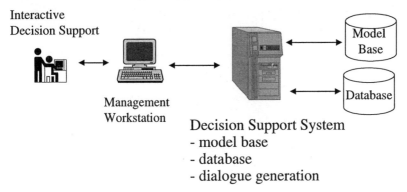

Management
Workstation

Model
Base

Database

Decision Support System
- model base
- database
- dialogue generation

tions that call for intervention. In the design and choice phases, decision support systems can be used to develop solution alternatives quickly with the built-in analytical models and databases. Furthermore, decision support systems will help decision makers explore the alternatives by performing "What-if" analyses, for example, experimenting with different plausible scenarios. Figure 10.2 depicts the structure of a typical decision support system.

A subsidiary of a large American metals company, whose primary mission is to carry bulk cargos of coal, oil, ores, and finished products to its parent company, employs a powerful decision support system for voyage estimating (Laudon & Laudon, 1997). The firm, which owns and charters vessels, also bids for shipping contracts in the open market to carry general cargo. Such voyage-estimating decision support systems aid managerial decisions by providing answers to a wide range of questions such as which vessels should be used at what optimum speeds to maximize profits, given a customer delivery schedule and an offered freight rate.

With the dramatic advancement of information technology, current spreadsheet and database software for the personal computer platform make building small and yet powerful decision support systems within the reach of individual employees. Recall from Figure 10.2 that the two key components of a decision support system are model base and database. Today's personal computer spreadsheet and database software delivers sophisticated features that were only available for larger computers not long ago. Individuals can derive tremendous benefits from exploiting spreadsheet and database software for decision-making purposes. The remaining discussions will first turn to the process of building spreadsheet models, followed by illustrative examples.

Figure 10.3
The General Structure of Business Spreadsheet Models

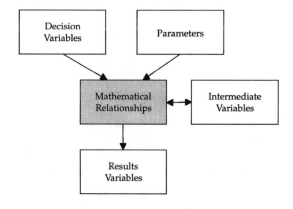

BUILDING SPREADSHEET MODELS FOR DECISION MAKING

Overview

A model is a representation of reality. Most models are simplifications that capture the most relevant features of a problem. Models are useful to describe a problem, discuss the problem, explore and analyze the problem, and solve the problem. Spreadsheet models are simple mathematical models implemented by using spreadsheet software, such as Microsoft Excel. There are numerous business applications of computer spreadsheet models, including, but not limited to, portfolio selection, options pricing, capital budgeting, demand forecasting, production scheduling, and strategic planning. Business spreadsheet models have a general structure as shown in Figure 10.3.

To build useful spreadsheet models for decision support, one must first identify decision variables, parameters, and result variables. Result variables are those we want to optimize, for example, the profits to maximize or the costs to minimize. Decision variables are those for which we must make decisions, for instance, the quantity to produce of a product or the price to charge for a new product or service. On the other hand, the parameters are those beyond decision makers' reach or control. Parameters are most likely due to the environment or the market as a whole, such as interest rates. More often than not, intermediate variables are introduced to improve the readability of a spreadsheet model. After the decision variables, parameters, and result variables are identified, they are tied together by mathematical relationships in a model usually in the form of equations, inequalities, or functions. Spreadsheet models are most useful for decision making in that we can find the optimal values of result variables by using the "solver" feature or perform "What-if" analyses by varying the values of parameters. We can best appreciate the usefulness of spreadsheet models by the following business case adapted from *Lotus* magazine in which the objective is to find economic order quantity (EOQ).

Spreadsheet Modeling of Economic Order Quantity

Imagine that you are the inventory manager for Uncle Bunko's Nifty Trick and Novelty Wholesalers. Your job is to make sure the company never runs out of, say, Groucho Marx noses. You must figure out *how often* to order noses from your supplier and *how many* noses to order each time (Cranford, 1989).

You could order a week's worth every week to keep the supply of noses topped off. But each time you order Groucho noses from the supplier, you incur expenses called *ordering costs* (e.g., the cost of the order form and the labor involved in placing and receiving the order). Ordering too frequently therefore increases your ordering costs since you incur ordering costs *each time* you place an order.

Perhaps, you are thinking, order a year's worth every year. While this might be appropriate for plastic novelty items, it presents some obvious problems for businesses that deal in oranges or perishable groceries. Although funny noses fall into the nonperishable category, it's still risky to order a year's worth at a time. Groucho Marx noses may become passé. Besides obsolescence, there are costs (called *carrying costs*) associated with keeping inventory in stock. Determining carrying cost is tricky, and the result is usually just an estimate, but many people hold that the annual carrying cost of an item ranges between 20 percent and 30 percent of the item's cost. Ordering infrequently saves ordering costs but increases carrying costs since, on average, the amount of inventory on hand will be larger (if you order a year's worth once a year, on average you'll have one half of the annual demand on hand every day, whereas if you order every week, on average you'll have one half of the weekly demand on hand every day).

Obviously, the amount to order is the amount that strikes the best balance between ordering costs and carrying costs. In other words, the appropriate reorder amount incurs the lowest total cost, the sum of ordering costs and carrying costs. This amount is the EOQ (Cranford, 1989).

In order to determine the EOQ, we set up a spreadsheet (see Figure 10.4). Note that only the major portion of the worksheet is displayed. Cell C2 contains the cost per Groucho Marx Nose, which is $0.50. The total quantity needed in one year is 1,600 and stored in cell C3. Each time you reorder, it costs $10, as shown in cell C4. The rate of inventory

Figure 10.4
Economic Order Quantity (EOQ) Model

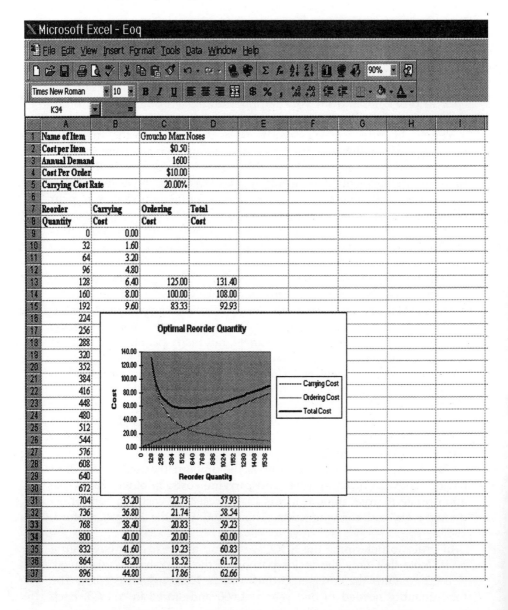

	A	B	C	D	E	F	G	H	I
1	Name of Item		Groucho Marx Noses						
2	Cost per Item		$0.50						
3	Annual Demand		1600						
4	Cost Per Order		$10.00						
5	Carrying Cost Rate		20.00%						
6									
7	Reorder	Carrying	Ordering	Total					
8	Quantity	Cost	Cost	Cost					
9	0	0.00							
10	32	1.60							
11	64	3.20							
12	96	4.80							
13	128	6.40	125.00	131.40					
14	160	8.00	100.00	108.00					
15	192	9.60	83.33	92.93					
16	224								
17	256								
18	288								
19	320								
20	352								
21	384								
22	416								
23	448								
24	480								
25	512								
26	544								
27	576								
28	608								
29	640								
30	672								
31	704	35.20	22.73	57.93					
32	736	36.80	21.74	58.54					
33	768	38.40	20.83	59.23					
34	800	40.00	20.00	60.00					
35	832	41.60	19.23	60.83					
36	864	43.20	18.52	61.72					
37	896	44.80	17.86	62.66					

carrying cost is set at 20 percent according to past experience. Cells C2 to C5 store the values of parameters (Cranford, 1989).

The spreadsheet in Figure 10.4 is constructed as follows. We first entered a zero in cell A9. Each of the remaining formulas in column A takes the value above it and adds one fiftieth of the annual usage of the item. When we create the graph, as shown in Figure 10.4, we plot the carrying costs, ordering costs, and total costs associated with 50 different reorder quantities. Carrying costs on column B equal the product of the rate of inventory carrying cost and the cost of the *average* inventory resulting from reordered quantity. Note that the average inventory is calculated as one half of the reorder quantity because the on-hand amount is assumed to alternate between the amount you order and zero. The calculations of the ordering cost and total cost should be obvious.

The chart clearly shows the behavior of total cost as a function of reorder quantity. Neither ordering too frequently nor ordering too much is optimal. The best amount to order each time is between 480 and 600 noses, showing a range of leeway for reorder quantity. Although there exists abundant rigorous academic literature on economic order quantity, the spreadsheet model in Figure 10.4 is probably more easily understandable to most managers and employees

Spreadsheet Model for Retirement Funds Allocation

Spreadsheet software can be employed for enhancing the quality of making decisions not only on difficult business problems but also on relevant personal issues. The following example shows how the "solver" feature of spreadsheet software can be exploited to determine the optimal allocations of a person's 401(k) retirement funds.

Suppose we are contemplating the optimal allocation of our 401(k) plan. We have selected a mutual fund company, say TIAA/CREF, and we are interested in investing in the following fund categories: International Equity Fund, Equity Growth Fund, Real Estate Fund, and Bond Fund. According to the advice from most financial planners, in our mid-career, we need to observe the following rules for our portfolio: (1) At least 20 percent in International Equity and at least 30 percent in Growth Equity; however, no more than 65 percent in Equity funds; (2) at least 25 percent in Bond, but no more than 40 percent in Bond and Real Estate. These rules aim at creating a portfolio of investments that will balance the rates of returns and volatility risks of different funds.

Figure 10.5 implements a spreadsheet model to find optimal allocations of our 401(k) plan considering the above rules. cells A5 to A8 in Figure 10.5 lists the fund categories. The corresponding rates of returns are in cells B5 to B8. The decision variables in this model are the recommended investments in each fund, in cells C5 to C8. The rules of

Figure 10.5
401(k) Retirement Funds Allocation Model

	A	B	C	D	E
1	**401(k) Pension Portfolio Planning**				
2					
3	**Investment**	**Projected**	**Recommended**	**Projected**	
4	**Opportunity**	**Rate of Return (%)**	**Investment**	**Return**	
5	International Equity	0.2888	0	=B5*C5	
6	Growth Equity	0.3596	0	=B6*C6	
7	Real Estate	0.0986	0	=B7*C7	
8	Bond	0.0975	0	=B8*C8	
9		**Totals:**	=SUM(C5:C8)	=SUM(D5:D8)	
10					
11	**Investment Constraints:**		**LHS**	**RHS**	
12	Maximum Allowable Contributions by IRS		=SUM(C5:C8)	9500	
13	Minimum investment in Int'l Equity		=C5-0.2*C12	0	
14	Minimum investment in Growth Equity		=C6-0.3*C12	0	
15	Maximum investment in Equity		=C5+C6-0.65*C12	0	
16	Minimum investment in Bonds		=C8-0.25*C12	0	
17	Maximum investment in Real Estate&Bond		=C7+C8-0.4*C12	0	
18					

investment are captured in rows 12 to 17. For example, the maximum allowable contribution to a 401(k) by the IRS is $9,500 in cell D12, an amount to be increased to $10,000 in the 1998 tax year. An inequality to express such a constraint will be C12 < D12. Figure 10.5 shows appropriate formulas in cells C13 to C17 for the investment rules.

To find the optimal allocations conforming to the investment rule, one then invokes the "solver" feature available in today's spreadsheet software. For example, Figure 10.6 shows the solver parameters for the Microsoft Excel spreadsheet. The optimal allocations found by the spreadsheet software are shown in Figure 10.7.

TO OBTAIN INFORMATION FROM DATABASES

Overview

The second and equally important component of a decision support system, as shown in Figure 10.2, is the database. Data are a critical resource to any corporation. Failure to have a solid grasp on essential business data could prove disastrous. Bristol-Myers Squibb, a major pharmaceutical company, found its competitive position weakened because of fragmented and inconsistent data on doctors, their prescription-writing habits, and managed care facilities (Sentry Market Research, 1996). Databases have become the standard approach for defining, storing, maintaining, and retrieving critical business data. As opposed to the traditional file environment where data are stored in separate files for each application, the database approach organizes data so that they can be accessed and shared by many different applications.

There are three principal models for logical database designs—hierarchical, network, and relational. Most current database software implements the relational model where data are represented in simple two-dimensional tables called "relations." Microsoft Access, the most popular database product for the personal computer platform, follows the notion of relational databases. Although large corporations have database specialists, titled database administrators (DBAs), to lead the database analysis, design, and maintenance efforts, individual employees can benefit from learning how to obtain information from databases for decision-making purposes. Most of today's personal computer database software has the Query by Example (QBE) feature that is extremely easy to use for ordinary users without resorting to the standard database query language, Structured Query Language (SQL). Essentially, a query is a question you ask about data stored in databases. To obtain the needed information from databases, a user can construct a query with ease by specifying an "example"—hence the term "query by example." The following section demonstrates the QBE feature of Microsoft Access.

Figure 10.6
401(k) Retirement Funds Model Solver Parameters

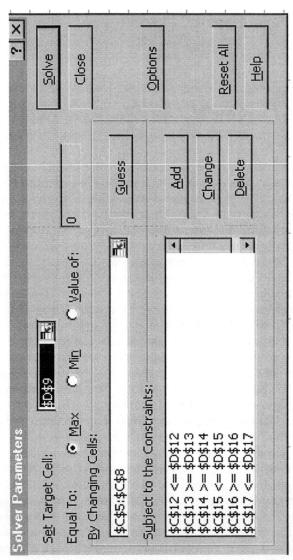

Figure 10.7
401(k) Retirement Funds Solver Results

	A	B	C	D	E	F	G	H	I
1	**401(k) Planning**								
2									
3	**Investment**	**Projected**	**Recommended**	**Projected**	**Allocation**				
4	**Opportunity**	**Rate of Return (%)**	**Investment**	**Return**	**Percentage**				
5	International Equity	28.88%	1,900	549	20.00%				
6	Growth Equity	35.96%	4,275	1,537	45.00%				
7	Real Estate	9.86%	950	94	10.00%				
8	Bond	9.75%	2,375	232	25.00%				
9		**Totals:**	9,500	2,411					
10									

Query by Example to Obtain Information from Databases

Queries are commands for retrieval of specific records that meet stated conditions. They provide details to answer a question the user has. There are two ways to obtain needed information from databases for the personal computer platform, either by writing SQL code or by using the QBE user interface to relational database systems. The basic idea of QBE is to express a query by creating *examples* of the items being requested. There is no programming experience required to use QBE. QBE is a powerful tool for most managers and employees to retrieve information for decision-making purposes.

In a relational database system, all data are arranged in the form of two-dimensional tables. Each table has columns (>fields') and rows (>records'). Columns appear vertically on the screen, containing data of the same kind throughout. Columns are given names, which appear at the top. Rows appear horizontally on the screen, containing different kinds of data about a single entity.

To illustrate how to use QBE of Microsoft Access, three sample tables (see Table 10.1)—Supplier Table, Parts Table, and Order Table—are created as the basis for demonstration in this section. The Supplier Table stores information regarding the unique supplier number, the name, the status, and the city of all suppliers. The Parts Table contains the part number, name, color, unit price, and weight information of parts. The Order Table shows what part (identified by Part Number) is ordered from which supplier (identified by Supplier Number) and its quantity ordered on each order.

Based on these three tables, scenarios are constructed to imitate realistic situations where intended users of such databases, including both managers and employees, are in need of certain information relevant to their decision making. Each scenario includes a question likely to be asked by users, followed by detailed instructions for using Microsoft Access to answer such a question.

Scenario 1: What is the STATUS of all suppliers?

QBE Solution: The screen after opening the file that contains the three sample tables, Supplier, Parts, and Order, is shown in Figure 10.8.

To create a query, first click the query tab, then click the "new" button on the right. Select the "design view" to create a query. Add Supplier Table to the Query window, double click SUPPLIER NAME from the Supplier field list; SUPPLIER NAME will be shown in the first Field cell in the output grid. Then double click STATUS from the Supplier field list; STATUS will be shown in the second Field cell in the output grid. Click the Datasheet View button or the exclamation mark on the tool bar

Table 10.1
Sample Tables Created Using Query by Example

Supplier Table

SUPPLIER_NO	SUPPLIER NAME	STATUS	CITY
S1	Smith	20	London
S2	Jones	10	Paris
S3	Blake	30	Paris
S4	Clark	20	London
S5	Adams	30	Athens

Parts Table

PART_NO	PART NAME	COLOR	UNIT	WEIGHT
P1	Nut	Red	$12.00	3
P2	Bolts	Green	$17.00	9
P3	Screw	Blue	$17.00	9
P4	Screw	Red	$14.00	2
P5	Cam	Blue	$12.00	12
P6	Cog	Red	$19.00	10

Order Table

ORDER_NO	SUPPLIER_NO	PART_NO	QUANTITY
O1	S1	P1	300
O2	S1	P2	200
O3	S1	P3	400
O4	S1	P4	200
O5	S1	P5	100
O6	S1	P6	100
O7	S2	P1	300
O8	S2	P2	400
O9	S3	P2	200
O10	S4	P2	200
O11	S4	P4	300
O12	S4	P5	400

to see the results. Figure 10.9 shows the QBE screen for scenario 1, whereas Figure 10.10 shows the result of such a query.

In Scenario 1, certain fields (columns) of a table are selected for display. More often than not, end users need to retrieve records from databases to meet some specified conditions. Scenario 2 imitates such requirements.

Scenario 2: Who are our suppliers in the city of Paris?

QBE Solution: Add Supplier Table to the Query window; add SUPPLIER NAME and CITY from the Supplier field list by double clicking them to the output grid. In the Criteria cell for CITY, type "Paris." Figure 10.11 shows the screen for such a query.

Figure 10.8
Microsoft Access Main Screen

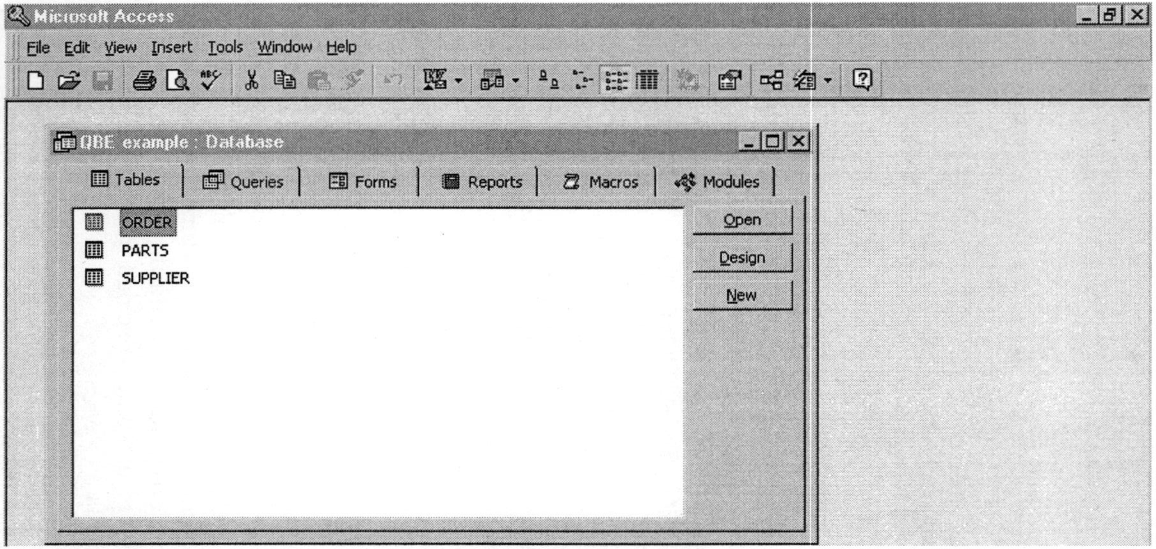

Figure 10.9
QBE Screen for Scenario 1

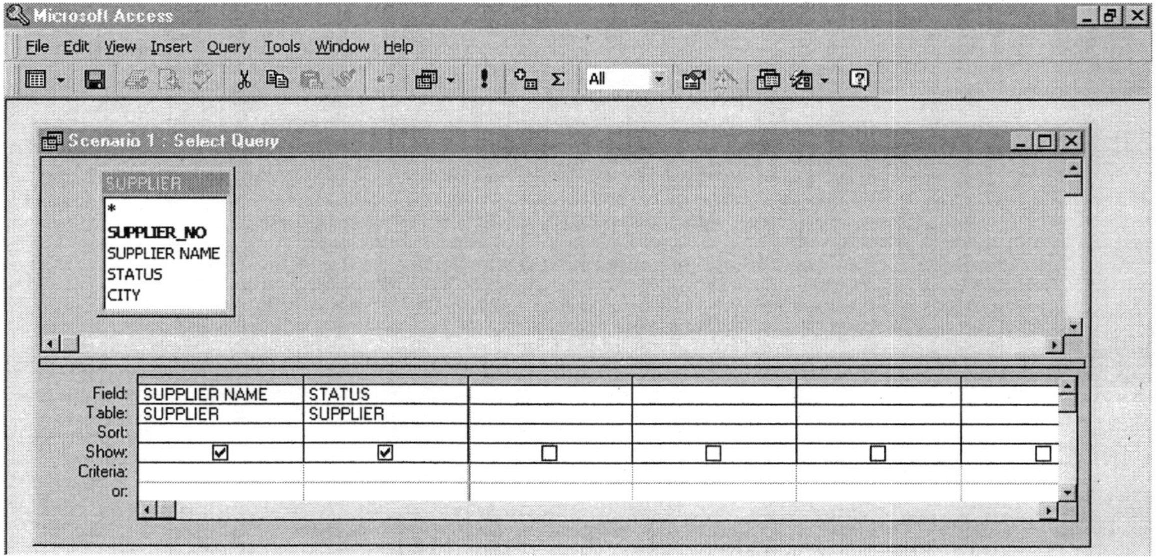

Figure 10.10
QBE Result for Scenario 1

SUPPLIER	STATUS
Smith	20
Jones	10
Blake	30
Clark	20
Adams	30

Many kinds of conditions can be inserted in the Criteria cell to retrieve the desired records from databases. Table 10.2 gives a summary of commonly used conditions.

There are situations where multiple conditions under different fields must be satisfied simultaneously. Placing all conditions in the same criteria line can accomplish this requirement, to be demonstrated in scenario 3.

Scenario 3: Who are the suppliers in Paris with status >20?

QBE Solution: Add Supplier Table to the Query window; add SUPPLIER NAME, STATUS, and CITY from the Supplier field list to the output grid. In the Criteria cell for STATUS, type >20. In the Criteria cell for CITY, type Paris. Figure 10.12 shows the query screen for scenario 3.

Apparently, some situations require either one of the multiple conditions being satisfied, but not simultaneously. This "either or"–type requirement is achieved by placing conditions in separate criteria lines. Moreover, today's database software has useful operators built in the QBE feature to provide summary information, for example, SUM to calculate the total value of a field, AVERAGE for the average, COUNT to count the number of instances. The following scenario shows an example where summary information is needed.

Scenario 4: How many different part types does each supplier supply?

QBE Solution: We need the Order Table to answer this question. Add Order Table to the Query window, then add SUPPLIER_NO and PART_NO from the Order field list to the output grid by double clicking them. Add the Totals row by clicking the E button in the tool bar. In the Total cell associated with PART_NO, choose Count from the drop-down list. Figure 10.13 shows the query screen for this scenario.

The previous four scenarios involve obtaining information from a single table. QBE enables end users to answer questions that require information to be extracted from multiple tables, a task achieved by linking multiple tables together. In such cases, the linked tables must have a

Figure 10.11
QBE Screen for Scenario 2

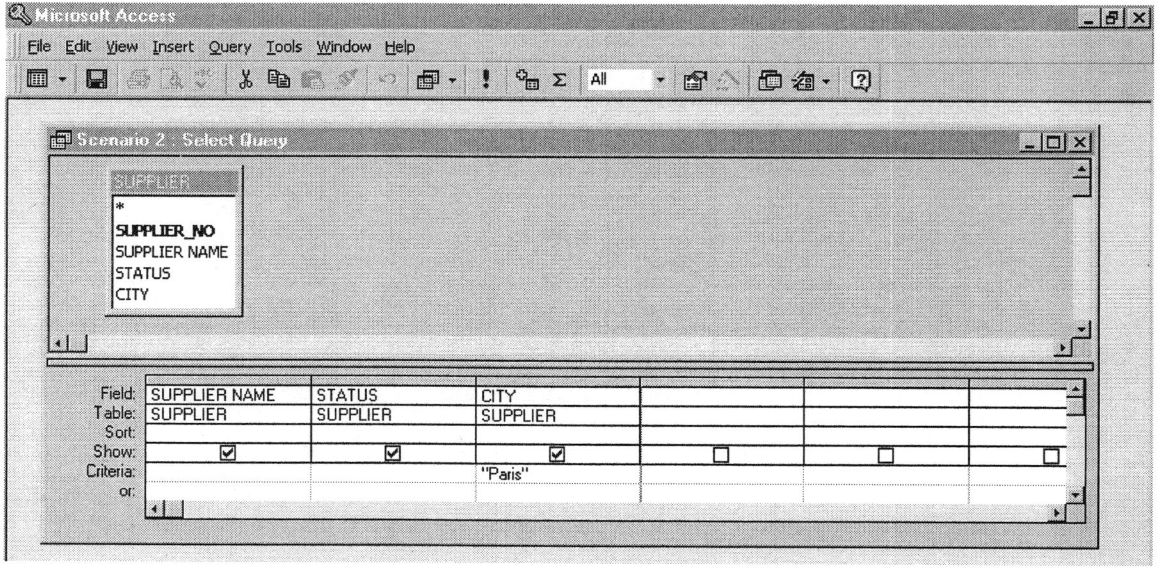

Table 10.2
Commonly Used Conditions

When you enter	Microsoft Access displays	And retrieves records where
New York	"New York"	Value is New York
<'30-Jan-93	<'#1/01/93#	Date value is on or before 30-Jan-93
100	100	Value is 100
>15000	>15000	Value is greater than 15000
Between 15-Mar-94 And 30-Mar-94	Between#3/15/94#And#3/30/94#	Date values are between 15-Mar-94 And 30-Mar-94, inclusive
In (Hall, Seeger)	In ("Hall", "Seeger")	Hall or Seeger
Sm?th	Like ASm?th"	Smith, Smyth, Y, etc.
*th	Like A*th"	128th, Perth
on	Like A*on*"	Condiments, Confections
10/*/93	Like A10/*/93"	All dates in October 1993

common field in terms of the same meaning and structure. For instance, suppose one needs to find out the names of suppliers who supply the part >Cam'. The Order Table contains the information regarding which supplier supplies what parts. However, this information is represented in the Order Table in terms of supplier number and part number, a common practice in database design. To manually answer the above question, one would need to use the part name >Cam' to find its corresponding part number from the Parts Table, which is P5 in this case. The next step is to retrieve all those records from the Order Table whose PART_NO field contains P5, resulting in S1 and S4. Finally, S1 and S4 are used to find the corresponding supplier names from the Supplier Table. This seemingly complicated task can be easily completed by linking the Supplier Table, the Part Table, and the Order Table together, as in the next scenario.

Figure 10.12
QBE Screen for Scenario 3

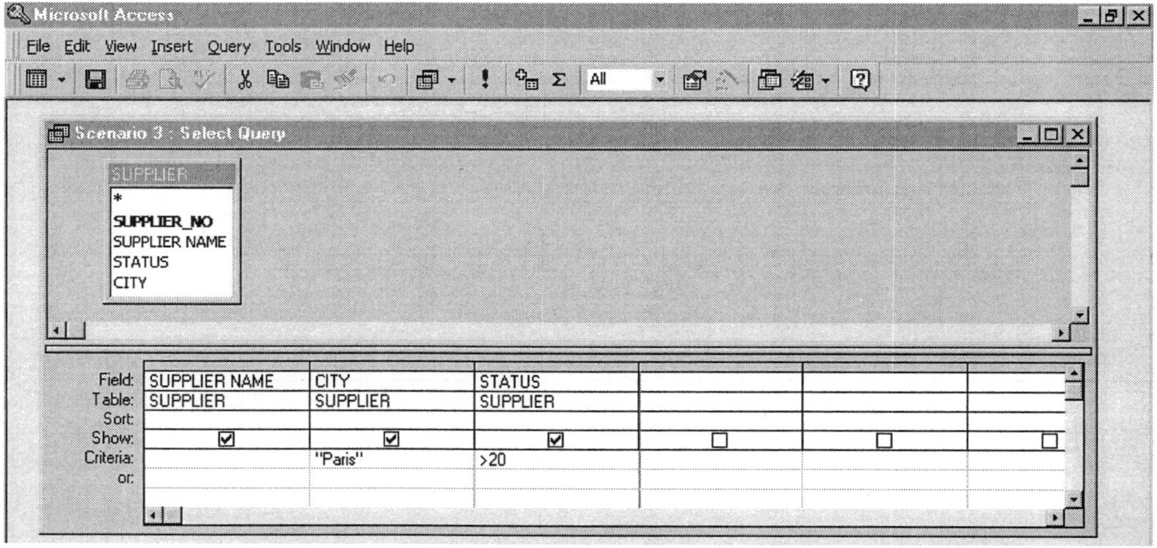

Figure 10.13
QBE Screen for Scenario 4

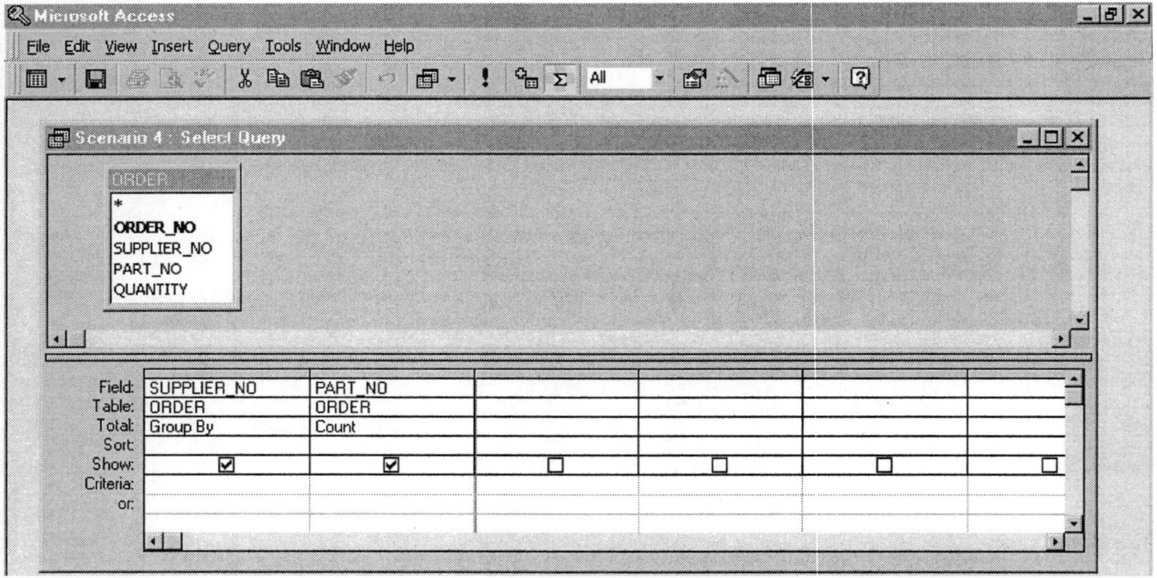

Scenario 5: What are the names of suppliers who supply the part >Cam'

QBE Solution: Add Supplier Table, Order Table, and Part Table to the Query window. Click and drag SUPPLIER_NO from the Supplier field list to SUP-PLIER_NO in the Order field list in the upper half of the screen. Click and drag PART_NO from the Order field list to PART_NO in the Part field list in the upper half of the screen. Add SUPPLIER NAME from the Supplier field list and PART NAME from the Part field list to the output grid by double clicking them. In the Criteria cell for PART NAME, type Cam. Figure 10.14 shows the QBE screen of this scenario.

CONCLUDING REMARKS

This chapter describes the clear trend of our society toward an "information economy" where information technology dominates the majority of economic activities. The shift toward an information economy is not only unmistakably evident but also overwhelmingly favorable. From individuals' career perspective, the implications of the information economy are too significant to ignore. It becomes apparent that individual employees today, whether or not choosing information technology as their career, need to take advantage of information technology to ensure their success tomorrow.

This chapter explores the critical role of two common productivity enhancement tools—spreadsheet and database software—for employee success. Specifically, the discussions focus on (1) why spreadsheet and database software is essential for enhancing individuals' decision-making quality, thereby ensuring their success in the workplace, (2) how the spreadsheet software can be employed to solve realistic business and personal problems, and (3) how to use the user-friendly QBE feature of database software to obtain information for decision-making purposes.

REFERENCES

Dyer, J. Lasdon, L., & Ruefli, T. (1998). The Tech-MBA. *ORMS Today* (February): 32–36.

Gleckman, H. et al. (1993). The technology payoff. *Business Week* (June 14): 57–79.

Laudon, J. P., & Laudon, K. C. (1997). *Essentials of management information systems: Organization and technology.* Upper Saddle River, NJ: Prentice-Hall.

Mandel, M., & Reinhardt, A. (1997). The new business cycle. *Business Week* (March 31): 58–68.

Mandel, M., et al. (1997). How long can this last? *Business Week* (May 19): 30–34.

Naisbitt, J. (1982). *Megatrends: Ten new directions transforming our lives.* New York: Warner Books.

Sentry Market Research. (1996). Quibb needed a single view of managed care: Data warehousing directions. *Software Magazine* (October): 30.

Figure 10.14
QBE Screen for Scenario 5

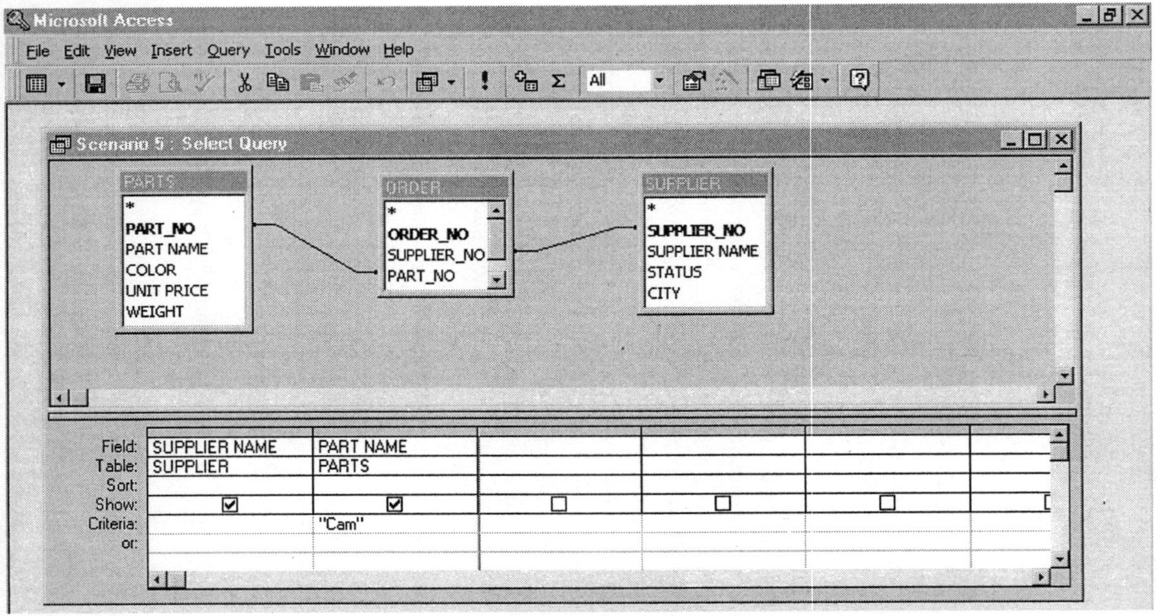

Simon, H. (1960). *The new science of management decision*. New York: Harper &
    Row.
U.S. Department of Labor Statistics. (1986). *The distribution of the U.S. labor force*.
    Washington, DC: U.S. Government Printing Office.

11

The New Employer-Employee Contract: A CEO's Perspective on Employer and Employee Success

WILLIAM DONALDSON

[T]he employment "contract" has shifted from paternal and permanent to individualistic and transactional.
                    —Thomas A. Stewart, *Fortune*, March 16, 1998

INTRODUCTION

Much has been, and continues to be, written about the "new contract"
between employees and employers that has emerged as we approach the
end of the decade. The vast majority of this new thought has been de-
rived and written by academics and consultants. Howard Stevenson
(1994) of Harvard Business School describes the "atomistic man"—the
smallest independent unit of the corporation—who is the building block
of the new organization. This individual is perceived to be, at best,
fiercely independent and, at worst, mercenary. Douglas T. Hall and Jon-
athan E. Moss, in an article in *Organizational Dynamics*, write of the new
"Protean Career Contract." This new career is highly variable and assumes many different shapes, roles, and structures (Hall & Moss,
1998).

While these scholarly notions are very thought provoking, and appeal
to me as both an academic and a consultant, they leave me somewhat
mystified as a business owner and employer. Was there ever really an
old "contract" to change? Is the new one any better or more robust? Has
human nature changed—or just the nature of employment? And what
should employers and employees do about it?

A Historical Perspective

Organizational theorists of the 1960s and 1970s wrote about the existence of the "original" contract. Its bonds were made up of loyalty and commitment from the employee to the employer in exchange for ceding control of one's career to the (hopefully benevolent) employer. In a time when American industry was dominant and emerging markets carried the hope of eternal growth and opportunity, this contract of convenience appeared to work well. Employers benefited from a constant stream of willing new entrants who signed on for a secure career of growth and opportunity. Employees under this model received a predictable, if not inspiring, job that provided for growth and development with little personal risk, although within a closely circumscribed corporate environment. The common-man terminology used to describe the old contract had each participant implying something like this: "I'll take care of you, if you take care of me!" Each party ceded a certain amount of sovereignty in this exchange. We now know that as time passed this state of affairs was unrealistic and unnatural for both parties. It took the advent of intense competitive pressure and global markets to reveal just how unworkable this contract had become.

Lessons of History

There is some question as to how real and pervasive this old contract was. Hall and Moss (1998) calculate that "fewer than 5 percent of Americans worked under any implicit agreement regarding long-term security" (p. 23). Regardless of how many American workers were covered under implicit or explicit contracts of this nature, it is clear that the leading light companies of the day that promulgated the basic terms of the old contract acted as proxy for a vast number of smaller firms and entities, as they do today. In fact, the fundamental tone of the old contract is revealed in and enabled by the common language that has been adopted in the workplace. One regularly hears an employee say, "I get paid $12.00 an hour," or "I make $90,000 a year." Conversely, employers advertise positions starting at $8.00 an hour. Yet these statements are patently false. They reveal that employees and employers have lost sight of the most basic element of a free market economy. Employees get paid for the value they put into the time they spend, and employers pay for that value, not just the time. The legacy of the "old" contract was an entitlement mentality and the erosion of the value-added element of a free economy. Employees felt entitled to a job, raises, and security, and employers came to expect loyalty and subservience. Without the basic value proposition the inherent worth of each partner became distorted, and labor inefficiencies crept into the system—the predictable result of which is competitive intrusion directed at the inefficiencies. The consequences have been played out in the business press for the last decade as pocket after pocket of distortion—read non-value-added entitlement layer—was attacked, either from within or without.

The "New" Contract

The relentless pace of change evidenced in the latter part of the twentieth century has brought with it new, emerging requirements for employers. Companies today must be more flexible, more adaptable, and more tolerant and inclusive of disparate markets, backgrounds, technologies, cultures, and the like. As a company is merely an assemblage of individual employees, by extension these employees must be more flexible, adaptable, and capable. In light of these new requirements, it is easy to see how the old contract lost its applicability. But what has replaced it, either implicitly or explicitly?

Perhaps Hall and Moss have captured the new contract best with their Protean Career Contract, the elements of which are listed in Figure 11.1.

The common-language version of this new contract I would like you to consider is Jim Rohn's (Nightingale-Conant, 1993) "I'll take care of me for you, if you take care of you for me!" This subtle shift of emphasis puts the responsibilities where they belong. All participants must independently maintain their capabilities, capacities, and attractiveness. It is a contract of mutual respect and contribution, and it fully reflects the open and free markets we all are subject to. The new contract clearly shifts the responsibility for career development squarely to the shoulders of the employee. He or she must take the initiative to acquire new skills and capabilities in order to be able to add more value to the enterprise or risk losing continued employment and opportunity. Conversely, the employer must make these learning, capability-expanding opportunities available or risk losing the value and capability of the employee.

The "New" Loyalty

So where does that leave loyalty? Is the new contract really atomistic and barren? Do the vast majority of workers yearn only for new capabilities, learning, challenges, and money without regard to binding, human ties? And do the vast majority of the employers in this new order view themselves as mere "docking stations" where employees fill up, input capabilities, and depart at will? Do they feel comfortable viewing employee contribution as a series of transactions?

The answer has to be no. Certainly there are employees, employers, markets, and situations that will adopt these rather sterile elements of the new contract. However, the basic human need of affiliation is far

Figure 11.1
Protean Career Contract

1. The career is managed by the person, not the organization.

2. The career is a lifelong series of experiences, skills, learnings, transitions, and identity changes. ("Career age" counts, not chronological age.)

3. Development is
    —continuous learning,
    —self-directed,
    —relational, and
    —found in work challenges.

4. Development is not (necessarily)
    —formal training,
    —retraining, or
    —upward mobility.

5. The ingredients for success change
    —from know-how to learn-how,
    —from job security to employability,
    —from organizational careers to protean careers, and
    —from "work self" to "whole self."

6. The organization provides
    —challenging assignments,
    —developmental relationships, and
    —information and other developmental resources.

7. The goal: psychological success.

Source: Hall & Moss, 1998.

more powerful than the implications of this new, emerging contract. The basic desire of people to participate in a sense of joint destiny is a powerful force that will drive employees to find those employers whose enterprise is rewarding on both levels, the professional-atomistic and the personal. Conversely, the need for a corporation to maintain continuity and developed knowledge and capacity will be a strategic imperative. In the new "knowledge economy," to lose such coin of the realm will be to lose real strategic position.

So the loyalty embodied in the old contract—that of longevity, rank, and entitlement—is being replaced with one of contribution, of mutual respect, and of fit—fit with values, culture, direction, and goals. What an exciting and uplifting change for those participants who grasp the implications and seize the initiative. However, it will continue to be a scary and unwelcome world for those employees and employers who continue to seek security and entitlement.

QUESTIONS FOR PARTICIPANTS

If the foregoing is true, there are two questions that are fundamental to a discussion of the "new" contract and its implications for both employees and employers. These are questions I believe every employee and employer should be asking on a regular basis.

- *Employees*: Is it possible to add to my skills, capabilities, and knowledge, thereby becoming more valuable and "attractive" to an employer, and therefore be paid more for the value that I put into the time I am at work?
- *Employers*: Are my employees continually gaining new skills, capabilities, and knowledge, therefore becoming more valuable to the corporation—and what am I doing to enable this value enhancement so that I remain "attractive" to my employees?

The Law of Attraction

My law of attraction states: To attract attractive employees a firm must be attractive to them. We know that attractive employees are those that take control of their careers and mirror the needs of the new external environment—they are flexible, capable, independent thinking, adaptable. And we know that as humans there is an inherent longing for affiliation and desire to contribute to something meaningful. Douglas Hall and Associates (1996) in their book *The Career Is Dead—Long Live the Career: A Relational Approach to Careers* indicate that the major sources of learning for employees under the new model will be the challenges they encounter at work and the relationships they build there. Consequently, they will seek employers that will provide them constant opportunities for growth, learning, autonomy, and contribution in an environment of like-minded employees. Attractive employers must, by extension, be those that make these things available. (Note: This will be fundamentally easier for employers in growth markets and industries. In flat or declining industries the ability to offer continuing growth and challenges may be limited by market attractiveness. In these cases the employers may have to adopt the following methodologies but be resigned to losing employees to other more attractive industries or markets. In cases such as these, do not despair. One strategy is to adopt the methods used by certified public accountant [CPA], law, and consulting firms and proselytized by Tom Peters (1994) of "being known by your alumni." This involves constantly bringing in new low-cost entrants and sending the higher-cost employees out to other divisions or to complementary companies.)

These questions and the law of attractiveness drive the discussion that follows about the implications of the new contract for employers and employees. While this is a text designed to guide employees in this new environment, the following discussion starts with the implications for employers. My hope is that it will be illuminating to employees and act as a guide for understanding and choosing your future employer(s) wisely.

THE NEW IMPERATIVES FOR EMPLOYERS

Under this new contract two broad imperatives for employers arise—heightened leadership and a more strategic role for the human resources function.

The Need for Leadership

The need for leadership in this new environment cannot be understated. Leadership must constantly see to the task of making the company attractive to these more independent employees. There are two parts to this requirement. The first requirement for leadership is the development and refinement of the softer, more humanistic elements of attractiveness. These include:

A clear, powerful vision of the future for the company and its participants. If the two greatest elements of being attractive as a company are (1) offering continuous opportunity for growth and learning in the future and (2) offering an environment in which employees are compelled to stay affiliated in the longer term, a company and its leadership must be able to elucidate a clear vision of the future that can act as both a guide and a magnet—a guide that directs the employees' continuing development and a magnet that pulls at them and deflects other alluring opportunities outside the company.

A culture that is in evidence that clearly demonstrates support for the continuation of the contractual bond. The leadership must see to it that there is evidence of a supportive culture that fosters the new mind-set required by the new contract—that systems, policies, and procedures enable the new protean contract, not conflict with it.

Max DePree of Herman Miller refers to these as the "covenanting" elements that leaders must tend to. They make up the covenanted bonds that are implicit in the new contract. The second requirement of leadership is communication (DePree, 1989).

"It's Communication, Stupid!" I have this statement proudly displayed in my office, and yet how often the tyranny of the urgent causes me to

Developmental and training mechanisms. Again remember that traditional training has less impact as a learning tool and must be augmented with experiential and situational training. Formal mentoring and teaming assignments can help greatly in this area. Additionally, the traditional review process must be rethought. Increasingly firms are using 360-degree reviews to determine whether employees are sensitive to, and successful in, the new environment. Traditional performance reviews are being replaced or supplemented with results reviews, success planning, and team-based planning. All of these incorporate more employee involvement and self-direction.

Benefits. Increasingly benefits are being tailored more closely to lifestyle. On-site day care, spousal and extended-family benefits, merged career and life planning, and other "beyond work" employee benefits are emerging as important discriminators in increasingly tight labor markets.

Physical environment. In an article summarizing the elements that distinguish the 100 Best Companies to work for in America, *Fortune* magazine writer Ronald B. Lieber (1998) sights three fundamental similarities between these attractive employers. The first is *inspiring leadership*, and the third is *a sense of purpose.* We have discussed the importance of these in the previous section on leadership. The second element was *knockout facilities.* What better way to visibly show your commitment to existing and potential employees than having great facilities that are attractive in and of themselves? This does not mean palatial or opulent. *Gracious, clean, well kept,* and *inviting* are the operative words. Also, can you really be committed to ongoing development, training, and learning without dedicated time, resources, and space? If these are not readily visible to prospective employees, will they seek them elsewhere?

Organizational structure and design. In light of the fact that employees are looking for increased opportunities to learn and develop within the totality of the business system, leadership must ensure that there are not rigid boundaries that hinder the fluid nature of employment the new contract demands. It seems to me that we must view our structures as having "semipermeable" membranes through which employees can easily pass as they gather capabilities, knowledge, experience, and skills. I believe these must extend even to the outside boundaries. With increasing regularity, employees are being placed within customers' or vendors' facilities requiring that these previously hard boundaries, with their attendant turbulent boundary conditions, be made softer and more easily traversed. Even the ultimate boundary of continued employability needs to be softened. In the case of capable contributors who leave because the organization cannot provide them with the desired challenges, management needs to think carefully about an appropriate philosophy. Does one adopt the stance of welcoming the change, wishing the employee the best, and be content to be known by its alumni, or should one sever all ties with the past employee and move on to the next atomistic occupant? What will you do if this individual is available to you again and you need their capabilities?

Your Company as a Product

Since the new contract implies a breaking of the old methods and mind-set for attracting, developing, and retaining employees, the first implication is that an employer must adopt a new mind-set for thinking about the changed environment. Employees of today are much more independent and are much more inclined to demand empirical evidence of a company's commitment to upholding the company's part of the new contract—providing opportunities for growth, learning, development, and advancement. Similarly, companies are seeking employees who have demonstrated a willingness to participate, if not evidence of success, in this new environment. What can an employer do with this arrangement? How does it/should it shape your thinking? These two independent entities must come together in a mutually beneficial codependent reality, where each is investing in themselves for the benefit of the other. The description of this exchange is remarkably similar to the exchange between customer and supplier in long-term transactions. Can we as employers use this similarity for guidance?

In the companies I run as well as those that I consult with, I have suggested that employers view their company as a product and apply traditional marketing discipline to the problem. To do this, one must define each job position and opening as before but must now think of each position as a product in your product line. As with any product, this requires clearly defining the benefits of your product (the company and the position) *in terms of your customers'* (current and potential employees) needs and desires. One then employs the P's of marketing (place, promotion, price, positioning, etc.) to place the product (the company) in front of the customer (the employee). This implies determining the "position" your product should occupy relative to your competition—are you a leader in pay, technology, training, international, and so on? It implies determining the "promotional" vehicle(s) you should use to reach your target customers and the language you should use. The "place" of your product means where you are going to look for these new entrants and where they are going to find you, and so on.

I have found that this discipline causes the companies that use it to think much more strategically about attraction and retention issues and to do it from a customer (the employees) perspective. Gone are the days when we as employers could merely be "as good as the other guy." Now we must distinguish ourselves in increasingly competitive, fluid, and transitory markets for top talent.

Final Thoughts on Hiring

While some or all of the foregoing techniques can be used to prepare existing employees for the new realities inherent in the new contract, the most obvious method for effecting a change to the new reality is during the new-hire process. There are three powerful steps for ensuring that new entrants are prepared for the new realities.

Select for the characteristics. In the recruitment and selection process, look for evidence of both the personality elements required for success—adaptability, curiosity, a desire to learn, fit with the prevailing culture, alignment with the vision—and the professional elements—demonstrable skills, accumulation of capabilities and experiences, and evidence of past professional development and past success in the new environment. An emerging trend is considerable preselection screening done by peers from within the company. Techniques include: "new pal" lunches that pair an aspiring entrant with an existing employee for experience sharing; employee bonuses for successful referrals; intense group interviews that focus on attitude and fit more than skills; and test batteries that seek to determine an aspiring entrant's fit with the new environment.

Indoctrinate early and often. It is never too soon to begin the dialogue on mutual expectations, required and restricted behaviors, cultural observances, mutual success planning, and the metrics for analyzing success. A useful technique here is the use of what I call an "Owner's Manual" instead of an employee manual. The traditional employee manual devotes the bulk of its time to discussions of benefits and policies circumscribing behavior that is undesirable. Consider writing the "photo-negative" of this document. Prepare a document that describes all of the fantastic ways employees can contribute to the success of the enterprise, all of the available knowledge they can tap into and add to, all of the ways that they can share in the success and the rewards they contribute to. Try to inspire them. Remember you cannot berate people to do great things. Tell them what you expect of them, that you have great faith in their ability to deliver (if you don't believe that, why did you hire them?), and tell them what they can expect of you. Only as an afterthought tell them what they can do to get fired—most people know!

Reward and promote based on successful gains in capabilities and contribution. It is key to link the rewards and promotions to achievements along the dimensions of mutual success. As the Towers Perrin survey points out, employees are increasingly expectant of gain-and-profit-sharing mechanisms and other methods that share the success of the enterprise.

The foregoing implications for employers represent a sea change in philosophy and mind-set. Such transformational change is very difficult to grasp and make sense of. Hall and Moss (1998) indicate: "[I]t appears that it takes on average about seven years for an organization and its members to arrive at an understanding of the new relationship" (p. 31). Seven years! That is an eternity in today's fast-moving markets. However, just because it is difficult and time-consuming does not excuse us from its effects. Enlightened owners and managers will undertake the discipline of reacting to the new environment and learn to thrive in it, thereby seizing strategic advantage over those who wait. Can you afford not to respond expeditiously and orient yourself in the new reality?

A Final Note for Employers

By definition, a work such as this has to simplify a complex and multidimensional labor market into some broad generalities that act as proxy for the larger body. This is useful for disseminating as broadly as possible the ideas and concepts covered by such a work. However, it is also dangerous. No two industries, markets, segments, much less companies are the same. The labor markets available to these markets are no different. They are heterogeneous and maturing at different rates in different industries and in different locations worldwide. Please use these concepts and principles only as a spur for deeper thought on the applicability of them to your company, segment, market, industry, or country.

THE IMPLICATIONS FOR EMPLOYEES

By first illuminating the implications and actions for employers, I am confident that the employee and potential employee readers of this text will now have gleaned sufficient wisdom to seek with anticipation and knowledge those employers that are well advanced in adopting the new contract. However, there are some key considerations and fundamental questions you must ask yourself.

For Every Action, There Is an Equal and Opposite Reaction

Just as employers have to adopt a new philosophy or mind-sets for coping with the new contract, so too do employees. No longer do employees have the safety of allowing their employer to shape their career.

> *Perhaps the most important driver of learning for the employees is the fact that the new contract is not with the organization; it is with the self and one's work.*
>
> —Hall and Moss, 1998, p. 30

This reality begs the question of employees: Have you thought deeply and longitudinally about your life, personality, and career? At least deeply enough to accept the terms of this new contract or to seek opportunities in fields where the new contract is less pervasive or demanding? Being in charge of one's career is a heavy burden for certain individuals, especially young entrants into the labor market that may not have enough life experience to make informed decisions. Hall and Moss caution that "early career and life choices may not necessarily be the best fit for a person in mid-career" (p. 30).

Similarly, long-term employees brought through the vestiges of the old contract are experiencing a diminution of all the old patterns of thought, behavior, and reward. Many of the old methodologies that have served them well in the past now betray them. Relearning late in life and changing personal and business philosophies are wrenching, time-consuming transitions that require disciplined thought and patience.

And just as there are markets that are more or less affected by the new contract, there are employees who are more attracted to and prepared for it as well as those who are not. If through the process of assessing your career goals you determine that you are less comfortable with these new terms and conditions, do not despair. Seek those markets or industries where the new contract is less prevalent. Alternatively, seek positions that do not require the "Bedouin" elements of the new contract. As an employer, it is comforting to have individuals who know their desires and are willing to master a certain element of the business and command it for a significant time. However, be constantly mindful of the need to add incremental value at least in proportion to your incremental cost.

Be Careful What You Wish For—You Just Might Get It

The independence that is inherent in the new contract can be seductive. While employers who adopt the new contract encourage the gathering of skills and capabilities for independent use and contribution, and while the old ties of selfless loyalty have been broken, there is still a need for employees to remain aligned with the direction and culture of the company. Employees must resist the temptation to "get all they can while they can" under this new order. The operative question should not be "What am I getting here?" but rather, "What am I becoming here?" Are you becoming more valuable, more contributory, more capable? And if so, are those equities paying a return to the company or only to you?

While carrying exciting freedom and opportunity, this new independence carries with it implied obligations. I refer to them as the Three Rs of Expectation.

Respectful. Employees must be respectful of the enterprise. They must be respectful of the history, values, culture, beliefs, and other constituents that make up the extended enterprise.

Responsible. Employees must be responsible for themselves and the position they occupy while at the company.

Resourceful. Employees must be resourceful in discharging their responsibilities and obligations while in the company.

I do not consider these to be unidirectional. I believe the company owes its employees a return of these same expectations.

Specific Techniques for Employees

The most obvious technique an employee should use is to look for companies and leaders who are exhibiting these traits. The new contract heightens the requirements for employees to do their own "due diligence" on future employers. The key is to look for both hard and anecdotal evidence of the attractiveness of your potential employer. Is there evidence of inspiring leadership and a clear vision? Is their evidence of care and commitment in the facilities, tools, resources? Does a sense of purpose show through in the writings, actions, and plans of the firm? How deep does this evidence go in the organization? How do current employees view the company? Fortunately, technology has greatly enhanced this exploratory process. Company web sites and the World Wide Web are teeming with information on companies. Powerful search engines can mine huge amounts of data about your target. And even the smallest of companies have chat rooms and bulletin boards dedicated to them.

Once inside your new company, take full advantage of all the opportunities available to you. Seek out enabling superiors and team leaders that will allow you to gain experiences and capabilities. Befriend the human resources department and enlist them in your quest to grow and develop. However, remember the Three Rs of Expectation and seek to become someone of value and substance. Finally, share. Share your knowledge and experience. Share your enthusiasm and goals. Share your successes. Mentor others in their quest to grow and succeed.

A very useful technique is to seek out and form your own personal board of directors. Find individuals who will agree to help you guide your career. Seek out people who will not hesitate to challenge your thinking and your direction. Find individuals who will inspire you to grow and gain in capabilities, capacity, and contribution—and who will provoke you when you slack off. Don't settle for easy, casual directors. Choose individuals who will challenge and inspire you to be as good as you can be. After all, you are, as several business gurus put it, "a corporation of one."

Finally, a caution: Do not become overzealous. The new contract requires that employees take control of their own careers. It might appear that this means seizing every opportunity to grow and learn and contribute. While this is partially true, indiscriminate action is not what is called for. Do not confuse action with progress. Successful employees will take time to reflect on their direction and desires—to measure progress against plan and to reevaluate the plan if necessary. You are the helmsman of your destiny, and it is imperative that you pause long enough, often enough, to ensure that the course you are on is the right course for you.

FINAL THOUGHTS

Is this really new? Have employers just realized how valuable and free employees are? Have employees just awakened to the fact that they need to guide their careers with what Confucius calls "reverential care"? I do not believe so. I believe that enlightened companies have long recognized the inherent interdependency described in the new contract. And I believe that employees, given the choice, have always sought those entities that exhibit a fundamental respect for human dignity and choice. Hall and Moss (1998) found that certain companies have been promoting the elements of the new contract for years.

In the process of competitive adaptation, they have managed to maintain their core *values* about people through difficult economic and environmental changes. Companies in the continuous learning group have a fundamental respect for the individual. (pp. 28–29)

These companies tend to be those that end up on the lists of the "100 Best Places to Work," and so on. This should not be surprising; it is, after all, a human enterprise we are talking about. The new contract is all about mutual respect and benefit. An easy concept to grasp—but if you want to do it right, "the devil really is in the details."

Why do all of the above? Why should employers bend over backwards to attract and retain employees? Why should employees stay up late doing due diligence on future employers and managing their career? The short answers are performance for the firm, pride and security for the employees, and reward for both. Collins and Porras in their groundbreaking book *Built to Last* (1997) delineate the empirical link between companies that have adopted many of these precepts and those same companies' ability to deliver returns that are significantly better than those of the nearest competitor. Hall and Moss (1998) observe, "Data from Bain's [Bain Consulting] research show that the longer a company's relationships are with its employees and customers, the more profitable the firm is". Finally, Heskett, Sasser, and Hart in their definitive book on service management, *The Service Profit Chain*, (1997) show the clear links between employee capabilities, job satisfaction, customer satisfaction, and higher profit.

Perhaps the better question is, *Why not?* Why not create an organization that is more attractive than your competitors'? Why not become a more attractive employee, capable of delivering more value to your employer? What have you got to lose? And finally, why not *now?*

REFERENCES

Collins, J. C., & Porras, J. I. (1997). *Built to last: successful habits of visionary companies.* New York: HarperBusiness.
Covey, S. R. (1989). *The seven habits of highly effective people.* New York: Simon & Schuster.
DePree, M. (1989). *Leadership is an art.* New York: Doubleday.
Hall, D. T., & Associates. (1996). *The career is dead — long live the career: A relational approach to careers.* San Francisco: Jossey-Bass.
Hall, D. T., & Moss, J. E. (1998). The new protean career contract: Helping organizations and employees adapt. *Organizational Dynamics* (Winter).
Heskett, J. L., Sasser, W. E., & Hart, L. A. (1997). *The service profit chain: How leading companies link profit and growth to loyalty, satisfaction and value.* New York: Free Press.
Lieber, R. B. (1998). Why employees love these companies. *Fortune* (January 12): 72–74.
The new workplace paradox. (1998). *Management Review* (January): 7.
Nightingale-Conant. (1993). Audiocassette script of J. Rohn, "The art of exceptional living."
Peters, T. (1994). *The pursuit of wow: Every person's guide to topsy turvy times.* New York: Knopf/Vintage.
Stevenson, H. H. (1994). Power: A Harvard expert reveals how to win. *Success,* 41(5): 36–38.
Stewart, T. A. (1998). Gray flannel suit? Moi? *Fortune* (March 16): 76–82.

12

Staying Sane in an Ever-Changing World

WILLIAM I. SAUSER, JR.

INTRODUCTION

Powerful forces for change in today's work environment—including time compression, the technology explosion, relentless competition, globalization, and incessant calls for "downsizing" and "reengineering"— are causing high levels of stress for many employees and managers. Some have been broken by the strain, whereas others are expending huge quantities of energy resisting change and fighting against the surging tide.

This chapter, prepared by an industrial psychologist with considerable personal experience in guiding groups and individuals through the difficult waters of change, proposes a different approach—using the forces of change to provide positive momentum to one's own career enhancement. Pragmatic advice for sensing the direction of change and using its force to one's own advantage is drawn from the author's experience as a psychologist, business professor and administrator, agent of change, Christian lay pastor, and—perhaps most important—fellow struggler in maintaining sanity in today's challenging career environment.

This chapter is based on ideas shared during a series of seminars the author has led for employees and managers on this very topic. It is somewhat lighthearted, but its content has been validated by the author's personal experience and the many "amens" provided by workshop participants, who found the ideas to resonate with their own experience as well. The chapter follows an "outline" format, providing an overview of a strategy for using the forces of change for one's own benefit. Those desiring deeper coverage of some of the ideas presented in this chapter are encouraged to consult such excellent works as those by Albrecht (1979), Beer (1980), Blanchard and Johnson (1982), Burke (1982), Covey (1989), Drucker (1967), French and Bell (1990), and Hellriegel, Slocum, and Woodman (1992), all of which influenced the thinking provided herein.

The heart of this chapter is a presentation of ten key tips for staying sane in the work environment: (1) Raise your antenna, (2) audit the situation, (3) build your skills, (4) use the power of the force, (5) surf the waves of change, (6) be good to yourself, (7) break through depression, (8) smell the roses, (9) grow spiritually, and (10) be a tower of strength. Putting these ten proven tips to use in one's own life will help alleviate stress, maintain a sense of sanity and control, and enhance one's opportunities to enjoy a productive and rewarding career in business, government, or community service.

Before getting to the heart of the matter, however, let us first review briefly five forces for change in today's world of work and five reasons why human beings resist change. As we peruse these lists, ponder the following questions for yourself: What changes are you facing at present? What are your sources of stress? What are you doing to maintain sanity? How well is it working? What do you need to implement, revise, or delete in order to improve your plan to maintain sanity? The more you tailor the ideas presented herein to your *own* personal situation, the more valuable they will be to you. Let's get started, shall we?

FIVE FORCES FOR CHANGE IN TODAY'S WORLD

Among the many forces for change we are experiencing at present, five seem particularly to stand out in importance for today's employees and managers. See if you are being pressured by any of the items on this list.

Organizations under Siege

Fueled by intensified global competition, increasing customer sophistication and demands for improved quality at lower prices, and a growing cynicism toward "big" business, government, and labor, we have witnessed of late a major attack on many of the venerable old institutions and organizations of the past. Government, universities, the military, financial institutions, major manufacturers, utilities, and mainline churches have all become targets for scrutiny and change. "Downsizing" and "reengineering" have emerged as worldwide trends for large organizations as a result of intense global competition and its attendant needs for efficiency. These days, even experienced technicians and managers are losing their jobs as organizations seek to "streamline" operations. This has led to considerable insecurity and stress among groups of workers who were protected from such pressures in the past.

A Technology Explosion

All of us have been affected by the seeming explosion of new technology that has entered the workplace. Personal computers, fax machines, scanners, cellular telephones, fiber optics, radar detection systems, graphics design software, the Internet, web pages, and all the other new wonders we are experiencing can be quite intimidating to those of us who still have trouble programming our VCRs! Yet new technologies enter the workplace daily, in wave after wave, version after version.

It has been said that if you understand your computer software, it is most likely obsolete, having already been surpassed by a newer version. Trying to keep up with technology, use it effectively, make cost-efficient decisions about its deployment, and the like, are issues that are straining even the most sophisticated employees and managers. Securing our information and protecting our technological investments and sensitive data are growing problems for many of us. And let's not forget the "year 2000 problem," which many of us are trying to deal with as of this writing. New technologies are wonderful, but they can be challenging and stressful as well.

Standards, Laws, and Procedures

Most of us value "playing by the rules" and seek diligently to comply with the law, with professional standards, with regulations and specified procedures, which we see as the rules of the game. Staying in compliance, though, becomes difficult when the "rules" are constantly changing. This is the way of life for many managers and employees these days: New statutes and administrative rules, new case law, new professional standards, and revised organizational policies and procedures are issued every day as the pace of change in the workplace accelerates.

It is stressful for us to keep abreast of the legal and regulatory environment we work in these days because it seems to be in a constant state of flux. No sooner do we get ourselves straight on one set of procedures than we find ourselves scrambling to respond to a new set of rules. Those of us with years of experience as employees and managers have learned to adapt over time, but the need to change our ways of working time after time in response to newer and newer, more and more rules, laws, and standards becomes tiring after a while.

Time Compression

"The check's in the mail," we used to say, knowing that would buy us a few days' time. But with, first, overnight delivery services, then fax machines, then e-mail, everything sped up. Now we can be buzzed, beeped, paged, and prodded no matter where we are or what we are doing. As the means of communication have become more efficient and the exchange of messages has stepped up in time dramatically, we often feel as if time has become compressed. Some employees and managers are feeling considerable pressure to do more and more, faster and faster, and are beginning to break under the strain.

Litigiousness

Our nation is strong due in part to our freedom to seek justice and reparations in the courts. This constitutional right is dear to all of us. However, most readers will no doubt agree with me that the mood of litigiousness that pervades our society today can make the task of management—and even employment—at times very unpleasant. We must constantly be on guard not to say or do anything offensive, lest we find ourselves in court as a defendant in a lawsuit. "Working in a fish bowl" can be tiring and annoying, and I frequently hear fellow managers express their private frustrations with being constantly vigilant in all they say and do.

Altogether, these five factors—which are just a sampling of all we could identify and list—can make our jobs very daunting. So what are we to do? Before exploring ten tips for maintaining sanity, let us first review briefly five reasons why we human beings often resist change. Armed with this knowledge, we can better understand how to master change and channel its forces to work on our behalf.

FIVE REASONS WHY HUMANS RESIST CHANGE

Why do human beings resist change? We know that resistance is often a natural human reaction to change, but why is this? Hellriegel, Slocum, and Woodman (1992, p. 729) list five aspects of human nature that cause us as individuals to resist change: (1) selective perception, (2) habit, (3) dependence, (4) fear of the unknown, and (5) economic reasons. Let's explore each in turn. When we realize why we as humans tend to resist change, we will be better equipped to begin to understand how to channel the forces of change to our own benefit.

Selective Perception

We are bombarded every moment with information pouring into our brains from our sensory organs—our eyes, ears, nose, taste buds, and various touch and balance sensors. We cannot possibly attend to all of this information, so we screen out much of it through a process called "selective perception." What this means is that we pay attention to those sensations that we judge to be important, while ignoring the rest. Selective perception occurs both intentionally and unconsciously.

How do we choose those messages to which we pay attention? Selective perception is a very complex psychological process with many variables, but quite often when faced with messages signaling a change in the air, we attend to those that reinforce our current beliefs and maintain our present comfort level. In other words, we too often see only what we want to see and hear only what we want to hear. Through selective perception, we frequently "protect" the status quo by filtering out troubling signals that a change is needed or may even be on its way.

Similarly, we often read only those articles containing information we already know and approve, hear those commentaries with which we already agree, and listen to those persons whose ideas resonate with our own. "Dangerous" messages—those that somehow threaten our comfort level—are "tuned out" and ignored.

Our natural human tendency toward selective perception can sometimes do us great harm. When we block out all information with which we do not agree, we often miss clear signals that change is on the horizon. Thus, when change comes into full view, we are surprised by it, unprepared for it, and afraid of it. Can you see why our tendency toward selective perception can put us at a disadvantage in mastering the processes of change? If we cannot see change coming before our very eyes, how can we possibly become its master? You will note below how several of the ten tips seek to overcome our natural tendency to resist change by ignoring its troubling signals.

Habit

Habit is a wonderful thing for human beings. Can you imagine how difficult life would be without habits? Imagine if you had to think consciously about every little movement needed to drive an automobile. Would you ever make it to work in the morning? When we drive "by habit," our mind is free to think about other things, secure in the knowledge that our senses will warn us when something is the matter.

Many of the things we do, we do by habit: routine household chores, rituals of hygiene and dressing ourselves, greeting one another, sorting our mail—many, many things. We like this because it frees our minds to focus on other, more important things. Habit is comfortable to us, and we don't like to give up our routine habits. Furthermore, habits are often difficult to change—just reflect for a moment on your own experience when you tried perhaps to alter your "morning routine" or consciously drop a "bad" habit.

One very important reason we resist change, then, is that change often forces us to alter our habits. Even if a new software system or other "labor-saving" device promises to yield more efficiency once mastered, we often resist it because we do not want to change our safe, secure, habitual way of doing things. Even though I've been a writer for many years, I have resisted until recently the use of a word processor, preferring instead my habit of writing with pen upon yellow pads of paper! My old habit was hard to break, but I must admit that the editing capabilities of modern word processing programs have made me more efficient, now that I have finally "joined the twentieth century"—just in time for the dawning of the twenty-first, I might add. Habits run deep.

Dependence

We've already considered the fact that we are constantly being bombarded by more messages than we can possibly handle. One way we have learned to deal with this in the world of work is to *specialize*. We gravitate to our own spheres of knowledge and interest and depend on others for information and insights about areas beyond our scope of knowledge. When I want my car to run better, I take it to a trusted mechanic, since I am not knowledgeable in the workings of the modern automobile. Someone seeking knowledge about industrial psychology might in turn consult me, since that is my own area of specialty.

The point is that each of us has persons on whom we depend for advice and guidance. This dependence serves us well to a point, but what if the person on whom we are dependent is not truly informed as we had believed? We can be given misinformation, poor advice, improper guidance. I am not advocating that you immediately become suspicious of all your advisers, but you do see, don't you, how too much dependence on others can become dangerous?

Often we resist change because those on whom we depend for advice have *told* us to resist, since the change may adversely affect us. Trusting in this advice, we fail to seek out for ourselves the true nature of the situation. Again, this sets us up to be "blindsided" by change we fail to see coming our way.

Fear of the Unknown

When finding yourself in the presence of an unknown insect, do you typically choose to kill it by swatting it or stepping on it? Certainly many of us (myself included) have this very natural reaction. When called upon to explain our actions, we typically rationalize, "Better safe than sorry." It is indeed a natural reaction to fear the unknown. However, when we let that fear paralyze us into inaction, we can become vulnerable to destruction by the forces of change. One of the best ways to deal with this fear, of course, is to become *knowledgeable* about what is going on. We will see how this plays out in the ten tips to follow.

Of course, it is possible to fear the *known* also, but in this case we are acting not through ignorance but rather through insight. When we know the power of adverse change that disaster can bring, we can begin limiting possible disaster through positive action. This, too, is the basis for some of the tips to follow.

Economic Reasons

People tend to resist anything they view as punishment. When a potential change is known to have very real possibilities to cause you harm, you will likely resist it with all your might. That is why it is so important when in the role of change *agent* to consider any adverse effects others might experience as a result of your proposed organizational change. If others perceive that they will lose money, influence, clout, or status as the result of the change you are seeking to implement, you can expect strong and active resistance. Likewise, I am very likely to resist any change in my own situation that I believe could harm my economic standing within society. This is not irrational resistance; it is action in protection of one's own self-interest.

Having considered these five reasons why human beings resist change, let us now turn our attention to the ten tips for maintaining sanity in an ever-changing world. Note as we consider these tips their close relationships to the factors influencing change and resistance we have just discussed. As we examine each tip, consider how you might tailor it to suit your own personal circumstances. Naturally, you will find some tips more helpful than others; we are not all in the same circumstances, after all. However, if you find yourself rejecting a particular tip out of hand, go back and reconsider it. Could you possibly have been practicing selective perception, and "tuning out" an important message you simply "chose" not to hear?

TEN TIPS FOR STAYING SANE

Tip One: Raise Your Antenna

As noted above, we often wall ourselves off from important information by employing selective perception, habit, and specialization/dependence to keep ourselves from being exposed to ideas we might not want to hear. While this is human nature, it is not a good strategy for mastering the forces of change. Instead, we should seek to *broaden* our sources of information, even to the point of risking some fear to explore ideas heretofore unknown to us. By raising your antenna and seeking broader information that might signal oncoming change, you will have a distinct advantage over those who tend to isolate themselves. Here are a few suggestions in this regard.

Become aware of your situation. What is going on in your immediate situation? Don't know? Then you'd better take steps right now to find out! What is the mission of your unit? What is the purpose of your job? What are your key responsibilities and assignments? What does your supervisor expect of you? What obstacles stand in your way? What resources do you have at your disposal? How well are you performing? How does the citizenry view the importance and performance of your unit? What changes are blowing in the political winds? If you are unable to answer questions like these, you had better begin immediately to "do your homework," for you are in a prime position to be overwhelmed by unexpected forces of change.

Read broadly. Reading is a good, quick way to gain information. I recommend broad reading—reading that stretches your horizons and helps you gain facility with previously unfamiliar ideas. Read the newspaper, perhaps a news magazine or two, some classics, a few biographies and histories, some fictional novels, some fantasy and science fiction, some nonfiction books on current topics, and some scripture. You will be amazed how ideas from a variety of sources like these will open your mind to new ways of thinking, thus increasing your adaptability when change is needed.

If reading is "not your thing," you can accomplish the same objective through a variety of media: pop an informational cassette tape into your car stereo while driving or listen to a news channel or public radio. Watch films and videotapes or tune your television to a news channel, an educational channel, or my personal favorite, A&E (Arts and Entertainment). You'll be amazed what you can learn about what's happening in the world from such sources.

Set up a network. One excellent way to broaden your access to knowledge is to set up a network of friends and colleagues, all of whom keep one another informed of important happenings and tidbits of news. I'm not advocating here a "gossip grapevine" of false information but, rather, a set of informed individuals who care enough about one another to share valid information that may be helpful to all.

Many successful professionals have learned "the art of networking." Whenever they attend a professional conference or social gathering, they seek out interesting, well-informed people and exchange business cards. A week or two later they telephone their new acquaintances and share with them some important tidbits of information, being careful—of course—not to violate any confidences. In this manner, they begin to establish a strong network of persons who are willing to share valuable information that might give them an "edge" in the workplace. Civic clubs, professional associations, and other such groups are a natural foundation for networking and are typically employed for this purpose with excellent results.

Find out for yourself. Specializing in a particular field and depending on others for information and help in less familiar areas is, as noted above, a natural human behavior. It works well *as long as those upon whom you depend give you accurate information.* However, unfortunately, not all persons can be counted on to supply the truth. When you are in doubt about the validity of information you have received, *find out for yourself.* Do an independent investigation of the situation and see if the facts support what you have been told.

Seek information, not noise. Psychologists classify as "noise" false or random signals that do not provide useful information. Sometimes we call such noise "idle gossip." It is not a bad idea to spot-check periodically the veracity of the sources in your network. If you discover that one or more of your sources for some reason cannot be trusted to supply accurate information, then revise your network by replacing that individual with a more trustworthy source. Accurate information can help us spot trends and prepare ourselves for change; idle gossip, or "noise," is of no use to us and may even do us significant harm when we base decisions and actions upon it.

See the forest and the trees. Which is more important, the "big picture" or the details? Why waste time pursuing that question? Instead, seek out both types of information! Don't become so involved with the details that you miss the overriding concept, but also don't get so enamored with "the big picture" that you ignore important details. Too many people have been burned by failing to "read the fine print." The key here is to *balance* your information-seeking behavior and your interpretive thinking. Pull back and see the forest, but also step forward and examine closely some of the trees.

Look for trends. This is the point of seeking information—to spot the trends that may be signaling change on the horizon. Look for seemingly isolated facts that begin "fitting together" like the pieces of a puzzle. When you think you have spotted a trend, begin to "check it out" and to project into the future the changes that trend may bring for the way you do business and conduct your life. All of us like to "be on the inside." This is a good way to get ourselves there. Gather broad information, ponder it carefully, search for trends, project what is about to happen, then plan your moves accordingly. Don't just react to change; anticipate it and prepare for it.

Any venture capitalist or "player" of the stock market will tell you that you won't be 100 percent correct in all your projections; that is impossible. However, if you don't start training yourself to look for trends and prepare to capitalize on them, you will never be a success. In professional baseball, someone who can hit major league pitching once out of every three or four times at bat is likely to retire a millionaire. Babe Ruth struck out far more often than he hit a home run, but it's his homers we remember.

Spot the perfect wave. I'm not a surfer, but those who are skilled in this sport tell me, "The key to a good ride is to spot the perfect wave, then go!" The whole point of raising our antennas and searching for trends is to spot that perfect wave. When you see a wave of change coming your way, prepare yourself for the ride. We'll look at this idea in more detail below as we consider Tip Five.

Tip Two: Audit the Situation

For those of you familiar with the thought processes of investigators and auditors, here is a tip for you! If these ways of thinking are not familiar to you, pay close attention; you will learn something new and valuable. The ideas presented here will help you sort out quality information from trivial noise and thus help you improve the base of knowledge with which you deal with change.

Get the facts. See "Find out for yourself" above. Before taking any action, be sure you have the facts. Make sure you understand the situation thoroughly; get several points of view if the matter is in doubt. Don't put yourself at risk by acting before you have the necessary facts.

One caveat is necessary here: Realize that you will never have *all* the facts. Don't become obsessed with the process of gaining every single point of information that may exist about the situation before taking action. If this becomes your habit, you'll never be able to make a decision, because there will always be "one more thing to find out." The proper stance is to position yourself somewhere between these two old proverbs: "Look before you leap" and "He who hesitates is lost." Remember: Keep your balance.

Take an independent stance. If you are not independent but are instead biased in your search for information, you are quite likely to fall prey to selective perception, seeing and hearing only those items that support your predetermined solution. This, of course, defeats the very purpose of your audit! Keep an open mind while investigating; consider various points of view; be broad in your search for facts. Don't be overly influenced by those who are seeking to "slant" your findings; instead, remain independent and unbiased while seeking the facts.

Consider scope and materiality. When you have obtained a piece of information, consider its importance in the larger scheme of things. Information narrow in scope—that is, of limited significance in the broader picture—should not be allowed to assume undue importance in your decision. "Materiality" likewise refers to the relative importance of the fact in view of the decision to be made. Immaterial facts that have no real bearing on the matter at hand should not be allowed to "sidetrack" your investigation, decision, or action.

The ability to consider scope and materiality is a skill acquired through experience. One good way to build your skill in this area is to work through situations under the guidance of a mentor known for his or her ability to "sort out" issues and make sound decisions. Perhaps through your network you can identify such an individual who may be able to help you build this valuable skill.

Render an opinion. After gathering the facts, auditors are asked to "render an opinion" regarding the validity of the financial statements they have audited. The whole purpose of gathering the facts, of course, is to guide the making of a good decision. Once the facts have been gathered, you mustn't be afraid to reach a decision about intended action. One common trait of those unfortunates who seem always to be overwhelmed by change is their inability to make a decision when the time comes. You must be willing to risk making a *decision*, but you can certainly reduce the risk of making an *error* by gathering and reviewing the pertinent facts beforehand.

Formulate a plan of action. Once you have decided what must be done, it is time to formulate a plan of action to implement your decision. Some people prefer detailed plans, whereas others like a general outline, intending to "fill in the details as we go along." This is a matter of style. The key, though, is to make sure your plan is clear on the following essentials: who, what, when, where, how, and why.

If you cannot answer these classic "reporter's questions," you haven't yet done enough planning. In my business classes, I teach that a good plan will specify the key actions to be taken and their intended outcomes; will establish personal accountability, budgets, and deadlines; and will be flexible enough to change if feedback establishes that important goals and purposes of the plan are not being accomplished.

Tip Three: Build Your Skills

Adapting to change frequently requires the effective use of all your acquired skills. In some—perhaps most—cases, adapting to change will call for the use of skills that you might not yet have mastered or even begun to acquire! Since successfully dealing with change does require the use of many skills, it is important to build as many of them as you can before their use becomes essential for organizational survival. You don't want to be "caught short" in a crunch time. Here are some ideas to consider.

Keep on learning. There's a saying I like: "When you're through learning, you're through." The point of this saying is that we must always keep learning in order to survive in a changing world. Prepare yourself for a lifetime of learning, for that is what is necessary for success these days. If I had at my disposal only those things I learned while in high school and college, I'd be *lost* now—so much has changed since then.

Consider taking refresher training in your area of competence. Enroll in a college course that interests you, even one "not for credit." See if your professional association offers training sessions and workshops. Look into correspondence or "distance" education. If circumstances allow, pursue an advanced degree. If college is not an option, broaden your reading and personal study as described above. Join a group of others with similar interests and learn from them; form a discussion group or study team. Read a technical manual or recent review of research in an area of interest to you. The point is to keep your *learning* skills fresh; learning how to learn is too valuable a lesson to allow it to atrophy over time.

Embrace technology. One of the most important lessons for me to learn was to stop fighting *against* technological change and instead to embrace it and learn how to use it for my own benefit. Perhaps like me, you have been intimidated in the past by such devices as computers, cellular phones, fax machines, and the like. Don't run from them; instead, try them out. As you become more familiar with them, they will become less fearsome. You may even find that you enjoy using them, as I have. Sure technology is expensive; yes, technology seems to change all the time, with newer devices and models being released everyday; of course, some "labor-saving" devices aren't actually helpful in your circumstances. But how will you know what helps if you never try anything?

My mother-in-law cared nothing about computers until one day she received an e-mail message from her daughter while we were touring Japan. When she learned that networks of computers could be used like the telephone to send messages back and forth to loved ones, she became quite interested in them.

Sometimes we are afraid to try new technology for fear of "looking bad" in front of others—particularly those younger than ourselves, who might laugh at our "old-fashioned" ways. If you are uncomfortable with new technology, try it out in the privacy of your own home or in the presence of those you know to be trustworthy friends and teachers. Computer manufacturers and other purveyors of new technology have learned that "user-friendly" devices are much more popular with those who have not "grown up" in the information age; thus, they are now designing hardware and software with great appeal due to ease of learning and use.

If you can become at ease with new technology such that you are not afraid to try it out and innovate with it, you can become a role model for others seeking to master change. You may not want to purchase every new gadget that comes onto the market, but embracing new technology is a good way to prepare yourself for a future world that will likely be built around technological innovation. If you are having trouble "getting the hang" of things, seek the assistance of a young person who seems "naturally skilled" in this area. By learning from one another, we break down interpersonal barriers and gain respect for one another.

Shore up your weaknesses. The value of this idea is self-evident. If you find that you have deficits in important skills needed to survive in your workplace, begin immediately to enhance them. Use the ideas presented above to help you in your quest for excellence.

Try some new things. The point of this idea is to break ourselves out of our old habits, our routines. Mastering change often requires new skills and ways of thinking. You can sharpen your ability to adapt to change by proactively trying some things you have never done before. If you haven't done so before, go to the theater, the library, a nearby manufacturing plant, the zoo—something new. "Travel broadens the horizons," I've often been told, and the validity of this statement has been borne out in my own experience. Learn a new language, play some new games, visit a new place, make some new friends, study a new subject, learn a new skill—these are all valuable ways to prepare ourselves to adapt to change and to maintain our sanity when change occurs.

Discover your hidden gifts. Each of us has been given talents and gifts. Wouldn't it be a shame to live your whole life in ignorance of some special talent you may have and to let it go to waste? The main purpose of my suggestion to "Try some new things" is to help you avoid this unfortunate circumstance. It is only recently that I have learned that I have some modest talent to sing and to preach in church. I would never have discovered these hidden gifts, had I not tried some new things— in my case, joining the choir and enrolling in a lay pastor training course.

Once you have discovered hidden gifts and talents, you can turn them into new skills to add to your portfolio. The more skills you have, the more valuable you will be in a world that demands flexibility in adaptation to change. Who knows, you might just discover a new talent that opens the door for a whole world of positive change in your life. Don't be afraid to try new things or to discover hidden gifts.

Tip Four: Use the Power of the Force

One of my all-time favorite movies is *Star Wars*. I just love it when Obi-Wan Kenobi says to Luke Skywalker, "Use the power of the force." Indeed, those who can access and use "the power of the force" are destined to be the masters of change.

The great behavioral scientist Kurt Lewin was one of the first true theorists of the processes of change, and his ideas are very much in evidence today among master change agents. Lewin (1981) helped us to understand the concept of "force field analysis" and to employ it in the context of creating change. Borrowing ideas from physics, Lewin helped us see how such concepts as inertia, momentum, vectors, and opposing forces could be applied to direct positive social change.

Basically, Lewin taught us that the "status quo" represents a situation in which forces for change are equal to forces against change. When one or the other forces is strengthened or weakened—*or changes direction*—change will begin to occur. Thus an analysis of the force and direction of vectors for and against change can help us predict the speed and direction that change will take.

Armed with this knowledge, we can then begin not only to prepare for change but actually to *shape* change. By deploying our own forces strategically, we can *influence* the direction of change and use it for our own benefit. The ideas presented below represent a "step-by-step" approach to applying Lewin's theory. By following them, we can indeed "use the power of the force."

Marshal your muscle. Changing the momentum of a powerful force for change requires the expenditure of your own energy, so the first step is to assess and gather your own forces, or "muscle." What knowledge, skills, and abilities can you bring to bear? What key information do you have? Who are your allies, and what strengths do they possess? What other forces might you be able to rally to your cause? Now is the time to marshal them, to bring them near to hand. The more "muscle" you can marshal, the better your chances for shaping the direction of change. Here is where the time and energy you invested in following Tips One, Two, and Three will begin to pay off.

Don't fight change head-on. Trying to fight change head-on is like standing in the path of an oncoming freight train—you will likely get plowed under, or you will certainly be injured beyond repair. This is not the winning strategy. Even if you can "hold off" change for a while, its superior momentum will likely weaken you and wear you down to the point where you will eventually be swept along in its path. Instead, use your imagination to mentally picture the oncoming force of change and to determine in what direction you would like to see it move.

Know where you want to go. Continuing the thought begun above, imagine in your mind the direction you would like to see the river of change take you. Envision your destination, your ultimate goal. Is there some way you can combine your own energy with the forces of change so that you can be "swept along" to exactly your intended goal point? If you can envision a way, the next point is to "make it happen."

Be like a football offensive lineman, a sumo wrestler, a ballet dancer, a martial artist. What do these skilled athletes and artists have in common? They know how to apply their own energy to that of a moving body, thus sending that body in a new direction. The football blocker directs the tackler away from the point of the play; the sumo wrestler uses his opponent's own momentum to take him down or out of the ring; the dancer lifts the spinning ballerina into a spectacular leap; the martial artist flips her much larger opponent by directing his oncoming force into a different direction. All have demonstrated their practical understanding of force field analysis—they have marshaled their own muscle to direct another body into a predetermined desired direction. This is how one masters change.

Steer the forces of change. With a minuscule movement of her wrist, my tiny wife can steer her big, powerful sports car. She knows where she wants it to go and is able to use her driving skill and sense of direction to harness that powerful vehicle to take her wherever she wants. She has mastered the forces of that vehicle, she is "in the driver's seat." This is our own challenge in becoming masters of change: We need to put ourselves into the driver's seat. I hope the tips I have shared with you to this point are helping you to formulate a personal plan to use the forces of change in your own situation to your own advantage.

For example, what if your raised antenna has picked up signals that your unit is about to move from a manual to an automated operating system, and your audit of the situation has led you to the conclusion that a particular computer software system is most likely to be employed? You can then build your skills in the use of that system such that when the change is announced, you can be ready to demonstrate your mastery, thus positioning yourself for possible career advancement. Instead of wasting your time resisting the change, you have figured out how to use the power of the force to move you to a better career position. Congratulations!

Be a responsible driver. Let me end this section with a little plea for ethical behavior. Once you have become a master of change, you will have at your disposal powerful forces that can be used for great good or great harm. We deplore those who use their power to hurt others. Seek to be a responsible driver of change; never use the power of the force to inflict harm on others. Tip Nine below provides some good advice for those seeking to be responsible drivers of change, using its powerful forces to bring good things to humanity.

Tip Five: Surf the Waves of Change

This brief tip is simply a recap of the ideas presented above, but this time using the analogy of the surfer. My purpose here is to remind us all that being a change master can—and should—be lots of fun.

Spot the perfect wave. Be on the lookout for a good ride. Don't let the perfect wave pass you by, but don't sit still in the ocean waiting forever if you see an exciting wave rolling your way. You can't have fun surfing if you spend all your time watching.

Get into position, then go. Hey, what more needs to be said? Let's go!

Ride the wild surf. I love the music of The Beach Boys; it makes me feel so good. Jump on your board and ride that wild surf! Don't let it intimidate you. Go for it!

Have fun on the way. After all, isn't this why we came to the beach? If you're not having fun, get out of the game.

Paddle out for more. Even the perfect wave eventually breaks against the shore and is no more. Don't despair, just paddle out for another! This is the key to enjoying yourself as a change master. There's always another wave, another opportunity to use the force for your own fun and for the benefit of others.

Tip Six: Be Good to Yourself

Let us change our focus now from tips for mastering change to tips for maintaining sanity. This can be a pretty tough world in which to live at times, so we all need some ideas about how to make life a little more pleasant. That is the purpose of these last five tips: to share some of my own ideas for getting more pleasure and meaning out of life. The first set of ideas, listed in this section, are focused on taking care of your physical body. The stresses of life put a great deal of strain on our bodies. If we are not careful to take care of ourselves—to be *good* to ourselves—our bodies may break down under the strain. I offer the following for your consideration.

Blow off some steam. Our bodies are well designed to handle the stressors our cavemen ancestors faced—those that could be readily identified (such as a tiger or bear) and dealt with decisively through fight or flight. In fact, that is what our bodies are programmed to do when faced with a stressful condition. Physiologically we become *mobilized* to fight or flee when faced with a stressor. Once we have succeeded in dealing with the stressor, our bodies automatically *demobilize* and return to a relaxed state—until the next stressor appears!

Unfortunately, most of the stressors in the modern world are not *discrete* stressors like tigers and bears. They are more likely to take the form of money problems, family crises, work pressures, and the like. Our bodies know no better than to try to deal with these stressors, too, in the programmed manner. Thus we automatically gear up to "fight or flee" when under stress.

Maintaining a mobilized state for long periods of time with no relief can be very wearing on our bodies, leading toward mental or physical breakdown or exhaustion. Thus, it is highly important periodically to "blow off some steam" before we blow up like overheated pressure cookers. If we do not take proactive steps to relieve our own tension, we are likely to "lose our cool" in the presence of others and cause them mental or physical stress. It is for this reason that we are advised to find creative ways to blow off steam, then employ them regularly.

Aerobic exercise (rhythmic exercise of our large muscle groups during which we breathe steadily throughout, like swimming, biking, jogging, cross-country skiing, power walking, rowing, and rhythmic dancing) is an excellent way to blow off steam, since it also strengthens our physical stamina and conditioning. Other creative means for relieving tension include gardening, housework like vacuuming and ironing, singing, playing a musical instrument, engaging in a sport like basketball or tennis, sailing, hiking, and the like. One lady I know relieves her tension by "pounding out hymns on the piano," she tells me.

There are also creative ways of blowing off mental steam, such as diary keeping, writing, making lists, conversing with trusted friends, listening to stirring music, and losing oneself in a good book or film. The point here is to find some things you enjoy doing and that help you relieve tension in a benign manner. Do *not* allow tension to build up inside yourself such that it comes bursting out in ways that cause harm to yourself or other people.

Learn to relax. This goes hand in hand with the advice provided above. Help your body restore its natural stress-management cycle by learning how to relax. Deep muscle relaxation is a skill you can learn by taking a class or listening to a good audiotape. Relaxation tapes are available in most record stores. Meditation, prayer, and self-hypnosis are also good techniques to use when seeking to relax. If you don't know how to relax, or have considerable trouble doing so, you might wish to consult a physician, counselor, or clergy member for assistance. Some persons never truly relax, thus setting themselves up for stress-related breakdowns. Don't let that happen to you.

Watch what you consume. All of us need food and drink to survive, but too often we consume things that are harmful to us. (Consuming *too much* good food and drink can also be a problem, as can consuming too little.) The best watchwords here are *balanced* and *in moderation.* If you are not sure you are eating a healthy, balanced diet, consult a physician, nutritionist, or other dietary specialist. We truly *are* what we eat. Consuming too much fat, salt, sugar, acid, alcohol, caffeine, nicotine, tar, or other such substances can be hazardous to our health. Also, some of us have food allergies that can flare up when we eat or drink the wrong things.

A second aspect of this theme is to be careful with medications. Many of us are too dependent on painkillers, antacids, laxatives, antihistamines, and other "over-the-counter" medications. It is a good idea to consult your physician before taking any medications. Your primary care physician should be kept informed of all prescriptions and other medications you are using. In all cases, of course, take medicine exactly as prescribed by your physician. Avoid all illicit drugs—they are nothing but trouble and can lead to disaster and heartbreak.

Get some rest. Doesn't that sound like something your mother might say? It is good advice. Most of us do not rest enough, especially when we are under stress. This can lead to a myriad of health problems.

Exercise aerobically. This has already been mentioned in the discussion on "blowing off steam," but I reiterate it here to emphasize the importance of physical conditioning. Bodies that are in good physical condition can handle higher levels of strain and recover much quicker from periods of stress. Walking is the particular aerobic exercise I like best. The experts tell us to get at least 20 minutes per day of aerobic exercise at least three times per week to maintain fitness—more to increase fitness. Be careful, though, not to become "addicted" to exercise such that it becomes an all-consuming activity that throws your life out of balance.

See your doctor. To protect your health, make regular visits to your physician, dentist, optometrist or ophthalmologist, and other health care providers. Better safe than sorry.

Assert yourself. This is a suitable topic for another whole book, and in fact, there are a number of "self-help" books on this topic that can be found in any library or bookstore. Know that there is a big difference between *aggressiveness*, which can be harmful to others, and *assertiveness*, which is basically a process of taking responsibility for your own life and your own decisions, choosing to do only those things that you personally believe are good for you. Seeking clarification from your boss when you are not certain what's expected of you is a positive example of assertion. Taking control over the environment by adjusting the thermostat, rearranging your personal work space, or reducing the presence of annoying stressors—such as noise and interruptions—is also a progressive means of asserting yourself.

Let go of the baggage. Too many of us are hauling around backbreaking bags full of guilt, shame, and feelings of inadequacy. Bearing the crushing weight of such loads is unhealthy and unnecessary. If you find yourself in this situation, find a trusted soul—a mental health provider, clergy member, close friend or family member, or other such specialist in caring conversation—to help you become unburdened. This is very, very important in the struggle to maintain sanity. It is not a sign of weakness to consult a specialist for these problems. No, seeking help in this regard is a sign of strength and courage.

Tip Seven: Break Through Depression

This tip is an elaboration on Tip Six for those who have found themselves in a period of depression, perhaps as a result of grief brought on by change. Since virtually all of us will find ourselves in this situation one time or another (I certainly have), it is an important topic for all of us to consider.

Remember the common cold. Depression can be thought of as "the common cold of mental illness." It has many, many causes; is experienced at one time or another by virtually all human beings; typically "goes away" in time if not too severe; and can be treated with some sensible home remedies. Depression, like the physical ailment of the common cold, *can,* however, become a severe illness, so it should be carefully monitored. If depression persists beyond a few weeks; has no readily apparent cause; is accompanied by such symptoms as a dramatic diminution of hygiene or excessive sleep or insomnia; or is accompanied by stated desires for or attempted self-destruction, a professional mental health provider should be consulted without delay.

Establish a routine. This is one of the most effective home remedies for simple depression: Establish a routine and stick with it. Even if you don't feel like doing so, force yourself to get out of bed in the morning, maintain hygiene and dress yourself presentably, go to work, and follow through your regular routine for the day. Giving in to the temptation to stay in bed, feeling sorry for yourself, won't help matters and can only make them worse. (Of course, if you are physically ill as well, you should probably take sick leave.) We have all known persons who—upon facing a setback at work or perhaps even losing employment—have simply "let themselves go." This is not the thing to do when depressed. Instead, provide therapy to yourself by following through on your normal routine until the depression fades away. If it does not fade away, a visit to a capable mental health provider is warranted.

Force yourself to have fun. This is another "home remedy" for depression. Do not "wallow in the blues." Instead, force yourself to remain active by doing something you typically find to be fun. Go with friends to see a movie, invite friends over for a party, go for a walk with your dog, do something fun with your family, take a short vacation to the beach or the mountains. If you force yourself into situations that are fun for you, you are quite likely to have your spirits lifted.

Help someone else. This is great advice for someone who is self-absorbed in depression: Use your energy to do something good for someone else. When you change your focus to helping others in need instead of moping about in depression, you will do wonders both for yourself and for those you assist. You will often find that those you help will have a reciprocal skill that can lift your spirits.

Talk things out. I mentioned above the value of talking things out as a means for blowing off mental steam. I restate the idea here because mental health providers recognize it as one of the best techniques for dealing with depression. One of the greatest gifts one person can give to another is to *listen.* Find a compassionate listener—one who will hear you out rather than interrupt with intended "solutions to your problems"—then pour out your troubles. Believe me, you'll feel better. Perhaps there is someone among your network of close friends who cares enough about you to give you the gift of listening. If not, you can talk to your pets or even your plants! Remember, it's the *talking* that will be therapeutic to you; put your concerns into words and get them out.

Seek professional help. If the "home remedies" don't work, if you can't find anyone who will listen to you, if your depressive symptoms seem to be beyond the "common cold" stage, or if you *ever* feel self-destructive or suicidal, do not hesitate to seek professional help. That is what the professionals are for—to help you recover from the grip of a debilitating condition. Don't be dissuaded from consulting a capable mental health provider by those who might seek to stigmatize you. In these days of enlightenment, it is clearly better to seek help when you need it than to deny yourself the services of a capable therapist who could aid you.

Understand the role of medication. The human body functions through a variety of chemical, hormonal, and electrical processes. Medical research has found that many physical and mental ailments—including some forms of depression—can be the result of chemical imbalances within your body. There are many valuable psychotropic medications available these days that can restore the proper chemical balances and alleviate the symptoms of depression. If your physician prescribes such a medication for you, take it according to instructions, confident in the knowledge that it will most likely help you to recover from your feelings of depression.

Tip Eight: Smell the Roses

So often we become so enmeshed in the issues and pressures of our jobs that we fail to appreciate the good things that life has to offer us. Here are a few ideas for maintaining our sanity by "stopping along the way to smell the roses." These are familiar ideas, but too often they are forgotten or ignored, much to our regret later. Indulge me while I present them here.

Enjoy your family. Each of us is a member of a family. Families can be formed by birth, by marriage, or by choice. Enjoy your family. Take pleasure in the accomplishments and joys of your family members. Encourage them; spend time with them, for time is a precious gift these days. Help your children grow; honor your father and mother; enjoy your grandchildren; love your spouse. When times are tough, be there for your family.

Be a friend. "I wish I had more friends," people often tell me. My simple advice: To *have* a friend, you must *be* a friend. By being friendly to others, listening to them, spending time with them, doing little favors for them, showing them you sincerely care, you can quickly build your circle of friends. Reexamine your network of "contacts." How many of them are truly friends? Are there some names on your list you'd like to cultivate as close friends? If so, follow the simple advice given here: *Be their friends.*

Travel, experience, and grow. The value of traveling to new places, experiencing new things, meeting new people, discovering new ideas, and thereby growing as a person was mentioned above in the context of preparing yourself to deal effectively for change. It is restated here to remind us of its inherent value. Keep growing to keep going.

Focus on the journey, not the destination. We all will come to the final destination of our lives soon enough. Remember: Life is not a "dress rehearsal"—it is *for real*. Enjoy your life by focusing on the journey. Don't be in such a hurry to reach the end.

Get your priorities right. Know what things you truly value, then prioritize your life and times around them. My priorities include my family, my church, my work, the arts, my friends and neighbors, and my personal growth and development. What are yours? Would an analysis of how you spend your time reflect your true priorities?

Balance your life. If the answer to the question posed above is *no*, then start right away to bring some balance to your life. Audit your activities and eliminate those that do not fit your priorities, thus making time for more important things. I periodically follow my own advice in this regard, and I often find myself amazed at the time I waste on empty activities that are not in line with my true priorities. Balance, balance— that is what is needed. All work and no play will make Jack a dull boy— and Jill a dull girl!

Tip Nine: Grow Spiritually

It is often fashionable in intellectual circles these days to deny the importance of spiritual growth. Given my role as a religious leader, I dare to mention the need for spirituality as part of a balanced life. It is not my purpose here to proselytize or to attempt to force my particular beliefs on you. Rather, Tip Nine is a call for all of us to recognize the need for spiritual growth to be part of the balance of our lives.

Perhaps you are not a religious person. If "organized religion" is not appealing to you, then build your spiritualism in other ways that are meaningful to you. The ideas I have listed here are those that have worked for me and that a number of the people I have spoken with have endorsed as meaningful.

Embrace a faith tradition. Perhaps you grew up in a particular religious faith, or have found a faith tradition that appeals to your needs, or maybe you are in the process of actively searching among a variety of traditions. It is not my purpose here to argue the merits of any particular system of faith. Rather, I simply want to inform you that millions of people throughout the world have found that embracing a faith tradition has helped them enormously in maintaining their sanity while dealing with the stresses of change.

Attend worship services. If your faith tradition conducts worship services, attend them as often as you are able. Regular corporate worship builds faith, strength, and character.

Read the scriptures. If your faith tradition has a book of holy scriptures, spend some valuable time reading them. For many, they are a source of comfort and inspiration. Discuss your faith's scriptures with others and seek out a better understanding of their meaning and application to your own life.

Get involved. It is likely that your faith tradition has programs of service to a variety of people in a variety of conditions. Get involved in one or more of these programs. Through such involvement, you will build friendships as well as faith and become a part of something larger than yourself.

Walk the walk. This is one of the most important aspects of building spirituality. No one respects a hypocrite. If you have embraced a faith tradition, then by all means, let your life be a testimony to it.

Tip Ten: Be a Tower of Strength

I hope the advice I have provided to this point is meaningful to you. I hope you have found some ideas to implement that will help you with the difficult task of maintaining sanity in an ever-changing world. I hope the thoughts shared here were as meaningful to you as they have been to me and to the many employees and managers I have worked with over the years. Now for the final tip: Be a tower of strength for others. Once you have mastered the forces of change, weathered the storms of life, and somehow have even maintained a semblance of sanity, be prepared to share your *own* ideas with others who may be able to benefit from them. Here is my final offering: a simple list to remind you of things *you* can do to help others who may be struggling with change alongside you. Please share generously.

Realize that others are hurting.

Know that you are needed.

Use your gifts.

Pull others through.

Enjoy your rewards.

Thank you. And may your life be blessed.

REFERENCES

Albrecht, K. (1979). *Stress and the manager: Making it work for you.* Englewood Cliffs, NJ: Prentice-Hall.

Beer, M. (1980). *Organization change and development: A systems view.* Santa Monica, CA: Goodyear.

Blanchard, K., & Johnson, S. (1982). *The one minute manager.* New York: William Morrow.

Burke, W. W. (1982). *Organization development: Principles and practices.* Boston: Little, Brown.

Covey, S. R. (1989). *The 7 habits of highly effective people: Powerful lessons in personal change.* New York: Simon & Schuster.

Drucker, P. F. (1967). *The effective executive.* New York: Harper & Row.

French, W. F., & Bell, C. H., Jr. (1990). *Organization development: Behavioral science interventions for organization improvement* (4th ed.). Englewood Cliffs, NJ: Prentice-Hall.

Hellriegel, D., Slocum, J. W., Jr., & Woodman, R. W. (1992). *Organizational behavior* (6th ed.). St. Paul, MN: West.

Levin, K. (1951). *Field theory in social science.* New York: Harper & Row.

13

Keys to Employee Success: What Skills Are Really Important for Success in the Future?

JOHN G. VERES III AND RONALD R. SIMS

INTRODUCTION

As we have seen from preceding chapters, the traditional functions, roles, and skills of employees are changing. For example, consider the fact that 20 years ago a textbook in organization behavior would not have been considered complete without a discussion of the concept of "how to motivate employees." Traditional approaches to motivating employees implied that key requirements for a successful career in management include competitiveness, a desire to lead, and a desire to dominate others. According to the prevailing theories of the time, managers needed to be in charge and to be willing to control others. Operating employees, on the other hand, were expected to follow orders—not to think. A favorite expression was, "Use their backs and not their brains." We are discussing motivation, not because it is considered central to management success any longer (since in our view employee self-motivation is what is really important today) but because it provides a good illustration of the changes in one type of employee role, management. Let's take a closer look at how the role of management has changed before we turn to a more detailed discussion of the skills important to employee success in coming decades.

RETHINKING EMPLOYEE RESPONSIBILITIES

In order to plan, organize, lead, control, and have full accountability for results, managers do need control and a strong desire to be in charge of others. However, to be successful in today's and tomorrow's organizations, the central role of managers is providing leadership and direction. The functions of planning and organizing are done either by teams of employees or by the manager along with full consultation and cooperation of employees. Furthermore, managers are not only supervising others; many are expected to produce themselves, whether it is by handling their own accounts or being involved in the building or the design of the product or the service. In many of today's organizations, managers are required to perform any function that is necessary. If a baggage handler is overloaded with work at Southwest Airlines, any manager around will need to chip in and load baggage into the planes. Even the president of Southwest, Herb Kelleher, has been known to load luggage on some busy days. Of course, Mr. Kelleher is still engaged in leading the organization but plays a lesser role in the other functions.

Even the controlling and monitoring functions, which for many years had been the exclusive domain of management, are now being done by teams of employees who check on their own progress and take corrective action as needed. One of the precursors of the quality movement, which is central to all of today's organizations, is the concept of *quality circles*, where groups of employees identify their own work problems and devise solutions. In many manufacturing organizations, *quality control*, which is the formal function of monitoring production and checking for defects and errors, is now being done by the teams of employees who make the products. For example, at Ford, any group of employees that sees a defect in a car is now allowed to stop the production line and fix the problem on the spot. Previously, only high-level supervisors were allowed to stop the line, no matter how many defective cars were passing by.

One of the recent changes in the controlling and monitoring functions of manager is *total quality management (TQM)*. TQM means that everyone in the organization will engage in any activity that is necessary for producing a high-quality product or service and delivering it to the customers. In effect, managing quality becomes everyone's job and not just the managers'. The Japanese car manufacturers used the TQM concept, which was developed by W. Edwards Deming in the United States, very successfully in producing high-quality, low-cost automobiles. TQM relies on the principles of continuous improvement. Everyone engages in regular incremental product and process improvement.

Ford has relied on TQM to produce its Ford Taurus line of cars. It brought teams of managers, engineers, suppliers, and other key people together to design and build this car. They aimed to improve every single process that is involved in building a car, from its design to its testing to its manufacturing. Managers and employees involved in Team Taurus took pride in the fact that they were designing a state-of-the-art, high-quality automobile at a cost that would be able to compete with its Japanese competitors. Taurus was such a well-designed product that it quickly became the best-selling brand in the United States. Ford relied on its teams to plan and implement the new product, and all team members were given the responsibility of producing the highest-quality car. At Ford, teams took on the traditional managerial roles of planning, organizing, and controlling the Taurus design and manufacturing process.

As you can see, the traditional functions that were traditionally the domain of managers are now being shared by managers and employees. Next we will discuss some of these new roles for employees.

NEW EMPLOYEE ROLES

How we view and define the roles of all employees has changed. Both sides of team skills are absolutely critical in today's world. That is, employees at all levels must be skilled team players. Managers must also acquire team-building skills.

One of the key changes has been the addition of the role of team player and facilitator. A team player/facilitator is a team member who is responsible for helping the team move forward and is responsible for the outcome. The team facilitator is in charge of the process but may not always be in charge of the product or outcome. So the new employee–team facilitator may at times have the traditional responsibility for helping to get the work done by the team along with facilitating the teams process. In today's organization, all team members share accountability.

The role of team player/facilitator is fast becoming one of the key ones for today's employees. Employees are being asked to manage themselves and teams of people they are a member of and not rely on a traditional manager to take on these responsibilities. Taking on the role of team member and team facilitator poses a special challenge for today's and tomorrow's employees. Employees need to know how to facilitate team processes and more than ever how to help create a truly cooperative team. The new team management roles that employees must possess are helping to assess team skills, counseling and encouraging other team members, helping the team define its tasks and goals, helping the team develop an implementation plan, helping the team manage conflict and relationships, helping the team to clarify its boundaries, determining and obtaining necessary training, and continuing to do real work. These new roles focus on the process of helping the team do its job and meeting its goals, rather than simply being a member of the team. For example, the whole team determines what training is needed by team members, helps the members get the training and resources they need, and takes an active role in conflict resolution and goal setting.

Today's managers must also be skilled team players—often playing on several management teams. But they must also know how to build teams. This includes selecting team members, training members to be effective team players, helping them to meet the goals of the organization, and continuously diagnosing the needs of the group.

All the new organizational structures hinge on teamwork. Those who do not possess strong team skills will quickly see themselves becoming obsolete in the new workplace. To be successful, then, employees must know how to be valued team players (i.e., be a contributing member of the team).

Although not all organizations are implementing these new responsibilities or employee roles, many are incorporating various aspects of these new roles into the traditional employee roles. For example, Honeywell trains all its employees in team facilitation. Although the facilitation may not be central to all employee jobs, the role and skill are important in being a successful team member in the many teams that function in Honeywell. Like many other organizations, Honeywell is using self-managed teams (SMTs) to address many issues and problems. The self-managed teams are groups that function without a formal manager and are trained to analyze various situations and propose alternatives and implement solutions. Leadership of these teams often rotates among members, and the primary leadership role is facilitation.

The new role of employees requires them to use their technical skills actively, since they are more than ever before expected to produce and demonstrate how they contribute to team, department, and organizational productivity and success. Interpersonal or human skills are central to working in teams. Conceptual skills are also more important than they would be in traditional employee roles, since teams are actively involved in problem identification and solution planning. The next section describes in more detail the skills we believe are necessary for employee success in the coming decades.

NEW EMPLOYEE SKILLS FOR TOMORROW'S ORGANIZATIONS

The new skills required for employee success in coming decades are managing/creating change, being flexible, managing one's career, managing diverse relationships, managing one's empowerment, being creative, thinking conceptually, being a strategic manager, being a role model, being information technology (IT) literate, and managing continuous improvement.

New Skills	Description
Managing/creating change	Ability to recognize (and create) change and trends

Being flexible	Ability to be flexible in adapting to change
Being IT literate	Ability to use technology effectively to enhance performance
Managing one's career	Ability to take responsibility for one's career by taking advantage of training and education (being a lifelong learner) and by thinking creatively about career track
Managing diverse relationships	Ability to successfully participate and work in diverse relationships and personal relationships inside and outside the organization
Managing one's empowerment	Ability to be empowered (i.e., accept the responsibility, accountability, and authority for tasks both individually and as a member of a team)
Being creative	Ability to "think out of the box"
Thinking conceptually	Ability to see the big picture
Being a strategic manager	Ability to understand and employ strategic management techniques
Being a role model	Ability to be a good role model for others—both inside and outside the organization
Managing continuous improvement	Ability to use critical thinking skills
Building trust	Ability to build trust between themselves and others

We will discuss each of these skills below. You have also read about each of these skills in some form or another in the other chapters in this book.

Managing/Creating Change

As the world of work continues to change rapidly, so too must employees if they are to succeed in coming decades. The constant changes in organizations all over the world make it essential for employees to be receptive to, and know how to manage and create, change. Managing change is the ability to recognize trends and to have the flexibility to adapt to them. Today's employees need to stay informed about business, social, cultural, and political trends, understand their implications for their organizations, and be ready to adapt to the changes. This management of change is a highly complex skill that cannot be taught in one training session. Fundamentally, today's employees need to learn to roll with the punches.

Those who work to maintain the status quo may quickly become obsolete. The key today is to challenge the status quo tactfully. Change is the order of the day. As organizations continue to diagnose the need for change, they want employees who can and will change—those who embrace and even create it are valued members of the organization. People cannot cling to old beliefs and ways of doing things. To remain the same is to fall behind quickly.

Being open to change requires that employees go one step further in today's world of work. It means also looking for ways to change. The old adage "If it ain't broke, don't fix it" is obsolete. The new perspective is, "If you haven't fixed it, you probably haven't looked hard enough." A failure to critically assess and change means to fall behind the competition.

Being able to roll with the punches, critically assess, create and manage change are critical themes and skills highlighted in Chapters 1, 2, 7, 11, and 12.

Being Flexible

One of the greatest challenges presented to all employees today is dealing with uncertainty. To better manage uncertainty and change, employees must be flexible. To be rigid opens the door for failure. Only by being flexible can people adapt to uncertainty and deal with information as it becomes available. Flexibility enables employees to adapt to changes as well. Rigidity breeds resistance to change. Chapters 2 and 12 articulate the importance of employees being adaptable and flexible if they are going to respond successfully to a more chaotic and demanding workplace.

Some of the most innovative companies have turned "failures" into tremendous successes (such as the classic example of 3M's Post-it Notes from a failed glue). This kind of success, however, requires that organizations and their employees be flexible, be willing to take risks, be able to learn from mistakes and be able to spot opportunities.

Part of this flexibility requires that people be comfortable making mistakes. Fear of failure is a rigid stance that harnesses an individual's ability to learn.

Nothing remains the same. Technology is rapidly changing the face of most of the jobs performed in our organizations. People must be ready to accept these technological changes and adapt. The computer age is said to only be in its infancy. The radical redesign of companies has only begun. With that, people must become more flexible to adapt to the changing world.

Being Information Technology Literate

Exciting advances in information technology have dramatically increased employees' abilities to communicate with others as well as to access information quickly to make decisions. For employees to be successful in the new millennium, they need to keep up-to-date on advances in information technology.

Computers, microchips, and digitalization are dramatically increasing an employee's communication options. Today, employees can rely on a number of sophisticated electronic media to carry their communications. These include electronic mail (e-mail), voice mail, electronic paging, cellular telephones, mode-based transmissions, video conferencing, and other forms of network-related communications.

Employees are increasingly using many of these technological advances. E-mail and voice mail allow people to transmit messages 24 hours a day. When an employee is away from the office, others can leave messages for them to review on his or her return. For important and complex communications, a permanent record of e-mail messages can be obtained by merely printing out a hard copy. Cellular phones are dramatically changing the role of the telephone as a communication device. In the past, telephone numbers were attached to physical locations. Now, with cellular technology, the phone number attaches to mobile phones. Employees can be in constant contact with their other team members, supervisors, and key members in and outside of the organization, regardless of where they are physically located. Network-related communications also allow the employees to provide updates on their work when their jobs are done on computers in remote locations (e.g., telecommuters discussed in Chapter 5), to participate in electronic meetings, and to communicate with suppliers, customers, and interorganizational members.

For the new millennium employee to be successful, he or she also needs to keep up-to-date on other advances in information technology such as groupware (i.e., computer software that enables members of groups and teams to share information with each other), intranets (i.e., a company-wide system of computer networks), and the Internet (i.e., a global system of computer networks). Chapter 10 on information technology offers examples of the importance of technology to improved decision making by employees in organizations. To be successful in the coming decades, employees must understand that they should not adopt these or other advances without first considering carefully how the advance in question might improve communication and performance in their particular groups, teams, departments, or whole organization.

It is important for the new millennium employee to understand that technological advances in communications have disrupted old ways of working in organizations. Formerly closed bureaucracies and command and control systems are being pressured to open up. Further, it is important for employees at all levels of the organization to keep focused on the aim of all communication: coordinated and cooperative action that achieves a team's, department's, and organization's goals and mission. The guidelines presented below are offered to provide employees with some insights that will increase their potential for success in the "wired" environments of today's and tomorrow's organizations.

If you are going to be successful in the ever-changing wired environments of organizations, you should keep the following in mind:

1. *Don't fight the net.* Information networks are here. Avoiding or escaping the use of increased speeds in information exchange causes negative reactions and skill obsolescence.

2. *Learn to trust.* Networks open up information and force the sharing of resources across functions. Trust becomes a key ingredient for cooperation and doing business inside organizations.

3. *Manage yourself and your career.* With information networks, more attention must be given to one's contribution to overall performance and career enhancement. Professionalism and commitment are necessary for employee's success.

4. *Build and manage diverse relationships.* Paradoxically, people need more, not less, face-to-face interaction in electronic communication environments.

5. *Be a team player.* Teams do more of the "real work" of the entire organization in integrated, wired organizations. Team members must, therefore, be committed to taking advantage of ongoing learning and training opportunities and sharing of knowledge and supportive of other team members.

6. *Do the things leaders do.* Work in wired organizations also emphasizes the need for leadership—at *all* levels. A study of over 170 teams of knowledge workers found that teams "are most successful in an environment where decisions spring from rigorous evaluation of costs and benefits, development and implementation of organizational strategy is an organization-wide effort, and each individual understands the organization's vision and direction. All [of this] depends on every employee being a leader (Stewart, 1994).

Managing One's Career

Along with the ability to manage change and be flexible and technology literate, today's employees have to *manage their own careers*. Managing one's career, as defined by several contributors in this book, means actively guiding one's career through taking advantage of training, education, and new learning opportunities. Thus, one must be self-directed when it comes to managing his or her career, as stressed in Chapter 4 on self-directed careers. Active career management also involves thinking creatively about one's career. The traditional vertical career ladder simply does not exist in many organizations, particularly in the United States. Few organizations promise their employees stable, long-term employment these days. However, many attempt to keep their employees "employable" by constantly updating their skills, as highlighted in Chapter 11 on the new employer-employee contract.

To accomplish that goal, AT&T, DuPont, Johnson & Johnson, GTE, TRW, Lucent Technologies, and several other companies recently formed the nonprofit Talent Alliance, an organization designed to help employees plot their careers. The Alliance is headed by Jeanette Galvanek whose goals include helping employees find continuous employment—but not necessarily with the same company. The Alliance offers career counseling, bulletin boards, a web site, and chat rooms, all to help employees find jobs that match their skills and interests. Employees can be matched with training and education programs available through its member companies and through various universities. Galvanek believes that the Alliance's unique and unprecedented collaborative effort among many companies provides employees with timely, real, and relevant information about jobs. She also considers Alliance's focus on balance between work and family to be one of the group's assets.

Bill Applegate, the CEO of AG Communication, bluntly states that his organization cannot guarantee anyone a job. However, he promises that AG employees will maintain high technical competence that will make it easier for them to find new jobs when needed. It used to be that many employees stayed with the same organization throughout their careers. However, now due to the ever-changing business environment, employees need to manage their careers in such a way as to be employable by many organizations. AT&T, for instance, always prided itself on providing lifetime employment; however, since laying off more than half of its work force just in the past few years, it has become obvious to its employees that they need to manage their own careers so that they have the option to change jobs at will.

As you have read in previous chapters, changes in organizations provide opportunities for creative employees to craft their own path. An employee's knowledge and experience and intellectual capital are becoming the focus. Employees of the future are less and less either service or manufacturing workers. They are knowledge workers whose value for the organization is based on their expertise and knowledge. They have advanced skills, creativity, a desire for autonomy, and self-motivation, and their success depends on their active management of their career.

The need to take an active role in managing one's career is evident in a number of chapters in this book. Chapters 3, 4, 6, and 9 all emphasize the importance of individuals taking responsibility for managing their careers, given the fact that organizations no longer see this as one of their commitments to employees.

Managing Diverse Relationships

One key aspect of career management is having well-established relationships with people inside and outside your organization. Managing relationships involves the ability to develop personal and work relationships effectively. Today's employees not only manage their relationships with fellow team members (and supervisors); they are also increasingly in constant interaction with their external customers, suppliers, and many other outsiders. They are often expected to take active roles in their communities through charitable organizations, and many are also expected to keep abreast of political developments, at home or abroad, that may affect their organizations.

Imagine how an organization in your community can be affected by the revertment of Hong Kong to China. What will be the long-term impact of this political move on your organization, no matter where it is located? Savvy employees need to think ahead and be able to predict the impact of political events on their business. Maintaining a network of diverse acquaintances across the globe to keep abreast of world events allows employees to become more valuable to their organization.

With the strong focus on cultural and global issues, the management of relationships is even more complex in a culturally diverse and global environment. Cultural diversity means that many different cultures interact. It is hard enough to manage relationships when people share your values and beliefs. The process becomes considerably more complex when people hold different views of the world and what is appropriate and what is not. Chapter 6 on being successful in Asia clearly articulates the importance of understanding and appreciating cultural differences for success in Asia.

The active management of relationships requires strong interpersonal skills to successfully manage internal and external relationships. With technological advances, the workplace has changed the way communication is performed. But the importance of communication remains a top priority/concern. Remember the importance of communication to the success or failure of the new wave of "teleworkers" discussed in Chapter 5 on telecommuting. Without good communication, telecommuters, their supervisors, coworkers, and valued customer interactions are ineffective, thus resulting in poor relationships and less-than-quality service and products.

Employees in teams get things done with others. With the rise of teamwork, all employees need to work with others to perform the necessary processes. This means strong interpersonal skills are required of all employees.

Katz (1974) suggested that conceptual skills, technical skills, and interpersonal skills are required of all managers in today's organizations.

However, as one moves from lower to higher levels, the percentage of each of these skills changes. The one staple is interpersonal skills; these remain in the same proportion throughout the three organizational levels and are important in managing relationships in a more diverse and global work environment.

Managing One's Empowerment

Another skill required of employees is the ability to manage their empowerment—that is, accepting the responsibility, accountability, and authority for tasks both individually and as a member of a team. This is contrary to the traditional manager-employee role where managers delegate and empower employees and team members. *Delegation* refers to assigning various tasks to employees. Empowerment goes one step further than delegation. By empowering employees in the past, a manager not only delegated a task but also delegated the responsibility and authority to complete the task. The employee was therefore given power, or empowered, by the manager to be in charge of the job. In many of today's organizations, managers are left out of the education, which results in self-managed teams assigning tasks to team members who have accepted all that comes with empowerment (i.e., responsibility, accountability, and authority).

You have just read about the increasing use of teams and the new team facilitator role that employees are expected to play. No one team member can keep control of all the tasks. Employees need to be responsible and accountable for their own behavior and trust team members to do their job. This means that employees must be willing to become more involved in their work through greater participation in decisions that control the teams' work and accepting responsibility for work outcomes.

Becoming more involved in one's work through greater participation in decisions means that employees must be willing and able to act on behalf of the team and the organization. This also includes accepting the rights and obligations to perform and get the job done. Getting the job done means using the authority you've been given to get the materials, the equipment, and the support from others necessary to be successful.

While accepting responsibility means an individual is obliged to carry out assigned duties, accountability means that he or she will perform the assignments in a satisfactory manner. The importance of being receptive to and accepting the power that comes from being empowered in today's organizations is paramount to employee success in the coming decades, as Chapter 3 on making your way in the next century suggests via its "21 New Rules." Decisions and power are increasingly being pushed to the lowest levels in the organization. Along with this increased involvement in decision making and the power and authority that come from empowerment, employees are expected to do more with less and be valuable contributors to the organization. The rules offered in both Chapters 3 and 4 put a premium on managing empowerment and all that comes with it.

Being Creative

Organizations today and tomorrow require creativity and innovation. Businesses can no longer operate the way they did just ten years ago. Innovative processes and approaches to doing business must be adopted.

America has fallen behind in the development of the twelve emerging technologies moving into the new millennium. Without creative employees, America cannot remain globally competitive and regain success in technology transfer.

Creativity is the ability to combine ideas in unique ways to make unusual associations between them. Each of us has the ability to be creative, and more of us will need to be creative in coming decades. Thus, employees must use the right side of their brains. It is critical that creative problem solving be used to augment the traditional rational problem solving. Today's problems/issues require a more open approach than can be offered by logical processes. Creativity is necessary. This requires that people learn to "think out of the box" without placing artificial constraints on the possible solutions.

To become more creative, employees can follow these steps (Stevens, 1993):

1. *Think of yourself as creative.* Although it's a simple suggestion, research shows that if you think that you can't be creative, you won't be. Just as the little choo-choo train in the children's fable says, "I think I can," if we believe in ourselves, we can become more creative.

2. *Pay attention to your intuition.* Everyone has a subconscious mind that works well. Sometimes answers come where we least expect them. For example, when you are about to go to sleep, your relaxed mind sometimes comes up with solutions to problems you face. You need to listen to this intuition. In fact, many creative people keep a note pad near their bed and write down those "great" ideas when they come to them. That way, they are not forgotten.

3. *Move away from your comfort zone.* Every individual has a comfort zone in which certainty exists. But creativity and the known often don't mix. To be creative, we need to move away from the status quo and focus on something new.

4. *Engage in activities that put you outside your comfort zone.* Not only must we think differently; we *need* to do things differently. By engaging in activities that are different to us, we challenge ourselves. Learning to play a musical

instrument or learning a foreign language, for example, opens the mind and allows it to be challenged.

5. *Seek a change of scenery.* As humans, we are creatures of habit. Creative people force themselves out of their habits by changing their scenery. Going into a quiet and serene area where you can be alone with your thoughts is a good way to enhance creativity.

6 *Find several right answers.* Just as we set boundaries in rationality, we often seek solutions that are only good enough. Being creative means continuing to look for other solutions, even when you think you have solved the problem. A better, more creative solution just might be found.

7. *Play your own devil's advocate.* Challenging yourself to defend your solutions helps you develop confidence in your creative efforts. Second-guessing may also help you find more correct answers.

8. *Believe in finding a workable solution.* Like believing in yourself, you also need to believe in your ideas. If you don't think you can find a solution, one won't be found. Having a positive mental attitude, however, may become a self-fulfilling prophecy.

9. *Brainstorm with others.* Creativity is not an isolated activity. By bouncing ideas off others, a synergistic effect occurs.

10. *Turn creative ideas into action.* Coming up with ideas is only half the process. Once the ideas are generated, they must be implemented. Great ideas that remain in someone's mind, or on papers that no one reads, do little to expand one's creative abilities.

Thinking Conceptually

It is important that all new millennium employees have strong conceptual skills—that is, they must be able to see the big picture. This requires that employees see more than their small area/unit of the organization. Strong conceptual abilities will allow employees to see that the organization itself is part of a larger system that includes the organization's industry, the community, and the nation's economy. This will give the employee a broad perspective and contribute to creativity. By seeing the "whole" helps employees to fight suboptimization and create a sense of "we."

Thinking conceptually gives employees the mental ability to coordinate a variety of interests and activities. It means having the ability to think in the abstract, analyze lots of information, and make connections between the data. To think conceptually, employees must be able to think critically and conceptualize things regarding "how they could be."

Thinking conceptually is not as easy as you may believe. For some employees, it may be impossible! That's because to think conceptually one must look at the infamous "big picture" mentioned earlier. Too many times, we get caught up in the daily grind, focusing our attention on the minute details. Not that focusing on the details isn't important. Without that, little may be accomplished. But working with other team members to set long-term directions requires employees to think about the future. It requires the ability to deal with uncertainty and the risks of the unknown. To be successful in the future, then, employees must be able to make some sense of the changing world of work and envision what can be.

To develop conceptual skills means that employees must seek out educational opportunities and accept power. The more employees understand the overall functioning of the organization, the better they will understand how their part fits into the whole—and therefore, how to make improvements. They will also understand how their work impacts other areas and the possible ramifications. Additionally, they will be better at being a strategic partner and manager.

Being a Strategic Manager

Related to conceptual skills is the need to understand and employ strategic management techniques. As our organizations become more skilled in employing strategic management, the responsibilities are being delegated down the organizational hierarchy.

That is, each employee is expected to be a strategic manager. Each employee will be responsible for continually scanning the internal and external environment and conducting a Strengths, Weaknesses, Opportunities, and Threats (SWOT) analysis. Opportunity identification and problem identification are each organizational members' responsibility. In today's rapidly changing and uncertain world, organizational survival depends on every employee scanning the environment and watching for opportunities. These opportunities can ensure the long-run success of the enterprise.

Those closest to the "front line" often see changes in the environment first and can then signal the organization to make the necessary changes in strategic direction. To be able to signal the organization, employees in coming decades must increasingly understand the strategic management process from beginning to end. Organizations have moved to educate their employees about the strategic management process and have moved to increase the partnership between employees at all levels of the organization by way of "open-book" management (i.e., organizations essentially share all information with employees so that they are able to better understand current and future business decisions).

Being a Role Model

Each employee must be a good role model for others—both inside and outside the organization. Part of this includes simply doing the "right thing" as an employee and as a human being.

The longer employees are with the organization, the more important this role becomes. Other, "newer" employees learn vicariously by observing what others in the organization do. Highly visible employees want to be caught doing something right. They also want to be seen as loyal to the organization.

Being a role model can be especially important to the successful development of new managers like those discussed in Chapter 7. New entrant managers, like other employees, can learn a great deal from role models about the organization, various departments, and teams. They can learn what are acceptable and expected behaviors along with the values that are encouraged and rewarded in the organization.

Managing Continuous Improvement

The popular business press has emphasized the need for continuous improvement—both on an individual and on an organization-wide level. Senge (1990) has discussed the "learning organization." Many of these concepts can also be applied to individuals.

Continuous improvement requires critical thinking skills. Yet employees must learn these critical thinking skills and take advantage of opportunities to use them! The best performing organizations of tomorrow will reward critical thinking.

One common thread running through the skills is an awareness of the importance of continuous improvement—continuously improving as individuals. This means keeping up the appropriate mix of skills as well. Continuous improvement encompasses both the individual and organizational levels. That is, employees must focus on continuously improving their organizations and themselves.

The functions, roles, and skills of employees are clearly changing. The constant changes, the new organizations, the diversity among the employees, fast technological advances, and the global economy all require constant retraining and education. As employees are asked to work with others across the world, manage diverse relationships, work with complicated information systems, fill in for former laid-off workers as needed, and be fully competent to provide input in their companies' strategic planning, they are under increasing pressure to be versatile and to have considerable knowledge and skills about many different aspects of business.

Building Trust

Each individual employee will have an increasingly significant impact on a team's trust climate in coming years. As a result, employees need to develop their skills in building trust with internal and external members of the organization. The following summarizes ways you can build trust (Pascarella, 1993; Bartolomi, 1989).

Demonstrate that you're working for others' interests as well as your own. All of us are concerned with our own self-interest, but if others see you using them, your job, or the organization for personal goals to the exclusion of your team's, department's, or organization's interests, your credibility will be undermined.

Be a "true" team player. Support your work team through both words and actions. Defend the team and team members when they're attacked by outsiders. This will demonstrate loyalty to your work group.

Practice openness. Mistrust comes as much from what people don't know as from what they do know. Openness leads to confidence and trust. So keep people informed, expand your decisions, be candid about problems, and fully disclose relevant information.

Be fair. Before making decisions or taking actions, consider how others will perceive them in terms of objectivity and fairness. Give credit where it's due, be objective and impartial in performance evaluations (i.e., especially when you are participating in 360-degree evaluations), and pay attention to equity perceptions in reward distributions. These three points are especially important given the increased responsibilities self-managed teams have in conducting evaluations of individual team members and making recommendations for distributing rewards.

Speak your feelings. By sharing your feelings, others will see you as real and human. They will know who you are and will increase their respect for you.

Show consistency in the basic values that guide your decision making. Mistrust comes from not knowing what to expect. Take the time to think about your values and beliefs. Then let them consistently guide your decisions. When you know your central purpose, your actions will follow accordingly, and you'll project a consistency that earns trust.

Maintain confidences. You trust those you can confide in and rely on. So if people tell you something in confidence, they need to feel assured that you won't discuss it with others or betray that confidence. If people perceive you as someone who "leaks" personal confidences or someone who can't be depended upon, you won't be perceived as trustworthy.

Demonstrate competence. Develop the admiration and respect of others by demonstrating technical and professional ability and good business sense. Pay particular attention to developing and displaying your communication, team player and facilitation, and other interpersonal skills.

The importance of developing the skill of building trust is articulated in Chapter 1 on succeeding in the new millennium and in Chapters 3 and 11 on the changing employee-employer psychological contract.

Because of the changes going on in the workplace, if you plan to be successful in the coming decades, basic knowledge, skills, abilities, other characteristics and specializations will help you get a job. However, employees will regularly be expected to learn new skills, rethink their career, and adapt to new requirements and new organizations. We have just discussed many changes that will be expected of employees in coming decades. Although stressful, the opportunities for learning and growth are an exciting part of today's dynamic workplace. Another change for today's employees are changes in their personal lives. We consider these next.

Changes in Personal Aspects of an Employee's Life

Along with new roles and skills, the personal life of employees is also being transformed. The traditional employee of the 1950s and 1960s was a white male, with a wife who stayed home and managed the family. Organizations knew what such employees needed and how to get the most out of them. There really is no single profile any longer.

More and more employees come in all colors and shapes. They are males and females from different ethnic, cultural, and religious groups. Many are single; some are married without children. Many are married dual-income earners with kids. Many are part of what is considered nontraditional families such as single parents with kids. More and more women have entered positions in many organizations in the United States. Minority groups have also increasingly joined the ranks of employees in many U.S. organizations. No matter what their background and their family situations, the personal success of future employees depends on maintaining balance between work and personal life. As many organizations are requiring their employees to work longer hours or many different shifts and adapt to changing schedules, employees find it hard to manage their personal life.

Whereas 50 or even 30 years ago, men and women had clearly defined roles, and the world of business was almost exclusively male, today men and women, both at home and at work, are living more similar lives. Several studies have found that having strong personal relationships in addition to a good career are key to happiness and good mental health. The workaholic employees, whether male or female, married or unmarried, and regardless of their ethnicity, are bound to burn out. So while organizations are putting pressure and new demands on their employees, employees in coming decades must insist for balance between their professional and personal lives and more control over their own time. You read earlier about the Alliance's focus on balance between work and family in helping employees plot their career. Such focus is increasingly needed to retain valuable employees.

The changes from traditional roles and skills to the new ones we just described are brought about by macro- and global changes in organizations all over the world. These changes are one of the most distinct features of today's complex organizations that successful employees must understand in today's and tomorrow's workplace.

As evidenced by the authors throughout this book, all organizations and employees are being affected by major challenges. Whether large or small, almost all businesses are feeling the force of globalization and cultural diversity. All also are feeling the impact of rapid change, increasing customer demand for quality and value, and having to satisfy multiple constituencies.

As the world is shrinking while becoming more complex, organizations and employees around the world are following the same patterns. They are restructuring for more efficient performance and creating new, innovative, and complex structures to handle the perplexing problems they face. Employee roles and skills are changing, and the generation of future employees is facing increasing challenges and opportunities, both at work and at home, as individuals try to keep up with the demands of their jobs, and their roles as both parents and children of aging parents.

WHAT DO EMPLOYEES NEED TO KNOW IN THE FUTURE?

Along with other contributors to this book, we have discussed the skills necessary for employee success in the coming decades. We have also considered the challenges that organizations face and several steps that they and their employees are taking to manage their changing environment. In spite of all these changes, several themes also emerge. First, globalization and increased interaction among different cultures will continue to be an integral part of any employee's job. Second, change—whether it is in the way organizations are managed, in the structure of an organization, in the use of teams, or in the use of technology to interact with one another or to make products or provide services—will continue to be a part of everyday life for employees in today's and tomorrow's organizations. Third, there will be increased pressure on employees to be flexible, adaptable, efficient, and creative and to help the organization deliver high-quality products and services. Fourth, employees will need to have broad perspectives that allow them to consider multiple viewpoints and multiple stakeholders.

Accurately predicting the future is not an easy task. Few visionaries among us are able to do so. However, being able to understand trends and taking appropriate action to face opportunities are essential to all of us. Thinking in a global, cross-functional manner is essential. Understanding and managing and creating change and behaving in a socially responsible way are fundamental. Thinking strategically and thinking like an entrepreneur, whether you are your own boss or work for someone else, are primary to your success in the future. Being able to work in teams and being willing to be a lifelong learner who is able to learn new tools and techniques on a regular basis are an essential part of being a successful employee in coming decades. Finally, all employees need to take a proactive and creative approach to managing their own career.

Career management is now each employee's responsibility. While many organizations do still assist individuals in managing their careers, the primary responsibility lies with the individual employee. Therefore, each employee must be well aware of the skills that are required in the coming decade and those likely to be important in the new workplace of tomorrow.

Just as any other asset of the organization grows obsolete, so too do the human resources. As change sweeps our organizations, new knowledge, skills abilities, and other characteristics are required to remain valuable in the workplace.

The good news is that all of these skills can be learned. It's never too late to start acquiring these skills. Many of these skills are related. Personal development in one area often means improvement in another area.

Recognizing that skill requirements are changing and acquiring these skills are key to employees' success and keeping them employable in coming decades. The ideas presented by the authors throughout this book will help you succeed in the coming decades. You have the power to prepare yourself to meet the challenges that the new workplace has in store for you. The question is, Will you accept the challenge?

REFERENCES

Bartolome, F. (1989). Nobody trusts the boss completely—now what? *Harvard Business Review* (March–April): 135–142.

Katz, R. L. (1974). Skills of an effective administrator. *Harvard Business Review* (September–October): 90–102.

Pascarella, P. (1993). 15 ways to win people's trust. *Industry Week* (February 1): 47–51.

Senge, P. (1990). *The fifth discipline*. New York: Doubleday.

Stevens, T. (1993). Creativity killers. *Industry Week* (January 23): 63.

Stewart, T. A. (1994). Managing in a wired company. *Fortune* (July 11): 56.

Index

Abilities, 15
Acting ethically, 7–9
African-American women, 119–136
Agrarian sector, 140
Aggregation, 140
Agricultural sector, 158
Appreciative inquiry, 40
Aptitude Scales Quotient (ASQ), 11
Armoring process, 123–124
Asia, 123–124
Assessment center, 22

Baby boomers, 56, 108
BarOn EQ-i, 11
Boiling frog syndrome, 20–21
Building trust, 237–239

Career: anchors, 61–63; choice, 35, 55, 68, 126–128; counseling, 11, 45, 153; entry, 128, 130–132; forms, 62–64; goals and, 92; management and, 57, 67, 230, 241; mastery, 130–132; perspective, 157; paths, 73, 84; plans and planning, 55–57, 127; stages, 58–61; strategies, 113–114
Career success for women: childhood experience and, 121–126; early adult experience and, 126–132; future lessons and, 132–134; self-reliance and, 124–126
Careers, 55–56, 58, 62, 65–68, 72–73, 107, 116, 120–122, 126–134, 229–230, 239; employee contract and, 183–198; managing and, 231–232
Change, 185; managing and, 226–227; resistance to, 205–208, 228; uncertainty of, 228
Changing jobs, 3–4
Changing organizations, 2–3
Childhood experiences: armoring process and, 123–124; being a person and, 124; daddy's girls and, 122; education and, 126; self-reliance and, 124–126
Competence, 238
Conceptual skills, 226, 232, 236
Conflict, 44–45
Confucianism, 92–96, 99
Confucius, 91, 95, 99
Continuity, 23–24
Continuous improvement, 27, 36, 237
Continuous quality improvement, 38–39
Courage, 123
Creativity, 44–45, 234

Cultural diversity, 233
Culture, 188

Database: design and, 167; information and, 167–168
Database software, 158, 160–162, 179
Decision making, 160–162; effectiveness and, 158; information technology and, 160–162; phase of, 160; quality of, 165; spreadsheet model and, 160–167
Decision Support System (DDS), 161, 167
Delegation, 233
Dependence, 204–205
Depression, 217–218
Differentiation, 140
Discontinuity, 18–28
Diversity, 44–45, 47

Early adult experiences: career choice and, 126–128; career entry and, 128–130; career mastery and, 130–132
Economic order quantity (EOQ), 163–165; spreadsheet modeling and, 163–167
Education, 15–16, 48
Effective followership skills, 5–7, 13
Emotional intelligence, 9–13
Employee responsibilities, 223–225
Employment contract, 183, 238
Empowerment, 2, 36, 41, 52, 233–234
Entrepreneurship, 45–46
EQ-i test, 11
EQ-Map, 11
Ethical standards, 8
Ex-pat, 91, 93, 95, 100–101

Fear, 204–205
Feedback, 360-degree, 22
Force field analysis, 212
Forces for change, 200–202, 213
Fundamental Interpersonal Relations Orientation: Behavior (FIRO-B), 147
Future managers, 105–117; role of, 106–107
Future work, 142–144

Gender, 124
Glass ceiling, 120, 130
Goal setting, 25
Goals, 92, 153
Guan-xi (good feeling), 99–100, 102

Habit, 203–205
Human resources, 190–192

Ideal self, 19–28
Industrial age, 158
Industrial Revolution, 139–140
Information economy, 158–160, 179
Information sector, 158
Information technology: better decisions and, 160–162; literate and, 228–230; skills and, 226–227
Interpersonal skills, 232–233

Job: career of the future and, 142–145; history and definition of, 137–142

Kaizen, 38
Knowing yourself, 137–156
Knowledge, 1, 15
Knowledge-based organizations, 3
Knowledge, skills, abilities, and other characteristics (KSAOCs), 1

Leadership, 49–52, 188–191, 224; transformational, 51
Learning, 210, 215; self-directed change and, 16–19
Learning by objectives, 26
Lifetime employability, 57
Lifetime employment, 56

Management by objectives (MBO), 26
Managing/creating change, 227–228
Managing diverse relationships, 232–233
Managing one's empowerment, 233–234
Managing transitions, 144–145, 154
Mentor, 67, 131–132
Meta-competency, 15
Models, 162; spreadsheets and, 160–167, 179

New age entrants, 114–115

New employee contract: hiring and, 193–194; implications for employees and, 194–197; law of attention and, 187–188; need for leadership and, 188–190

New employee roles, 225–226

New future managers, 105–117; ethics and, 107–108; role of, 106–107

New loyalty, 185–187

New organizations, 106–107

New psychological contracts, 109–110, 231

New rules, 64–66, 233

Newcomers, 106–107

Old employer-employee contract, 183–185; loyalty and, 186–187

Organizational change, 71–74; employee relationships and, 72–74

Outsourcing, 142

Outspiraling, 131

Parameters, 162, 167

Permanent employee, 143

Personal computing, 158

Protean Career Contract, 183, 185–187

Psychological contracts, 15, 56, 238

Psychological factors, 141–142

Quality circles, 224

Quality control, 224

Query window, 170, 174

Query by Example (QBE), 167–180

Rationalization, 140

Real self, 18–28

Resistance to change, 202–205, 228

Retirement funds allocation, 165–167; spreadsheet modeling and, 165–167

Rokeach Value Survey, 148

Role model, 236–237

Selective perception, 203, 205

Self-directed career strategy, 66–68

Self-directed careers, 55–64, 230

Self-directed change, 2; learning and, 15–28

Self-managed teams, 226, 233

Self-reliance, 124–126

Skills, 2–13, 15, 209–211, 233; new employee and, 226–240

Spreadsheet models, 160–167, 179; economic order quantity and, 163–165; retirement funds allocation and, 165–169

Staying sane: forces for change and, 200–202; resistance to change and, 202–205; tips for and, 205–221

Strategic manager, 236–237

Strong Interest Inventory (II), 147–148

Structured Query Language (SQL), 167, 170

Success, 107

Succession planning, 57

System optimization, 41

Team building, 225

Team player, 225–226, 230, 238

Teams, 112, 114–115

Technical skills, 232

Technology, 201, 210–211, 228

Telecomutting: boundary issues and, 81–87; defined, 74; flexible work arrangement and, 73–74; future and, 87–88

Thinking conceptually, 235–236

Total Quality Management (TQM), 224

Training, 15–16

Transformation, 51

Transformational leadership, 50–51

Working smarter, 45–46

World of work, 111–112

Yin/Yang balance, 33

About the Contributors

ELLA L. J. EDMONSON BELL is Associate Professor of Organizational Behavior at the Belk College of Business, University of North Carolina at Charlotte. She received her Ph.D. in Organizational Behavior from Case Western Reserve University. Professor Bell's research has focused on the career and life histories of professional African-American and European-American women. She is currently coauthoring a book with Stella M. Nkomo entitled *Our Separate Ways: Black and White Women's Paths to Success in Corporate America*.

RICHARD E. BOYATZIS is Professor and Chair of the Department of Organizational Behavior and Associate Dean of Executive Education Programs at the Weatherhead School of Management, Case Western Reserve University. His current research focuses on adult development of abilities and values, self-directed change, and self-directed learning. His prior publications have addressed self-directed change and learning, power and affiliation motivation, alcoholism and aggression, and leadership and management competencies and development. Boyatzis is author of *The Competent Manager: A Model for Effective Performance* (1982) and *Transforming Qualitative Information: Thematic Analysis and Code Development* (1998) and coeditor of *Innovation in Professional Education: Steps on a Journey from Teaching to Learning* (1995). In addition, he has authored over 50 articles and chapters in scholarly publications. He received his B.S. degree (1968) from the Massachusetts Institute of Technology in Aeronautics and Astronautics and his M.A. degree (1970) and Ph.D. (1973) from Harvard University in Social Psychology.

M. RONALD BUCKLEY is a Professor of Management and a Professor of Psychology at the University of Oklahoma. He received his Ph.D. in Industrial/Organizational Psychology from Auburn University. He has published over 60 articles in scholarly and professional journals. His areas of interest are the selection interview, the accurate assessment of organizational change, the ethics of students in business, and the socialization process for newcomers to an organization.

HSING K. CHENG is currently with the Department of Decision and Information Sciences of the University of Florida. He received his Ph.D. from William E. Simon Graduate School of Business Administration, University of Rochester. His research interests focus on electronic commerce, computer clustering technology, and how to optimally price computer software. His work has appeared in *Computers and Operations Research, Decision Support Systems, European Journal of Operational Research, IEICE Transactions, Journal of Business Ethics, Journal of Management Information Systems,* and *Socio-Economic Planning Sciences.*

WILLIAM DONALDSON is Founder, Chairman, and Chief Executive Officer of MAXX Material Handling, a leading manufacturer of extendable belt conveyors and belt curves for the material handling industry. In addition, he is Founder and President of Strategic Venture Planning, a management consulting firm. He is an Adjunct Professor at the College of William and Mary, Graduate School of Business and a faculty member for the American Management Association's Management Course for Presidents.

ROBERT M. FULMER is currently the W. Brooks George Professor of Management at the College of William and Mary. Dr. Fulmer's research and writings have focused on future challenges of management, implementation of strategy, and leadership development as a lever for change agents. Fulmer is the author of *Crafting Competitiveness and Leadership by Design* (1998). He received his M.B.A. from the University of Florida and his Ph.D. from University of California, Los Angeles. He is Founding Chairperson of the Executive Education Exchange, President of the Board of Editors for *Executive Development: An International Journal,* and a past President of the Southern Management Association. He currently serves as Senior Adviser to the President of the Institute for East/West Studies.

PHILIP A. GIBBS is a Visiting Assistant Professor at the College of William and Mary. His teaching and research interests include corporate strategy, mergers and acquisitions, and corporate governance. Prior to entering academia, he was a principal at Hay Associates, where he consulted on strategic management, organizational development, and reward management. Other corporate experience includes managerial positions at FMC Corp. and Allied-Signal Inc. Dr. Gibbs has a Ph.D. in Strategy and International Management from Massachusetts Institute of Technology. He has published in the *Strategic Management Journal, Organization Dynamics*, and the *Journal of Career Development*. He is a member of the Strategic Management Society, Academy of Management, and the Southern Management Association and serves as a reviewer for the *Academy of Management Journal, Strategic Management Journal*, and the Business Policy and Strategy Division of both the Academy of Management and the Southern Management Association.

GIGI G. KELLY is an Assistant Professor at the College of William and Mary. She received her doctorate in Management Information Systems (MIS) from the University of Georgia. She teaches in the areas of systems analysis and design, decision support systems, database, and information resource management. Her research interests include telecommuting, collaborative work groups, and the integration of information technology and organizational development. She has extensive consulting experience in MIS and has published articles in the *Journal of MIS, Information Systems Management, Journal of Small Group Research, Computerworld*, and various conference proceedings.

KAREN LOCKE is Associate Professor of Business Administration at the College of William and Mary's School of Business. She joined the faculty there in 1989 after earning her Ph.D. in Organizational Behavior from Case Western Reserve University. She uses qualitative methods to pursue her research interests. Her investigative work focuses on the construction of contribution, the examination of emotionality in the workplace, and more recently, the issues associated with telecommuting. Her work has appeared in journals such as the *Academy of Management Journal, Organization Science, Journal of Management Inquiry*, and *Studies in Organization, Culture and Society*. Additionally, she coauthored a book with Karen Golden on writing qualitative research, titled *Composing Qualitative Research* (1997).

DANIEL F. MICHAEL earned his M.B.A. degree at the University of South Alabama. He is currently pursuing his Ph.D. in Human Resources at Auburn University while serving as a graduate teaching assistant. He is also serving as a graduate research assistant for the Center for Business and Economic Development at Auburn University, Montgomery. He has over twelve years of management experience and eleven years of teaching experience. His research interests include the individual and organizational factors influencing the information and feedback exchange process, and the causes of stress, commitment, and motivation in temporary employees.

KENNETH L. MURRELL is Professor of Management at the University of West Florida in Pensacola. He is also President of Empowerment Leadership Systems, a consulting firm working with a large variety of organizations. His most recent interest is in combining values of community and spirit in organizations He has traveled and worked in more than 50 countries and has been consulting with the United Nations Development Programs for more than ten years. He is coauthor with Judy F. Vogt of *Empowerment in Organizations: How to Spark Exceptional Performance* (1990) and author of over 80 articles, reviews, and technical reports. He is also a part of the Taos Institute and Chair Elect of the ODC Division of the National Academy of Management.

STELLA M. NKOMO is Professor and Chair of the Department of Management in the Belk College of Business Administration at the University of North Carolina at Charlotte. A former Scholar-in-Residence at the Mary Ingraham Bunting Institute of Radcliffe College and Harvard University, she is coauthor with Dr. Ella L. Bell of a research monograph prepared for the U.S. Department of Labor, Glass Ceiling Commission, *Barriers to Work Place Advancement Experienced by African-Americans* (1994), and the forthcoming book, *Our Separate Ways: Black and White Women's Paths to Success in Corporate America*. Her nationally recognized work on race and gender in organizations and women in management appears in management journals and has been cited in several popular press publications including *The Christian Science Monitor, USA Today, Essence,* and *Black Enterprise*. She is on the editorial boards of several management journals including the *Academy of Management Review, Work and Occupations, Organization,* and the *Journal of Management Education*.

MILORAD M. NOVICEVIC is a Doctoral student in the Management and Marketing Program at Michael F. Price College of Business, University of Oklahoma. He has fifteen years of managerial experience in European and U.S. companies. His research interests include strategic global leadership and staffing, norm-based governance in interorganizational networks, and management development issues.

DIANA PAGE, an Associate Professor at the University of West Florida, has published in the *Organizational Development Journal, Simulation and Gaming,* and the *Academy of Management Executive*. She has consulted with a wide variety of organizations in the private, public, and not-for-profit sectors.

MARK PAYNE is a Regional and Group Account Director for Saatchi & Saatchi. Mark has spent over five years in the Asia region, responsible for building Procter & Gamble brands and others in over fifteen different Asian markets. He has resided in Taiwan, Singapore, and now Sydney, Australia.

MILANO REYNA is Saatchi & Saatchi Asia's Regional Human Resource Director. He has spent over three years in Asia, working across fifteen different countries. He currently resides in Hong Kong.

WILLIAM I. SAUSER, JR. is Associate Dean and Professor, College of Business, Auburn University. He earned his B.S. in Management and M.S. and Ph.D. in Psychology at the Georgia Institute of Technology. Dr. Sauser is licensed to practice psychology in Alabama and is a board-certified specialist in Industrial/Organizational Psychology, having been granted a diploma in that specialty by the American Board of Professional Psychology. Dr. Sauser is a former President of the Alabama Psychological Association and a former International President of the Society for Advancement of Management, Inc. He is a member of the editorial board of the *SAM Advanced Management Journal* and has published extensively in the fields of psychology, management, and educational leadership.

THOMAS D. SIGERSTAD is a Doctoral student in the Management and Marketing Program at Michael F. Price College of Business, University of Oklahoma. His research interests include corporate social responsibility. He has served as an executive for a number of *Fortune* 500 companies.

RONALD R. SIMS is currently the Floyd Dewey Gottwald Sr. Professor of Business Administration at the College of William and Mary. He is the author or coauthor of fifteen books and more than 70 articles that have appeared in a variety of practitioner and scholarly journals. His current research focuses on the relationship between leadership, organizational culture, and ethics and improving managerial effectiveness.

SERBRENIA J. SIMS received her Ed.D. from the College of William and Mary in Higher Education Administration. Her research focuses on higher education policy, diversity, assessment, and human resource management issues in the public and not-for-profit sectors. She is the author or coauthor of four books on related topics.

JOHN G. VERES III has been Director of the Center for Business and Economic Development since October 1982. He received his Ph.D. in Industrial/Organizational Psychology from Auburn University in 1983.

Dr. Veres's research interests center on job analysis, test validation, and issues in equal employment opportunity. His most recent works include a book entitled *Human Resource Management and the Americans with Disabilities Act* (1995), coedited with R. R. Sims, and an article entitled "Investigating Newcomer Expectations and Job-Related Outcomes," co-written with Miki Buckley, Don Fedor, Danielle Wiese, and Steven Carraher and published in the *Journal of Applied Psychology* (1998).

DANIELLE S. WIESE is a Doctoral student in Management at the University of Oklahoma. She has an M.B.A. degree from Texas Christian University. Her research interests are historical issues in performance appraisal and interviewing, the ethics of students in business, and dual-career issues in an international context.

ISBN 1-56720-194-6

HARDCOVER BAR CODE